Sustainable
School
Leadership

An elegantly written book which analyses why so many talented school leaders leave their jobs early and why many others are not willing to take up their role. The sensitive and comparative approach used allows the authors to go beyond the superficial and trite attempts which have prevailed. The nuanced analysis and recommendations should be compulsory reading for Government ministers planning their next 'new' policy initiative.

Paul Morris, Professor of Comparative Education,
UCL Institute of Education, University College London, UK

A much-needed book that presents an eloquent portrayal of the challenges characterising 21st-century school leadership. It is also a clarion call for conventional approaches to educational leadership to be revaluated if leaders are to be sustained in their roles into the future. The argument is complemented by the 'lived' experiences of school leaders themselves. These portraits inject their own validity and assertiveness in conveying the complexity of contemporary school leadership, how individuals make sense of this complexity and the various ways they deal with it. Written with both passion and incisiveness, the commentary is a powerful entreaty for school leaders to engage in new ways of learning, new dispositions and new behaviours. As such, it is one of those rare expositions that carries sufficient weight to help nudge the field of Educational Leadership in a slightly different direction.

Simon Clarke, Professor, Graduate School of Education,
University of Western Australia, Australia

A powerful and well-written text on a topic of significant contemporary interest to practitioners, students and academics in the field of educational leadership. The writers are at the top of their game in exploring the many challenges that face school leaders across a number of countries.

Mark Brundrett, Professor of Educational Research,
Liverpool John Moores University, UK

This comparative study uses narrative and portraiture to uncover the deep dilemmas facing principals in the distinctive cultural contexts of Hong Kong and the United Kingdom. Many rich dimensions of sustainability are explored as these school leaders describe how this experience with narrative has transformed their thinking and action. The further vivid self-reflection of the authors makes this a compelling read for all who are concerned about schooling and the environment.

Ruth Hayhoe, Professor, Ontario Institute for Studies in Education,
University of Toronto, Canada

A book that all new senior leaders should be required to read. It is both well written and challenging. Taking a cross-cultural, research-focused approach, the authors have put together a challenging yet inspiring book, which offers leaders help in framing their own leadership sustainability and that of others.

Megan Crawford, Professor and Director,
Plymouth Institute of Education, University of Plymouth, UK

Focuses on school leaders as individuals but refreshingly is not just an individualised analysis. Instead, compelling accounts of particular school leaders and their experiences are matched with a deeply thoughtful commentary that locates leadership within cultural, political and organisational contexts, and locally, nationally and globally as well. The complexities of school leadership come to life through the portrait methodology used and the contextual specificities highlighted. In a timely corrective to standardisation, Bottery, Ping-Man and Ngai suggest that leaders often do their best work when their individuality is supported rather than suppressed. In defying easy answers, this book is chock-full of insights for leadership practice today.

Martin Thrupp, Head, Te Whiringa School of Educational Leadership
and Policy and Research, and Professor, Wilf Malcolm Institute of
Educational Research, University of Waikato, New Zealand

Bottery, Ping-Man and Ngai offer an in-depth analysis of the complexity of sustainable school leadership. Through the development of portraits of school leaders in the UK and Hong Kong, the authors reveal the wicked problems of sustainability. This book is essential to the study and understanding of school leadership.

Patricia A.L. Ehrensal, Assistant Professor,
Educational Policy and Leadership Department, Cabrini University, USA

Sustainable School Leadership

Portraits of Individuality

MIKE BOTTERY, WONG PING-MAN AND GEORGE NGAI

BLOOMSBURY ACADEMIC
LONDON • NEW YORK • OXFORD • NEW DELHI • SYDNEY

BLOOMSBURY ACADEMIC
Bloomsbury Publishing Plc
50 Bedford Square, London, WC1B 3DP, UK

BLOOMSBURY, BLOOMSBURY ACADEMIC and the Diana logo are trademarks of
Bloomsbury Publishing Plc

First published in Great Britain 2018

Cover design: Anna Berzovan

A catalogue record for this book is available from the British Library.

ISBN: HB: 978-1-3500-0524-2
PB: 978-1-3500-0522-8
ePDF: 978-1-3500-0525-9
eBook: 978-1-3500-0523-5

Typeset by Deanta Global Publishing Services, Chennai, India
Printed and bound in Great Britain

To find out more about our authors and books visit www.bloomsbury.com
and sign up for our newsletters.

CONTENTS

ACKNOWLEDGEMENTS

There are many people we need to thank for helping us in the writing of this book. First and foremost we need to thank all of those principals and head teachers who gave generously of their time and thought to talk with us about their job. Some have large parts to play in this book, others are only gently mentioned, but all contributed to the way we understood the complex and demanding job of school leadership; without their contributions this book clearly would not have been written.

Second, we want to thank all those who read drafts of chapters, or portraits, or the full draft of the book. In particular we want to single out thanks to Julian Stern, Nigel Wright, Peter Gilroy, David Oldroyd, Sarah James, Clare McKinlay and David Dixon.

Third, we want to thank the editorial team at Bloomsbury for their help, advice, understanding, making the publishing of the book such a supportive process.

And last but not least, we want to thank our families for putting up with us while we travelled, interviewed, wrote and re-drafted the manuscript. Without their help and patience this book would not have happened.

LIST OF TABLES

INTRODUCTION

Educational leaders currently inhabit a difficult and complex world. They face multiple challenges arising at many levels, and there is now good evidence that many are finding these pressures increasingly stressful, with greater numbers seeking to retire early, and fewer wishing to take on the role. Yet the study of individual and role sustainability in educational leadership lacks clarity and understanding. This book breaks new ground by throwing fresh light on these issues through both extensive empirical research and theoretical investigation.

This book suggests that part of the problem stems from the fact that a number of perspectives have not been fully addressed when leadership practice and its sustainability have been considered. This has resulted in what Truong, Hallinger and Sanga (2017, p. 93) described as the use of only a 'limited palette of colours'. Utilizing the experiences and outlooks of three researchers from Western and Asian backgrounds, the book develops insights into the problems of leadership sustainability, including those of individuality and cultural difference, organizational pressures, wicked theory and emerging forms of globalization. These understandings are underpinned by over a decade of research using a distinctive version of portrait methodology, which has yielded over three quarters of a million words from English head teachers and Hong Kong principals on how they deal with their pressures. This evidence does three things: it provides considerable depth of understanding on how individuals inhabit the leadership role, and deal with threats to their sustainability; it demonstrates just how personal and individual the leadership role is; and finally, the results suggest that the use of the methodology itself may well be a significant means of maintaining such sustainability.

Together, the theory and the empirical research suggest that there are at least eight threats to leadership sustainability. We also argue that the two threats most quoted – the lack of preparation for the role, and the increased volume of work associated with it – are largely the consequences of greater threats to sustainability, and in fact amount to the 'pollution' to the leadership role 'downstream'. We suggest that the key long-term polluting factors are in fact 'upstream': the damage over the last few decades to many government–

educator relationships; their different perceptions of the purposes of the leadership role; the increased accountability and surveillance of leadership work; the enlarged use of power rather than persuasion by governments to effect changes; the increased complexity of the role; and the growth of blame and guilt cultures in education. These threats are subtle, long-lasting, and ultimately can be very debilitating, and any preparation for the role which fails to address and remedy these threats, and any attempts to reduce workload which doesn't factor their remediation in, will fail to resolve many issues of leadership sustainability, and may even make the situation worse by their omission.

A further significant contribution of this book is its cross-cultural appreciation of the threats to leadership sustainability. Too often the literature in this area assumes that what threatens leadership sustainability in the West will threaten it similarly elsewhere. Yet cultures are underpinned by different views of what constitutes reality, and what constitutes the 'good life'. Both the authorship of the book, and the contrasting views of English and Hong Kong educational leaders, allow a greater appreciation of how sustainability is differently threatened in different cultures, and suggests that remedies in one culture are not necessarily appropriate to problems of sustainability in another.

Educational leadership is then increasingly complex and challenging, and there is much that may threaten the sustainability of those in the role. But there are also many things which can be done to facilitate such work, mediate such demands and remedy its problems. This book suggests that in a highly complex world, a greater embrace of an ethic of individual humility will allow a better understanding of other people's beliefs and perceptions, particularly when they work within different organizational, national and cultural contexts. It argues that the leadership role needs to be seen, not as providing the vision, the answers to everyone's problems or the charting of courses for others to follow, but as a role which creates intellectual and social environments within which they and others can cooperate to better deal with the problems faced. Leaders need then to become more the catalysts than the providers of solutions to difficult problems. And finally, the book suggests that leaders are individuals, and they do their best work when their individuality is harnessed to the role, and not suppressed by it. Leadership sustainability is then at least in part a function of personal fulfilment in the role, and this is unlikely to be attained if those within it feel that their views and visions count for little in its practice.

CHAPTER ONE

Leadership Sustainability:

Meanings and Threats

Introduction

It is clear that any book on leadership sustainability needs to discuss what it means by 'sustainability', and this book will address this issue in the subsequent pages. Surprisingly, perhaps, it is *not* going to discuss in great deal what is meant by 'leadership', other than to state that it is viewed in this book as more than something created within and by a formal hierarchy, as well as more than just the property of particular personalities. 'Leadership' is then something that can be exhibited at many levels of an institution, and of an education system, and between individuals and groups as much as something exhibited by just one person.

Now our disinclination to write at length on the meaning(s) of leadership may strike some as surprising, because there is much disagreement on the meanings of the term, and a great deal of time and space in many books on educational leadership can be taken up with this discussion. For much of its early history, leadership was described in highly individual and personal terms (see Western, 2010), and had a return to this form in education in the early years of this century with the assertion of the need for transformative leadership in an age of turbulence and change (Gunter, 2016). However, times have changed again, and to such an extent that Bush and Glover (2014, pp. 559–60) recently went so far as to claim that distributed leadership was now the 'normatively preferred leadership model in the twenty-first century' – at least in education – and indeed there is a large library of materials, and not a few careers, built around discussion of this issue (see MIE special edition, 2016). So it might be asked how a book with leadership central to its title can avoid such debate. Indeed, given that the research conducted by the authors reported in this book is concerned with individual leadership perceptions, it would not be surprising if it were assumed that the current authors espoused an individual, personal model of leadership.

Yet the research in this book did not emanate from concerns about such issues, whether that concern stems from interest in philosophic, pragmatic or power-based discourses on leadership. Instead, it came from a concern about the well-being of individuals in schools. All three authors have in the past been school practitioners in senior positions, two with experience as a principal, one with 14 years of deputy head teacher experience. From their own experiences, and then from subsequent personal links to schools and with the leadership in these schools, and from an ongoing familiarity with research in this area, they have all been aware of the way in which the sheer quantity of work expected of a person in the role in their respective countries has increased, at a time when low-trust legislation has been the norm in many countries, and a much more critical approach by policy-makers to professional practice has also become increasingly common (e.g. Hargreaves, 2003; Levin, 2004; Gronn, 2003). Moreover, while there was at the time of the inception of this research a limited literature on educational leadership sustainability, much of this was either largely theoretic (e.g. Hargreaves and Fink, 2003; Davies et al. 2007), or based upon samples of individuals who had already been identified as working successfully in the leadership role (for example, the research by Day et al., 2000, and by Gold et al., 2003). So our concerns about individual well-being did not diminish, but propelled us into seeing whether less high-profile individuals in schools might be rather less optimistic about their ability to cope with current pressures than this research seemed to indicate.

The point of this is to make clear that our initial interest lay in finding out how *individuals* were coping with these new demands, and as our ongoing research focus was on the leadership of institutions, the choice was made to investigate the perceptions of those individuals formally constituted as school leaders in our two countries: head teachers in England and principals in Hong Kong. We could have chosen other school 'leaders' – perhaps those slightly lower in formal school hierarchies, or those informally identified as 'leaders' by colleagues; but those individuals formally constituted as school leaders are clearly an important group to investigate, because so much flows through them, and so much responsibility is assigned to them through the designation of the role. Our interests do not of course exclude the investigation of other kinds of leadership groups – or indeed of the adoption of a distributed leadership model – but our concern was not with deciding whether individual or distributed forms of leadership are more appropriate descriptors of school leadership, but rather to simply ask the question: How are individuals in leadership positions reacting to the changes they are experiencing? And this interest was for two main reasons: first, because there had been up to that time so little written about the well-being of such individuals; and second, because it is an individual who goes into a meeting, it is an individual who takes home large amounts of work, it is an individual who goes to their doctor with stress, and it is an individual who has to retire early. And perhaps crucially, individual *perceptions* of what the role is like are at least as important for leadership sustainability as more 'objective' 'triangulated' views of the accuracy of such perceptions. For if individuals believe that the job is excessive in its demands, if it is seen as stressful and unfulfilling, and if individuals believe that they are not respected for the work they put in, then it will very likely impact on them in physical and psychological ways which will be very different from if they believed that the job was exciting, fulfilling and manageable, and that they were respected for the efforts they were making. Take, for instance, a remark made to one of the writers (Bottery, 1998, p. 36), before the research reported in this book began, by a UK curriculum area leader in the mid-1990s:

> It's profoundly dispiriting to come home after an exhausting and frustrating day, to know you've got another two or three hours work in front of you after you've finished your tea, to switch on the television, only to find you're watching a government minister telling you how you can't be trusted, how you're the cause of the country's educational and social problems, and to find your educational ideals are disparaged and belittled.

Regardless of how 'true' in any objective sense these comments may be, the anger and the frustration with which they were expressed left a strong impression on the interviewer, and gave deep cause for concern, not only about the interviewee's state of mind at the time, but about his longer term health, and his sustainability in the job.

So, it may well be the case, as Gronn (2016) argues, that leadership is probably a mixture of individual and distributed leadership thought and action along a continuum. However, this books' purpose is not to attempt the resolution of this debate. Rather, it is to try to understand how individual leaders across different cultures perceive a variety of pressures, located at a number of different levels. And if there is cause for concern here, and if the sustainability of the individual and the quality of role are threatened, then some of the remedies also need locating at a personal level – and an over-enthusiastic adoption of a distributed leadership model of leadership might then fail to appreciate the need for remedies at the personal level.

Is this important, and if so, why?

There are at least two kinds of reasons for suggesting that threats to leadership sustainability are important, even if they are not always easily separable. A first reason is pragmatic: there is now a strong body of literature demonstrating that strong and capable leadership is one of the most important influences on pupil performance (e.g. Leithwood et al., 2006; Robinson, 2007), and for a society to be in a situation where a sizeable number of such leaders want to leave the job, or where a sizeable number don't want to take on the role, clearly has important implications for attainment across that education system, and does not bode well socially, politically and economically for the future of that society as a whole.

But there is a second, ethical argument for concern about leadership sustainability, which is that there is likely to be something very wrong with a society if it neglects the welfare of its contributory members. Hubert Humphrey once said that

> the moral test of Government is how that Government treats those who are in the dawn of life, the children; those who are in the twilight of life, the elderly; and those who are in the shadows of life, the sick, the needy and the handicapped.

He was absolutely right, but there is also a wider argument which is similarly compelling: that a society's health will be endangered should any particular group of values be espoused which cause the welfare of groups within that society to be neglected. One of the dangers, then, of a dominance of business and free-market discourse, and a neglect of more caring social values, is that individuals and groups can too easily be conceptualized as no more than human resources, rather than as resourceful humans. When this happens, as Princen (2005) argues, they become little more than a consumable resource, replaced by younger versions when they are used up. This may seem a little extreme, but one should note, as Gronn (2003) does, the rise of 'greedy' organizations, where not only is a day's work expected from an individual, but so is their emotional commitment. Yet, such commitment doesn't seem to work both ways: many societies have experienced what Brown and Lauder (2001) called the democratization of insecurity, where no level of work is free from the threat of being laid off. Accompanying these threats has been the almost inevitable rise of 'function creep' (Starr, 2015, p. 130), as individuals have taken home more and more work on evenings and weekends, simply to keep on top of demands. And when examining the effects of these on leadership sustainability, much evidence suggests these pressures are very real for many leaders – and a consequent threat to both individual and role sustainability.

Prescriptive and descriptive meanings of sustainability

Now 'sustainability', rather like 'resilience', has become an increasingly fashionable term. It follows the use of a long line of other 'hurrah' words, like excellence, quality and effectiveness which all have the ability, if used as a recommendation, to smuggle in highly dubious meanings and values which the unsuspecting may fail to see. It is little wonder they appear in many political and management speeches, for it is difficult to argue with those who advocate the need to produce excellent results or a quality product, that systems should be highly effective, and produce products, actions or cultures which are resilient and sustainable. Yet it is very important to inspect to what values these terms are actually attached, because the uncritical reader may find themselves endorsing products, processes or people with which they really do not agree. So a new programme for preventing the extinction of the white rhinoceros may be seen as an excellent idea, if it is highly effective, and makes the species both more sustainable and more resilient. But one may not be quite so happy with a training programme for Mafia-hit men, which also produces excellent results in terms of the number of successful murders per individual attempt, and which therefore makes Mafia culture both more resilient and more sustainable.

The point may be slightly laboured, but it is very important to be aware that sustainability is a *prescriptive* term – that things may be taken to be 'good', and may be approved, simply because they are described as 'sustainable'. So it is essential to be clear about what 'these things' are. 'They' could refer to the sustainability of species of rhinoceros, or of organized crime, and while many would warm to the sustainability of the former, only a few would likely warm to the sustainability of the latter.

Now while there seems agreement currently that the greater sustainability of individual leaders and greater sustainability of the role are both 'good things', one still needs to be cautious about what purposes are assumed to be 'good' for the role, and what values and actions are assumed to be good for the individual in the role. One also needs to be sure that proposed remedies to threats to sustainability are personally acceptable, because these may well be underpinned by assumptions about the causes of unsustainability with which you may not agree. You may, for instance, think that the principal cause of leadership unsustainability is a lack of preparation for the role, and therefore better preparation is the way to resolve this issue. This is a fairly standard governmental response, but if the issue which actually makes the role unsustainable is the new set of purposes attached to it by government, then any amount of preparation for leading on such purposes will likely not resolve the sustainability problem. It is then essential to look at what have been suggested as threats to leadership sustainability, what are advocated as the most effective remedies to these threats, and what purposes such remedies would ascribe to individuals and the role.

Threats to sustainability

Now to some extent, what is suggested as making the leadership role unsustainable depends on whom you read, and what they think makes the role unsustainable. In other words, their focus, their values, their 'framing' of the problem, will affect what they see and do, or choose to see and do, and what they choose to report. As Carr (1972) argued many years ago, everyone necessarily works within such 'frames' of reality, and many of these frames, and the information within them, may well contribute something useful to a better understanding of leadership unsustainability. However, it may also be true that what is suggested in some frames may only apply to some individuals, in some cultures or political systems, and not to others. The research presented in this book suggests that this is very much the case: that precisely because people *are* individuals, they are likely to be affected by different combinations of pressures, and some may hardly be affected at all. In the same way, as we shall see, some cultures or political systems may be more affected by suggested threats to sustainability than others, and some may hardly be affected at all.

Now the research on threats to leadership sustainability is largely derived from Western studies, and is normally based upon a view that leadership is threatened when either (i) people want to leave the position before legal retirement age, or (ii) that they leave quickly after taking the role on, or (iii) that there is a shortfall in the number of people who apply for such posts, and it is assumed that people do not want to take up the role in the first place, or finally (iv) that those who were interviewed were still in the job, but increasing numbers of them said that the quality of the role was diminishing. The evidence for diminishing leadership sustainability goes back twenty years or so, and doesn't really vary in the message it is sending. Thus, one can go back to authors like Fullan in Canada and the US (1997), Williams in Canada (2001), Troman and Woods in the UK (2000), Hodgen and Wylie in New Zealand (2005), as well as Gronn (2003) and Chapman (2005) for largely Western international reviews of these phenomena, and then find that the same issues are occurring today in much the same countries (e.g. Berliner, 2011, Fuller, 2012, Doyle and Locke, 2014, *Times Educational Supplement*, 2013, Reames et al., 2014, Young and Szachowicz, 2014), but are also now being talked about elsewhere – as in Jordan and Saudi Arabia (Al Omari and Wuzynani, 2013), Iceland (Larusdottir, 2014) Indonesia (Gauss, 2011), and Chile (Galdames and Gonzalez (2016). Moreover, because leadership sustainability is but one variable in a complex system, the sustainability of one part of the system will likely generate problems in other parts. So, as Fuller (2012) in the United States points out, when principals don't stay in the job very long, teachers don't engage strongly with implementing needed changes, as they wait to see what the next principal will want – and how long he or she will stay in the post. In addition, when there is high principal turnover, there is normally a similar level of turnover of class teachers, and both of these trends tend to be associated with poor student attainment. So it is necessary to examine in a little more detail what the research says about the explanations for such threats.

There seem to be at least eight different kinds of threats to leadership sustainability, though as we shall see it is impossible to provide a neat linear list, as these threats are strongly interconnected, and feed back on one another. They are:

1 Damage to government/educator relationships;
2 Differences in perceptions of the purposes of the leadership role;
3 Increased accountability and surveillance;
4 Increased use of power rather than persuasion to effect changes;
5 Increasing complexity of the role;
6 Growth of blame and guilt cultures;
7 Excessive workload;
8 Insufficient preparation for the role;

Threat one: Damage to government/ educator relationships

We begin the discussion of threats by harking back to what the curriculum leader said earlier in this chapter about working really hard, yet switching on his television and finding a government minister telling him how useless he was. This is a deep level of disenchantment, almost certainly affecting his sustainability in the role, not only because of the apparent questioning of his competence in the job, and also because of the implicit questioning of his integrity, and in so doing damaging any trust relationship that might exist between him and government. Walker, Qian and Zhang's (2011) Chinese study is another very similar example, as the government there blamed the lack of success of new curricula implementation on a lack of competence by its school leaders, whereas Walker et al. strongly suggest the real problem was the cultural pressure for a greater focus on students' public exam performance. It seems very likely that such governmental expressions of blame on such leaders would do little for their morale, little for trust relationships and little for their sustainability. This experience is one example of probably many thousands of cases.

Now if a professional's *competence* is questioned, new measures for training (probably in terms of the specification of particular behavioural competences) may well be introduced, and inspections increased in scope and regularity, and speedier dismissal procedures introduced for those failing to meet these new standards. If professional *integrity* is also questioned, this will also constitute another reason for increased inspection procedures, and more testing – which all add to the volume of work asked for. Importantly and as argued elsewhere (Bottery, 2004), when individual professionals are told they are neither trusted nor have integrity, the reaction is likely to be – as it was with our curriculum leader – anger, frustration and a significant decrease in job fulfilment, probably leading to a decline in personal sustainability, with some not wishing to continue in the role.

Threat two: Differences in perceptions of the purposes of the leadership role

Recognition of competence and integrity are both important for the building of trusting relationships, but there is another quality upon which trust is normally constructed, and this leads into a second threat to individual and role sustainability. Much trust is based upon a relationship of shared values, and when educators and governments disagree on the purposes of the leadership role, some leaders may feel that the nature of the role has changed so much that it is no longer sustainable. In sum, when the purposes of the role are differently perceived by practitioners and governments, role sustainability may also be threatened.

Now a focus on differing purposes may lead one into a very different literature and set of explanations, for if one wants to understand the causes of at least some of the pressures on personal and role sustainability, then one needs to recognize that government purposes may lie beyond the realms of education, and may involve larger issues involving first, the functioning of the nation state, and second, the effects of culture upon these other issues.

Now when it comes to the functioning of the nation state, particularly Western nation states, many changes over the last few decades have been predicated on very different views from those held by social democratic theorists and governments, and indeed by many public sector professionals. Early writing on which much neoliberal thought was based (e.g. Hayek, 1944; Friedman, 1962; Nozick, 1974) led in the 1970s and 1980s to a fundamental reorientation of economic, political and social values in many of these countries, a realignment of societal priorities, and a different conception of

Table 1.1 Public sector work: Seven movements in values (after Stewart and Clarke, 1987)

- From the concept of citizenship, to the concept of consumerism;
- From the priority of the concept of the public good, to the priority of the concept of individual benefit;
- From professional service based on the priority of need, to service based on the priority of individual choice and the ability to pay;
- From the driving force of collective action, to the driving force of competition;
- From public sector professionals acting as service providers, public educators and policy contributors, to public sector professionals acting as implementers of governmental and institutional management policies;
- From professionals acting as contributors to various communal goals, to professionals acting as contributors to national and institutional competitive advantage;
- From viewing the public as clients and partners in communal and national goals, to viewing them as active consumers of services in a marketplace.

the work of the public sector professional. Thus, as can be seen in Table 1.1, social democratic concepts have been increasingly replaced by more market-based ones, which have led to the election of governments with very different value orientations from those of many public sector professionals.

Such change in thought and argument in government policies has also been increasingly steered by global changes, much of a similar free-market nature, and as writers like Levin (2004, 2010) and Fullan (2009) have argued, many nation states, since the 1970s, have either willingly or reluctantly felt the need to alter the purposes and practices of their education systems to better align with such trends, leading to national policies detailing changes in the practices and the roles of public sector professionals. In the process, marked difference in perceptions of the purposes of the role have been seen by governments and many public sector professionals, and in so doing have added to the threats to the personal sustainability of some of these, if they have felt they have become increasingly out of step with what their government wanted of them.

Threat three: The increased accountability and surveillance of the role

The decline in trust seen on both sides consequent upon the implementation of market-based legislative agendas may then lead many governmental agencies to increase accountability and surveillance levels. Such increases can happen in a number of ways; not only in terms of how often inspections are carried out, but also in terms of the number of areas inspected, and finally in terms of the depth to which such inspections dig. This not only adds to greater workload; it also necessarily leads to the greater surveillance of those being inspected, which will likely add to a decline in feelings of trust and competence. In addition, such increased accountability and surveillance will also probably result in individual leaders feeling that they have less private space within which to reflect upon issues and problems. This feeling of believing that whatever is said may be taken down and used against you, may then become a real threat to both personal and role sustainability.

Threat four: Increased use of power rather than persuasion to effect changes

While threats to sustainability described above can produce a difficult context for educational leaders, there is another threat which on some occasions is all that is needed to end a policy seen as sustainable, and that is the exercise of power by those senior in a hierarchy to close down particular leadership strategies or visions of educational development in order to achieve other strategies or visions. In some ways this is the most obvious of threats: a government withdraws funding from a particular curriculum project; another sets new priorities which become part of the remit of the national inspection regime; a local authority abolishes an advisory post as part of a cost-cutting and reorientation exercise; a senior management team sets new priorities within an organization and ensures that these are adhered to by staff. In all of these cases, what may have seemed to those individuals negatively affected by the change as highly useful, highly productive and highly sustainable practices are abolished, and in the process their day-to-day routines may become unsustainable, their personal visions no longer in tune with those of senior power-holders, and their positions may disappear. This form of threat to sustainability has always existed: but in countries with fast-moving political agendas, where the creation of educational policies is viewed as part of a political adversarial game, and where policy-makers feel less need (or feel they have less time) to consult those lower in such hierarchies – a description of the educational landscape in many countries currently – the personal and role sustainability of educational leaders become increasingly threatened. Moreover, as this process gets faster and less restrained, the more individuals are conditioned into accepting the notion of change for change itself, rather than in trying to conserve the best of what existed previously. In the process, approaches to leadership 'sustainability' may be transmuted into approaches to increasing their 'resilience', which make them tougher and more adaptable to constantly changing situations, rather than helping them to evaluate what may be the best and conserving these.

Threats five and six – the increasing complexity of the role; and the growth of guilt and blame cultures

Yet there are two more threats to sustainability, which are sometimes elephants in the room of leadership sustainability, and yet are suggested in much of the above. An excessive amount of work, consequent upon the implementations of rafts of different value-based legislation and accompanying accountability and surveillance measures; a decline in the relationships between governments and professional workers; and the conflicts between governmental purposes and resilient cultural values impeding such change, have all led to an increasing complexity to the role (Moller, 2009; Knapp and Feldman, 2012), and one major perception of teachers is that the principalship is more demanding and complex than the teacher's position (Pounder and Merrill, 2001, Bush 2011; Chapter 7 of this book). Part of this complexity has come from the sheer volume of problems that have been generated; part has come from the problems consequent upon dealing with legislation where governments and professionals no longer hold the same values or purposes; part has come from clash of values within a society; and part has come simply from the increasing complexity of the world in which we now live. This complexity has increased the number of levels of influence on legislative changes, and has generated many problems, formally seen as simple in nature and relatively easily resolvable, but which now are anything but. Instead they can create guilt and blame cultures if leaders fail to recognize that they are being asked to resolve problems that may be near to irresolvable. These then are important areas to consider, because they constitute the world in which educational leaders now work. A fuller consideration of how the complexity of leadership problems and the creation of guilt and blame cultures have both contributed to sustainability problems will be considered in the next chapter.

Threat seven: Overwork

The final threat, then, is the impact created by the sheer quantity of work now associated with the role. This can be produced by new legislative initiatives, and through exercises in greater accountability, in addition to the impact of the growing demands of Gronn's (2003) 'greedy organisations' on leadership work, and the kind of 'function creep' Starr (2015) talked about. The result that Young and Szachowicz (2014, p. 1) observe in the United States is this:

> Principals have always had mandates … but never have there been so *many* mandates being implemented simultaneously … . And doing all of this while managing previously existing mandates … can seem overwhelming.

This comment seems to apply to the situation of educational leaders in many countries and, as will be seen later, seems at least in part to be a product of the generation of 'fast policies' by governments, and of their desire to adopt a more muscular approach to the direction and practice of their education systems than before. Chapter 9 of this book describes in detail our research on the effects that these changes have had on educational leaders in England and Hong Kong, and while there were some genuine differences between the two education systems, one of the things that their leaders seemed to have in common was the feeling of drowning in a sea of paperwork. So while one head teacher in the low-trust English context said in an interview: '*I don't even have the time to think about the fact that I don't have the time,*' a Hong Kong principal, in a more supportive system, echoed the same feelings when he said that '*it's a tough job [being a principal], so no one wants to take up this position*'.

Threat eight: Insufficient preparation for the role

After some resistance by governments to the notion that the sustainability of educational leaders was threatened, the general response by governments has been to locate the problem in the degree of workload, and to a lack of preparation for the demands of the role. There has therefore been a proliferation of national colleges for the preparation of such leaders (see Bush and Jackson 2002) for such a role, the better identification and the fast-tracking of those who show particular aptitude for the role, and a retreat from advocacy of transformational models of leadership, where the onus seemed to rest strongly on the shoulders of single charismatic leaders. One has then seen the endorsement of more distributed models of leadership, so that work can be devolved to others lower in school hierarchies.

Now it is noteworthy that the first six threats described above have been largely ignored by governments as threats to leadership sustainability, their attention being mostly focused on overwork, and insufficient preparation for the role. Yet both of these, while clearly requiring remediation, could also be seen as essentially the 'downstream' effects of the previous six, and so attention here treats the effects rather than the causes. Indeed, when it comes to the last of these threats, insufficient preparation for the role, the focus has tended to be on practical measures, and for greater leadership effectiveness in implementing government reforms. Yet, this book argues that much of the threat to leadership sustainability stems from the changing world and challenges that leaders face, and little of this is addressed. It is therefore highly important to dig deeper into such issues, and to understand them better, and it is for this reason that we move in the next chapter to look at the increasing complexity of the role, at how this changes the nature of the role that educational leaders must adopt, and how this might change the nature of the pressures that governments bring to bear upon their educators.

Conclusion: Do we only want certain kinds of leaders to be sustainable?

It will not have escaped the attention of many readers that despite the focus in this book on maintaining or improving the sustainability of educational leaders, there will be more than a few policy-makers who do not want some principals or head teachers to be sustainable. They may be very happy to see those who disagree with them and their policies leave the leadership arena and make way for others more in agreement with their policies. Their relationships with these others are poor for a reason. As noted above, they may differ in perceptions of the purposes of the leadership role; and if they believe that such leaders are unlikely to implement their measures without some form of resistance or even subversion, they may feel they need to use power rather than persuasion, and to increase the accountability and surveillance of such individuals. It might then be suggested that this chapter must end largely where it started: that sustainability is a prescriptive word, and these policy-makers will not want to see such leaders being made more sustainable simply because they hold a different value position; they may then adopt positions and create legislation that deliberately make these others less sustainable. How would one reply to such a position?

Now it probably has to be acknowledged that sometimes it may be best for some leaders to leave: they may no longer have the energy, may have lost the drive, may in some exceptional cases be toxic to others. In these cases, their lack of sustainability in the role may actually be seen as a 'good' thing.

But for others, who still have the spirit, the drive, the desire to do the best for their students (and our research suggests that this comprises the large majority of those interviewed) then a desire for their unsustainability (or indeed their forced conformity) seems mis-guided and damaging to educational systems in at least the following ways.

First, as argued previously, it is a dangerous assumption to know or believe that you are right, full stop. In such a complex age, acknowledgement of the need for greater individual humility, and of an acceptance of the need for an appreciation of other approaches, is almost certainly the best way to negotiate an uncertain future. In evolutionary terms, variation is an essential survival tool. The same logic applies to education systems and their societies in turbulent times.

This pragmatic argument then is based on sound theory; in such an age, the drive to single-focus solutions is simplistic and ultimately highly damaging: we need to adopt strategies which enable the better appreciation of complexity. The restriction on thinking to single perspectives leads down roads which ultimately cause great harm to our adaptability. And ethically, there is something repugnant in the idea that one person knows what is best for another, when they do not know their personal challenges, or the contexts they have to work within.

Ultimately, though, this is not an educational problem but a human problem, a problem of people living together. Forcing one view of how to live in a society on others is abhorrent to most people, and history is full of examples of people who have risen up against such actions; if they have not, their society is likely to collapse from within. Education systems, and education leaders, who accede to the order to adopt the one view, are ultimately complicit in the creation of such societies. The essence of a healthy society, we would argue, lies in more than the toleration of other views, but in the recognition of the need for other views. Those who would make others of different views unsustainable in their roles need to be recognized for what they are doing to their education systems and their societies.

CHAPTER TWO

Sustainability and the 'Wicked' Reality of Educational Leadership

Introduction

The previous chapter described how increased demands on educational leaders in many countries over the last few years have led to threats to the sustainability of individual leaders, and in some people's eyes, to the role itself. There are a number of possible reasons for this phenomenon. One comes from the fact that demands now emanate not just from individual and local pressures, but from national, international and global levels as well, as international comparisons of student performance, such as PISA, have become primary government foci.

Another reason is that demands from different levels are not always comparable in nature: those at personal or local levels are likely to be easier to access and understand than those created at national and international levels, as intentions at these levels may be partly hidden from the individual, and/or partly mediated before reaching them, and so may not be easy to comprehend or fully respond to.

Furthermore, demands from and mediations at different levels may conflict: national pressures don't always cohere with local pressures, and neither necessarily do their mediations. In addition, many demands are likely to impact much quicker than previously, largely because of increases in speed of communication, and particularly through the use of information technology, which has also facilitated the removal of mediating layers (see Chapter 10 on this). Moreover, in an age of fast policies, the greater use of power to enforce change by those senior in hierarchies has increased in many countries. A final reason comes from the marked decline in many countries in the amount of trust extended to most public sector workers by their governments, being replaced by greater accountability and inspection of their work.

The increase in work stemming from most of these sources has led to concerns about the sustainability of the role, despite some governments' efforts to better prepare individuals for the role, through strategies like the advocacy of more distributed models of leadership in order to avoid work increases impacting upon just one individual. The result for those implementing such changes, however, is likely to be the creation of a professional dilemma. *On the one hand*, they may attempt to fully implement what is asked of them, and by working longer and longer hours, they may find that 'function creep' becomes part of their work reality. They may then be faced by workloads which make the job increasingly unmanageable. *On the other hand*, they may attempt to mediate and triage such processes in order to work in a personally sustainable manner, but which don't satisfy their wish to do the best by their students or their staff.

A further reason for concern over leadership sustainability is that any attempts at redressing the increased quantity of work almost certainly won't fully address the issue. The interactions between levels of demands create more than just simple additive work increases: they increase the *complexity* of the demands as well. This increase in complexity occurs in two different but related ways. The first increase occurs because much causation doesn't happen in simple linear patterns: very seldom are situations or problems found where A causes B, B causes C, C causes D, and so on. In reality, there are likely to be webs of variables affected by change, and A may cause B, but B may then affect M, which affects P and L jointly, before impacting unexpectedly once more on A. This necessarily results in many unpredictable and uncontrollable interactions. Educational leaders cannot then be concerned solely with events occurring at personal and local levels; they also need to be aware of the effects of levels above these (national, cultural, international, etc.). But as they try to do so, these add layers of complexity to the problems facing them, and the more difficult will be the achievement of an adequate response. As this happens, the sustainability of person and role is also more likely to be threatened.

But there is a further reason for the increased complexity of the role, which makes threats to leadership sustainability still more difficult to resolve. Even within the kinds of complex systemic arenas described, it is possible to have a general problem that all agree upon (e.g. greater creativity is needed in education systems), but there may be little agreement about the actual meaning of the term, as it can be, and usually is viewed from a variety of perspectives. This will probably happen because the meanings and the values behind such an apparently shared concern may be very different, and result in very different responses being proposed to what is apparently the same problem. Together, these two sources of complexity in the leadership role (system complexity, and different understandings of the nature of an issue) can combine to produce situations where problems may be hard or even impossible to define in any agreed sense, and therefore may not be resolvable in any final or definitive sense. When this happens, the resolution of educational challenges is going to be harder to predict, harder to control and harder to agree upon.

Yet much educational thought and practice in the West – both now and in the past – seem largely predicated upon assuming very much the opposite: that in most situations, one thing does cause another, and that we can get people to agree on the nature of a problem and the best responses to it. As we shall see later, such thought and practice may be heavily culturally determined, and may not be nearly as pronounced in other parts of the world. However, when such assumptions are made, when individuals fail to achieve problem resolutions, there is a very real danger that inappropriate assignations of blame will be attached to these individuals. In other words, if the complexity of many situations is underestimated, and if the differences of opinion as to what constitutes the problem are not appreciated, we may fail to realize that some demands are unfairly placed upon individual leaders, and cause greater unsustainability to them and the role they occupy, as they may then be blamed for not achieving the impossible. This then adds a new threat to leadership sustainability, pointing strongly to the need for a better understanding of the nature of complex problems, and of the blame cultures that may be produced by a lack of such understanding. To do this, we need to take a step back into the past of educational leaders' work, and trace the evolution of the role in one part of the world, to understand its increasingly threatened nature today.

A fabled golden past?

So far, then, it has been argued that it is not possible to fully understand the situation many educational leaders face without better appreciating the complex nature of the demands currently placed upon many of them. These processes began in many newly emerging Western nations in the nineteenth century, when they set up education systems with the express purpose, as Green (1997, p. 35) noted, being

> to spread the dominant cultures and inculcate popular ideologies of nationhood, to forge the political and cultural unity for the burgeoning nation states, and to cement the ideological hegemony of their dominant classes.

Thus it was that D'Azeglio declared after the Italian Risorgimento, that 'we have made Italy, now we have to make Italians' (Hobsbawm, 1990, p. 44). This was done by various means, a national language was imposed over local dialects, national standing armies were created, but probably most importantly education systems were constructed with the explicit intention of inculcating individual 'citizenship' loyalty to the nation state. This building of citizenship identity continued into the twentieth century with the decolonized nation states of Africa, the Middle East and Asia, and many aspects of these systems bore strong structural and curricular similarities to their former colonial masters (Bottery, 2003), even as they were strongly influenced by different cultural values. So, as these educational systems developed, most had a primary objective of creating a *national* identity to ensure that primary personal loyalty was to the nation state, at the same time as basic literacy and numeracy and other essential skills and behaviours were inculcated into individuals, to enable them to move seamlessly from the school into the workplace (Toffler, 1970, p. 354–5). In Asian countries like China, modern nation state education systems have reinforced an existing cultural tradition of focusing on the individual's contribution to group harmony, as much as on personal advancements (Nisbett, 2003).

Educational leadership has historically been a much less pressured position than it is in many parts of the world today. In Asian countries, this was in part because educational leadership was historically seen as a role situated within a hierarchy facilitating loyalty to the state and fostering group cohesion, and so any increased national interest in developing an education system ran with centuries-old traditions and values. In the West, at least until the third quarter of the twentieth century, much public sector educational leadership followed that of the private sector, and was situated in educational cultures of professional dominance, underpinned by a conception of professionals as possessing exclusive esoteric knowledge, who were eminently trustworthy, and who could therefore be granted considerable autonomy and self-regulation (see for example Durkheim, 1957; Tawney, 1921; Carr-Saunders and Wilson, 1933).

However, by the last quarter of the twentieth century, attitudes to professionals, particularly in the West, were changing, and from being described in highly altruistic terms, their role became more closely scrutinized, and viewed in much less complimentary terms. Handy (1978) in his typology of organizations described the kind dominated by professional bodies as 'Dionysian': organizations serving the wishes of the professionals, rather than serving larger organizational aims or the wider community. Handy went on to suggest (Handy and Aitken, 1990) that schools clearly fitted that description. Such comments were replicated in the equally unflattering view of professionals by Collins (1990), suggesting that they were largely motivated by the desire for ever greater 'occupational closure' – the limiting of those who could enter the profession, and the exclusion of others without their certification from engaging in such work. This, he argued, might be to the social, political and financial benefit of those already in such professional 'clubs', but had debatable benefits for the wider society. While many professionals would probably deny this characterization, they might still look back to former times as ones of greater autonomy and respect than currently.

New regimes, new demands

This critical literature coincided with and partly contributed to the reduced influence of welfare state ideology and related economic processes, and facilitated the rise in free-market values and practices, which not only rejected the notion that professionals could or should be the sole experts on appropriate practice, but also spurned the idea that they should be gatekeepers and guardians of welfare state provision. Writers like Hayek (1944) argued that welfare states not only maintained professional dominance, but also reduced the citizen's liberty, leading down roads to their ultimate serfdom. Largely neglected at the end of the Second World War, his line of argument rose to prominence with the decline in global terms of Western industrial dominance, as well as with the rise in energy costs in the 1970s. In this situation, a radical neoliberal economic philosophy then married well with concerns about the affordability of large welfare states, and there was a general political movement towards the tightening of public budgets, facilitated by control initiatives like New Public Management (Hood, 1991). Professional workers like educators were not the central targets of such reforms, but were rather more collateral damage consequent upon the pursuit of other societal projects. By 1993, Pollitt was noting that many professionals had moved from a position of being 'on top' in determining welfare and institutional visions and policies, to being 'on tap' to the demands of governments and institutional senior management teams – even if in many cases this left many head teachers and principals having to reconcile the wearing of various hats, their role increasingly changing from either autocrat (*L'ecole, c'est moi!*) or facilitator of a shared institutional vision, to one much more concerned with overseeing and enforcing external legislation, as well as implementing measures of self-regulation in their own institutions. Some of these leaders recognized the changes to come and took graceful retirement, others battled on, while a different breed of leader/manager came to be employed and shaped. In the process, the nature of desirable job specifications and subsequent training changed to match the increased oversight and inspection of both classroom and leadership performance, and by resultant threats to what had formerly been seen as an unwritten guarantee of a lifelong career.

There have been many variations on this story: continental European and Asian professional experiences of such changes have not been as painful as they have been in North America, Australasia or the UK (see Levin, 2003). Nevertheless, all have seen a ramping up of legislative demands, not only in terms of quantity and nature, but also in terms of speed of demand and response. Much international legislative change then has followed a paradoxical combination of increasingly neoliberal marketized policies combined with increased state-controlled direction of professional practice, seemingly irrespective of the political hue of the party in power. At the same time, the role of an education minister in most democracies in an age of 24/7 media coverage has been predicated on proposing plans to be implemented and realized within a single term of office, in order to demonstrate to an increasingly voracious news media that electoral promises had been 'delivered', and thus provided reason for re-election for another term. It is instructive to note that Gillian Shepherd, a former English Secretary of State for Education, commented that had she and her (UK Conservative) party known they would be in power for eighteen consecutive years 'the whole of the reforms would have been completely different' (quoted in Bangs et al., 2011, p. 48). Little was different on the other side of UK political divide: Michael Barber, adviser to New Labour while in government, talked explicitly, if inelegantly, of his role of driving an ideology of 'deliverology' (Barber, 2007).

Yet while many reflective politicians would probably admit that the profound cultural changes needed for genuine reform don't fit neatly into electoral timetables, the nature of much educational legislation has created greater demands and pressures on educational leaders and their role, which have hindered the realization of the nuances necessary for achieving authentic cultural change. Instead, as Fergusson et al. (1994, p. 113) have argued, a form of personal educational restructuring has increasingly taken place:

> As sceptical teachers ... comply with ... programmes of study, test their pupils, accept appraisal, as reluctant heads sit on sub-committees of governing bodies to apportion the school's budget ... they come gradually to live and be imbued in the logic of their new roles, new tasks, new functions, and in the end to absorb partial redefinition of their professional selves, first inhabiting them, eventually becoming them.

This is essentially debased Aristotelianism, as the repetition of practices create values, which lead to the replication of similar practices, rather than to careful and iterative reflection on the success of implementation so far. Educational cultures have then been remoulded, and in some cases short-term, simplistic and ultimately damaging mind-sets have been created, as both policy and implementation have underestimated the variety and complexity of responses required to resolve long-term intractable educational problems. And when such 'silver-bullet' policies are employed to meet policy deadlines rather than to properly address complex problems, they tend to ignore the need for nuanced implementations into different contexts. As we shall see in Chapter 8, Western cultural thinking has tended to take that road more easily than its Asian counterpart.

Importantly for leadership sustainability, the pursuit of such policies, practices and actions can also lead to the creation of 'blame' and 'guilt' cultures, particularly if those creating the policies see them only partially implemented, and blame practitioners for this apparent 'failure'. But 'guilt' cultures also follow if practitioners fail to realize the immense difficulty of their task, and believe they should still deliver a full amount to unreasonable legislative demands. As Fullan (1991) argued in a masterful overview of the relative failure of two decades of educational reform in North America, if a policy is to work, its implementers need to feel able to critique, mediate, and, if necessary, actively resist some policy developments, for good impactful policy stems not just from its initial conceptualization, but from those implementing it being able to translate it into their contexts and thereby provide new meanings to it. Once again, Asian cultures may better resist such threats: Nisbett (2003) suggests that a central characteristic of much cultural thinking here is the importance given to understanding the *context* of a problem as much as to the presenting problem itself.

An unrealizable need for certainty

The simplification and speed of educational policy can also threaten an important tacit assumption of the management of change. The essential core of much management is fairly straightforward: a plan needs to be managed well if it is to stand a reasonable chance of successful implementation. Yet the tacit assumption here is that one can – and should – be in control of such change. Control is indeed central to the larger Western worldview, as the relationship between human beings and nature has been seen as one where human activity is directed at gaining control of and dominating the natural world, and thereby ensuring greater predictability and certainty of outcomes. With such a perspective, and with the kinds of change management stemming from it, it is unsurprising to find managers and leaders being seen as, and seeing themselves as, needing to adopt a similar position with respect to the nature of their role. And one corollary of such belief is that if they cannot take such control, and ensure such predictability, they cannot be very good leaders or managers.

Once again, as Nisbett (2003) argues, Eastern views tend to be more accommodating: a more complex, less controllable world is assumed, where events are seen as occurring in more complex and systemic environments than they are in the West. This orientation helps reduce the likelihood that strong blame and guilt cultures will be fostered. World views then are important to these discussions, because leadership and the management of change are not stand-alone and context-free concepts. They are embedded within constellations of values and assumptions, which need examining and, if necessary, challenging, and it may be that there is much more than what is normally admitted in Western countries, and their education systems, that managers and leaders cannot and will never control. In addition, there is rather more of the management and leadership role than many would care to admit that is going to be unpredictable. Leadership and management, and particularly the management of change, then need to be at least as much about managing the unknown, the unexpected and the unpredictable as with putting into place systems to produce predictable results.

The greater Western embrace of predictability and control come largely from focusing on and dealing with the known world. As Rumsfeld (2002) put it, such leadership and management is concerned with dealing with the 'known knowns … things we know that we know'. This is a world of comfort and reassurance, but there is a great deal more, both in the larger external world, and in the more constrained world of leadership and management. First, 'known knowns' can very easily be 'unknown knowns' – where leaders (and just about everyone else) think they know something, only to be mistaken in this, and so many 'known knowns' actually belong to a second category, that of 'known unknowns'. A third category is of the 'known unknowns … things that we know we don't know': what Kuhn (1970) called the problems of 'normal science', where problems are worked out within a scientific paradigm and the answers conform to that paradigm. Thus, a behavioural psychologist works within a world described by the values of behavioural psychology, and only problems which conform to this paradigm are investigated. However, much more problematic for those wishing to cling to a world of the certain and controllable are a fourth category of 'unknown unknowns … things we don't know we don't know' – the stuff of Kuhn's (1970) 'scientific revolutions', where the world is now seen in an entirely different way.

Now the borders between these four categories are at least semi-permeable, and the distinctions between them are not always easy to define. Indeed, such semi-permeability is seen in many aspects of life, and largely explains the perennial fascination of organized competitive sport. Given the set of known rules within a sport, and given that one team is much 'better' than another in some agreed sense (the team cost ten times as much to assemble than did its opponents), it 'logically' should be the case that the former will beat the latter. And yet upsets are seen every week, as for some apparently inexplicable reason the underdogs triumph and the hot favourites are trounced. Many factors may come into such an unexpected defeat – a drunken party outside the favourite team's hotel preventing a proper night's sleep, a row over the phone by one critical member of the team with their spouse, the unexpected flu symptoms of another, a heavy thunderstorm during the match making slick play much more difficult, the unknown substitute who has no fear of failure, and has the match of his or her young life – so many unknown or unnoticed factors may come into play that prediction becomes that much more risky, and the sports headlines broadcast that evening are almost completely unexpected.

Of course, if the world is much less controllable than many would like it to be, then perhaps firefighting, instead of being seen by many as a consequence of the *failure* of leadership and management, may need in some cases to be viewed as the *consequence* of dealing with a particular problem. Its inevitability may then need to be built much more into any leadership approach. And if not firefighting, then perhaps as Verweij and Thompson (2011) argue, perhaps a fatalist approach to problems may have a greater role to play than most Western thinking would like to think, it normally being seen as little more than a counsel of failure, when an acceptance that little can be done in a situation currently, and that living with a situation, may in fact be the most rational and sensible approach.

The tame and the wicked

So far it has been argued that threats to leadership sustainability – both of the person and of the role – occur for a variety of reasons. One common feature of unsustainability is the increase in workload attached to the role, and this seems consequent upon rafts of new legislative demands, which in many cases take the form of a paradoxical combination of marketized, neoliberal agendas with increased state control of public sector practice. In addition, however, another cause of threats to leadership sustainability may come from the loss of trust between governments and public sector workers in many countries. This may be generated by the different purposes of these governments and their educators; it may also be generated by governments failing to recognize the true cause of a problem, and inappropriately blaming professionals for failure (see Walker, Qian and Zhang (2011)). These observations then suggest that another factor in threats to role sustainability is the increased complexity of the role.

A picture is also beginning to emerge of possible broad cultural differences between Western and Asian cultures, with the former tending to expect more control of problems through standardized responses, and the latter better recognizing the contextualized nature of many concerns. The danger with the neglect of context, and the promotion of standardization is that this can easily lead to the adoption of 'tame' approaches to leadership and management – ones which assume problems are relatively easy to define, and that there are, for many of them, clearly defined responses guaranteeing their resolution. Now it is important to note here that 'tame' problems are not being equated with 'simple' problems, even if they are sometimes confused with them. Certainly, tame problems are characterized by features which seem to promise an attractive degree of order, predictability and control, and they are formulated in definitive and easily understood ways, so that if an action is performed in the prescribed manner, there is a cast-iron guarantee that that the problem will be solved. Putting the correct key in a lock and turning it the right way is an obvious tame example, which is also a simple one. But a tame problem can also be quite complex: stripping down a car engine is not simple, but it is a tame problem, because if the car manual instructions are followed, the objective will be achieved. These two examples also suggest another couple of features of tame problems and solutions: that there are only a limited number of ways of understanding the problem faced; and that the responses will almost invariably be standardized, and so there seems little need to worry about the context.

Now this logic of the tame leads almost invariably to a very important conclusion for issues of leadership sustainability, for if a response to a tame problem fails, then the fault cannot lie with the response. Instead, it logically has to lie either in the manner of implementation, or with the person doing the implementing. If this is the case, then any shortcomings or failures necessarily have to be laid at the door of the implementers, which means that the response must be to either educate the implementer to better performance, or to find someone else to do the job properly. In this controllable world, a leader who engages in a lot of firefighting or says that a problem has to be endured for the moment will very likely be seen as someone who isn't coping, who hasn't read or understood the policy properly or who is not 'one of us', because they cannot have really signed on to the policy agenda, and so are deliberately undermining it. The fault, and therefore the blame, must lie with the implementer. And for those leaders who accept this definition of their reality, and these terms of the leadership role, the personal blame will be seen as appropriate, and guilt and feelings of personal failure will be seen as necessary consequences.

The limitations of the tame, the embrace of the wicked

Grint (2008, p. 12) has taken these ideas and argued that tame problems are the problems of managers rather than leaders, because they belong to a group of problems 'akin to puzzles for which there is always an answer'. On the other hand, he suggests that the problems of leaders are 'rooted in the distinction between certainty and uncertainty'. Because of these fundamental differences, then, he argues that the leadership role needs orienting much more towards the uncertainty end of any spectrum. Yet while one may agree with the general idea that managers should concentrate on one sort of task, and leaders on another, in reality much of a leadership role is determined by what 'leaders' are confronted by, what they are given to do and what they are able to do in the contexts they find themselves in. If much of what is given, or most of what is expected, consists essentially of tame problems (*'we have decided that the role comprises these actions, and your role is to implement them'*) then many 'leaders' may end up practising management, being practitioners and leaders of the tame, even if many possess the ability and mettle to see beyond this interpretation of their role. The danger is that if they come to believe that the worlds of policy, leadership and management are constituted mostly or wholly of tame problems, then that may be how they frame their role.

Yet much of what happens in the world is not very tame: much is a great deal messier, and cannot be framed by clear sets of rules. Many presenting problems are not found in textbooks, and don't have tame rules permitting the application of standardized responses. Many of life's messy challenges, and many of the problems of management and leadership are highly unique and highly personal. These are the 'wicked' problems suggested by Rittel and Webber (1973), which have been further developed by writers like Conklin (2006), Rayner (2006), Bore and Wright (2009), Wright (2011), Verweij and Thompson (2011), Barineau and Kronlid (2014), Bottery (2016), and Creasy (2017). Such writings suggest that wicked problems have a number of characteristics, the main ones in education being are listed below:

> First, and as noted above, there may be no definitive set of rules from which an individual can work to resolve a problem; each problem may well be unique.
>
> Second, this uniqueness is almost certainly due in part to the contribution of the levels of context which impact on the problem, as well as the manner and strength of such interaction; in most cases, this will lead to complex individual problems and the need for complex unique responses.
>
> Third, because human beings come to problems with different ways of understanding a problem, and likely with different values and views, it is very likely for there to be disagreement on how to actually frame the problem in the first place.
>
> Fourth, because of a problem's uniqueness and complexity, it may never be clear if a problem has been solved, or whether only its current symptoms have been eliminated;.

Finally, if a problem is misdiagnosed (which seems fairly likely, the more wicked a problem is) the more likely it is that only the nature of the problem to be solved is being altered – which may only be realized further down the line.

Leadership sustainability in a wicked world

If many challenges that educational leaders face are composed, at least in part, of such wicked dimensions, then the quality of individual and role sustainability may both be threatened, because if the wicked nature of much of the leadership role is not recognized, then tame problems and tame responses may be incorrectly utilized, and cultures of blame and guilt may be created. It is important then to ask how not only individual sustainability, but also the quality of the role, can be made more viable. What then makes for greater leadership sustainability in a wicked world? The previous analysis suggests a number of implications for the leadership role, and that by embracing them, both personal and role sustainability may be enhanced. Three areas seem particularly important. A first is in the framing of the leadership role; a second is in developing the role with stakeholders; a third is in implementing the role for students.

1 **Framing the leadership role.**
   a **Challenges should be seen as more about throwing birds than about throwing stones.** As Plsek (2001) argued, comparing wicked problems to tame problems is like comparing the flight of a bird to the flight of a stone when both are thrown. With the stone, the thrower normally has a sense of the direction in which they wish to throw the stone, and given the strength of the throw, they will usually have a fair idea of where the stone will land. While this is not exactly a 'tame' throw, for very few people have the abilities to land a stone precisely where they intend, nevertheless, it is a good deal easier than throwing a bird. For here, there is more than one mind and one intention at work. The thrower's intention may be complemented by the bird's intention, but it may not, and what occurs will probably be uncontrollable and unpredictable. Yet such understanding would seem to be an essential framing for policies and their implementation. While many may wish to think of policy implementation as having a stone's trajectory, the reality is more akin to the unpredictable and uncontrollable flight of a thrown bird, and the role of the leader is probably made more sustainable when the inevitability of at least some unpredictability and some uncontrollability are

better recognized. Once again, Western cultures may have much to learn from Eastern cultures in this respect.

b   **The role should be infused more with an ethic of humility than with an ethic of certainty.** Much Western leadership literature – particularly in business, but some also in education – begins with a transformative charismatic vision of the leader framing a vision (or accepting the vision from a source senior to them in the hierarchy) and leading others to its implementation. Yet while much educational practice now mimics the corporate nature of much business practice, it still has ethical questions to be asked. Are educational aims and purposes prerogatives for governments and managements, or should other stakeholders, including educational professionals have a participative voice in such decisions? And as Popper (1982) pointed out, if evidence, reason and logic are not the primary means of arriving at decisions, the alternative is likely to be one based on power and force. In the world of the complex and the wicked, the educator's role needs to be framed within such an understanding, which once more points to human limitations, and therefore to the framing of the role within an ethic of humility. It is also an ethic requiring embrace by those others involved in the same policy process.

c   **The leadership role should be as much about being able to live with uncertainty, as with having to move quickly to response.** In a world where the complex and wicked are better recognized, time would be needed in order to frame problems which reflected upon such complexity and wickedity. As Clarke (2015) argued, this requires that the leadership role is framed less within a belief about the ultimate control of all situations, and more within a frame of what the poet John Keats called 'negative capability', and what Durka (2002) p.1, called 'learned uncertainty' – the ability to remain comfortable with uncertainty, and to provide oneself and others with space for reflection, rather than with feeling the need to rush into action. In a belief system predicated upon control, decisiveness can often be little more than a hasty reaction to external pressure, and reflection viewed only as indecisiveness. In a world characterized by too much concern with acting quickly, the ability to remain comfortable with uncertainty and to resist the temptation to reify things until further clarity is acquired, are essential qualities to be nurtured for a more sustainable leadership.

d   **Ultimately, the role of the educational leader is as much about asking the right questions as providing the right answers.** It follows from this then that a major role for an educational leader lies in suggesting that there are not only tame and wicked problems, but that there are also tame and wicked responses, and that a crucial first thing is to identify what kind of problem

is being dealt with. This is critical because going for tame
options when wicked ones are required almost certainly leads to
damaging and unsustainable consequences.

2   **Developing the role with stakeholders.**

Given the nature of wicked problems, and the consequent framing of the
leadership role, there are a number of implications for other stakeholders'
involvement in school functioning and problem-solving.

a   **The leadership role should be as much about creating the right
    conditions for dealing with wicked problems, as with attempting
    to solve such problems.** If educational leaders need to embrace an
    ethic of humility more than one of certainty, they cannot expect to
    be, nor must they be expected to be, the sole creator of responses to
    wicked problems. They and all other stakeholders must recognize
    that their central role cannot be one of personally identifying the
    nature of a wicked problem, and then of leading others on some
    transformative and charismatic journey to the resolution of that
    issue. Instead, they and others must recognize the limits of (all
    of) their understanding, and the varieties of understandings that
    different stakeholders bring to the problem. Their role then is more
    about the use of words, actions and strategies facilitating problem
    identification and resolution among this larger community. Their
    role then must be as much about creating the right conditions for
    dealing with wicked problems, as with attempting to solve such
    problems themselves. And part of this role lies in educating others
    to recognize the different personal frames that stakeholders bring
    to bear upon a problem. As Datnow and Park (2009) suggest, in
    an age of increasing complexity, where multidirectional change is
    a given, co-construction is going to be the best way of developing
    adequate responses; and as Marion and Uhl-Bien (2001, p. 394)
    suggest, a leader's role will then in many situations be as much
    about 'creating transformational environments, rather than
    creating the innovation itself'.

b   **Part of the role of an educational leader must be to educate
    others to the limits of what can be promised.** This leads naturally
    to the recognition that responses need to be as complex and
    wicked as problems are. Such responses are likely to be 'messy'
    or 'clumsy', consisting not of silver bullets but of 'silver buckshot'
    (see Rayner, 2006; Grint, 2008' Verweij and Thompson, 2011).
    Such terms may initially not be that appealing: after all, they
    do not promise instant, universal or permanent solutions, but
    instead suggest that one does the best one can, but that a set of
    wicked circumstances necessarily limits the degree of certainty in
    a successful outcome. The role of an educational leader is then in

part to educate others to the limits of what can be promised. It is a lesson that certainly needs applying to most political cultures.

c   **They should however learn to recognize that different strategies are needed in arriving at responses.** However, despite the need for the frames that others bring to problems, and despite the almost essentially clumsy nature of most responses, this does *not* mean that leaders cannot and should not take a lead in dealing with specific kinds of problems. As Verweij and Thompson (2011) suggest, there are at least four different strategies for solving wicked problems: hierarchical, collaborative, individual and fatalist, and *all* may be needed at one time or another. Coming to appreciate which one of them – or which combination of them – is the most suitable for a particular problem is another step in creating the transformational environment in which problems can be properly addressed.

d   **They need to recognize that the role is as much inherently political as it is transformative.** So finally many will recognize that not only is the leader's role an educative one – a leading out from a simplistic and tame framing of problems to a better understanding of more complex and wicked one – but it is also an inherently **political** role. As argued elsewhere (Bottery, 2016) this is inevitably messy, inelegant leadership. There is no blank canvas upon which to paint a leadership portrait. Each leader comes to a particular context with a unique combination of skills and values, but is unlikely to find there problems which are mostly tame in nature, and that there are therefore few perfect responses. Leaders are by the nature of the role they play what Grint (2008) calls 'bricoleurs': individuals who must fashion out of an existing situation negotiated definitions of problems and responses, with inputs from many stakeholders. This is messy leadership, as leaders must judge when they have on board sufficient stakeholders to act in a timely manner. They are then more likely to achieve sustainable change by developing stakeholder relationships than they are by assuming that change is made through power-based or transformational compliance. Such an approach will not be perfect, and there will be few silver bullets, but it is more sustainable.

3   **Implementing the role for students.**

If educational leaders frame their role in the manner described, then a crucial element of this is going to be in educating their students towards such understanding in at least four different ways:

- in the tame and wicked realities of problems and responses,
- in the differences between the tame and the wicked,

- in the reality of the framing of problems and responses,
- on the limits of what can be promised and achieved in a wicked reality.

a **Student education must understand and reflect upon the nature of a wicked reality.** It then follows logically that the education of students must reflect the understandings described above. A beginning would be in educating students to consider the nature of causality, and in particular the consequences of holding linear as opposed to complex and systemic views of causal reality, and then of tame as opposed to wicked understandings of the world. A deeper appreciation of such differences would help students better conceptualize the nature of problems, and lead to a better understanding of the nature of the responses that are required.

b **Educational leaders must show students how equally important it is to listen to others' truths as it is to tell others their own.** A second understanding would then be in the difference between an ethic of certainty and one of humility. Schein (2013) argues that educating students into the former tends to lead individuals into telling others their 'truths', rather than in listening to others' 'truths'. Adopting the latter position would likely more often lead to a greater degree of tolerance of others' views; and in a world of many wicked problems, which require responses which may never completely resolve the problem, educating students into an ethic of humility opens up more of the space within which others' points of view can be viewed, and differences reconciled.

c **A third element of students' understanding then lies in appreciating the necessity of personal framing.** Without such appreciation, there is real danger of failing to recognize that all human beings, consciously or unconsciously, select different data, different information from that which surrounds and is available to them, and that others don't necessarily see the world in the same way, because they come to it with different experiences, different values and different frames. This once again has profound implications for the citizens of the future, and for toleration and reconciliation.

d **Educational leaders should educate students into the dangers of believing in too much certainty, predictability and control.** Given the above, part of a student's education should be in a greater awareness of the hubris of believing in an essentially predictable and controllable world. An epistemology of humility suggests that there are things that we know we know (though many others may doubt that we do); but that there is much that we know we don't know (though others may have useful answers here); and finally that there is very likely a great deal that we don't know we don't know. An embrace of a 'wicked' education is then an embrace of humility, provisionality and tolerance, and a rejection of the simplistic, linear and uni-dimensional, and the too-quick assignation to others of blame and guilt. This not only forms a vision statement for the sustainable leader in education: it frames a vision for a more sustainable world.

Conclusion: From conceptualizing to investigating the wicked reality of individual leadership

The tame and the de-contextualized are inadequate ways of solving the wicked problems of education and educational leadership. As Honig (2009) argues, it is not enough for policy-makers to ask, and for educational leaders to accept, that educational improvement and leadership sustainability can be attained by simply asking the tame question 'What works?' Instead of asking 'What works' we need to ask: 'What works for whom, where, when, and why?' (see Pawson and Tilley, 1997). This increases the complexity of the question, but it also increases the likelihood of a measure of success. As Yin, Lee and Wang (2014, p. 300) point out, when leaders accept, because of a strong compliance culture, that 'it is not the time to consider whether to implement this reform or not, but to think how to implement it well', they fail to sufficiently problematize the issue of implementation, and tame conceptualization adds to the wickedity of the problems to be faced further down the road.

The crucial question for this book then is to answer the question: What makes for greater leadership sustainability in a wicked world? The previous analysis suggests the need to frame the leadership role within this wicked world, and this then implies the need to develop their role with stakeholders, and to take this understanding into the education of their students. But this is not another prescription for another form of 'designer leadership'. One of the key understandings from over a decade of our research on leadership and its sustainability is how individual the nature of leadership is, and how individual the framing of the role needs to be. Much of this insight derives from the use of a method of investigation which interviews educational leaders, and from which a written portrait is produced of these individuals to describe how they function in the role. It is a methodology that not only provides insights into what sustains individual leaders, but may also provide one of the means of sustaining them. The next and final introductory chapter then explains how this approach works.

CHAPTER THREE

Portrait Methodology:

A Window into Understanding Leadership Sustainability

Introduction

The previous two chapters have examined the background to current concerns about the sustainability of educational leadership – both of the individual leader, and of the role itself. A picture has emerged of educational leaders over the last twenty years working in many education systems that are increasingly characterized by a paradoxical mixture of greater control and greater marketization. Some of these are low-trust cultures, which have increased the surveillance of individual practitioners, and thereby increased the pressures on them. Their sustainability has also been threatened by the tameness of some policy approaches in an increasingly wicked world, and when this happens, the ambiguity and paradox generated by centralist measures may not be appreciated. Sustainability is also compromised when policies fail to address the uniqueness of the contexts within which leaders work (Hoyle and Wallace, 2006). These then are strong contributory factors in problems of recruiting individuals to educational leadership positions, and in the retention of those already in such positions, particularly in much of the Western world.

It was against such a background that a research approach was sought which would help investigate the extent to which educational leaders were able to mediate governmental legislation within their local contexts. A variant of portrait methodology was thought well suited to these purposes. Portrait methodology is a qualitative approach, which uses the transcripts from standard semi-structured interviews to produce written descriptions, or 'portraits', of individuals dealing with the challenges surrounding them. It is an approach where a researcher goes one stage further than an ethnographer, who listens *to* a story, and instead listens *for* a story (Lawrence-Lightfoot and Davis, 1997, p. 13). For Hackman (2002, p. 54) this means that

> the portraitist searches for the authentic central story as perceived by the actors within the setting.

Of course, many different stories could be told by researchers using this approach, for portraiture is necessarily an interpretive exercise, which cannot assert any ability to penetrate to some objective reality, though the range of such stories is conditioned by the actual words spoken, and by how the subjects respond to their portraits. So there is always a fine balance between what the interviewee says and what they mean, and what the interviewer understands by what is said, and how they express that understanding. Yet the research team found it constantly surprising how often those whose portraits were written enthusiastically agreed that this was 'them' and perhaps as surprisingly, on occasions took considerable comfort from the fact that someone had 'seen' what or who they really were, and what they faced. The comment by one Hong Kong principal that *'in many ways the portrait comes back as a confirmation of what I was and what I always have been'* is not untypical of the reactions seen.

Portrait methodology is not new. A variant of it had been used earlier in the United States by Lawrence-Lightfoot (1983), and was later discussed in depth by herself and Hoffman Davis (1997). In the educational leadership field, the portrait approach has been described and discussed by Hackman (2002), and Waterhouse (2007), while English (2008) describes portraiture as one of twelve variations of forms of life-writing. Portraiture is a third-person rather than a first-person form of life-writing, and therefore sits in the qualitative research field with biographies, portrayals and profiles.

English distinguished between them by seeing portrayals as (p. 179) 'more biographical and more advanced on the birth-death axis', while profiles and portraits he suggested, were 'usually confined to a few contexts or one major context' (ibid.). As will be seen, we found that the portrait approach actually has more potential than is suggested here.

The distinctiveness of this variation

The particular variant the current team developed has a number of characteristics.

A first is that, in order to avoid leading interviewees in identifying particular challenges, the team used open-ended questions in semi-structured interviews, attempting to capture the thoughts, feelings and self-reflections of these individuals in particular contexts at particular moments in time. Interviews were then conducted where interviewees selected from a 'basket' of open-ended questions: '*What is your greatest satisfaction in the role?*' and '*What is the most prominent on-going problem you face?*' are examples of such questions, as the respondent is given the opportunity to supply the answer which is most appropriate to them, rather than selecting from a list supplied by the interviewer. It does not use the extensive and multi-method approach taken, for instance, by Lawrence-Lightfoot (1983). In our approach, while attention is paid to school literature, to the school's written policies, and where possible to short tours of the school by the individuals, these act only as background context, and as informal ways of getting to know the individual being interviewed. They do not make major contributions to the creation of the portraits.

Given that these portraits are based almost exclusively upon the perceptions of the interviewees, it might be argued that little confidence can be placed in them, because they are not confirmed by other kinds of data. Indeed, it might be argued that this is little different here from interview methods in other kinds of research, as they all seem to share the same problems: interviewees need not present a full picture of what they think and feel, may only provide answers which the interviewee thinks the interviewer wants to hear, or may simply not tell the truth to the interviewer. However, there are a number of strong reasons for believing that the responses given in this research were as truthful as the interviewees could be. One reason lies in the fact that all interviewees were promised confidentiality and anonymity at the outset. Indeed, at re-interview, a number of respondents commented that this allowed them to be more open about their real thoughts and feelings. As a Hong Kong principal said: '*It's a good chance for me to be myself.*' Only two interviewees – those of the portraits in Chapter 4 – were happy to be identified, and this is the only occasion in the book where anonymity is not utilized, and real names are used.

A second reason is that the respondents understood and were grateful that the interview was not part of a programme for monitoring their performance, particularly by Ofsted, the Office for Standards in Education, which was created in 1992 to inspect English schools. They were very clear to us that this allowed them to be open in their views. As one UK head teacher said: '*I would have been much more guarded to an Ofsted inspector, or anyone from a local authority, because you know they have another agenda.*' Such confidence is also supported by their behaviours at interview. Some had said that they had nothing to hide, and talked with great openness about sensitive issues (see for instance, the remarkably candid portraits in Chapters 6 of this book). Others talked and behaved as if the anonymity and confidentiality gave them a private space to discuss issues not available to them elsewhere. As another UK head teacher said '*You go on a management course ... and fill in a profile ... it's going to feed that agenda ... . As opposed to someone who is coming in and saying, ok, where do you think you are going? Such as you did.*' Finally, virtually all of the interviewees had something critical to say of themselves and their situation, and it seems very likely that had these individuals been acting self-protectively, they would have revealed less, and less convincing and complex portraits would have been created.

Moreover, even though the content of individual portraits lacked confirmation from other sources, they still have considerable potential and significance, as a person's perceptions and beliefs can on their own determine an individual's behaviour. If, for instance, it is strongly believed that a job no longer provides personal satisfaction, and that it creates too much pressure, such beliefs are quite sufficient in themselves to affect an individual's decision-making processes, to alter their relationships with others, to impact on a school's performance and to influence decisions on the timing of retirement. An individual's 'truth' may not accord with another external version, but it can be the deciding factor in an individual's sustainability in the leadership role.

A second characteristic of the approach is that the questions asked focused primarily on the situation that individuals were currently facing, even if some of this present needed to be understood in terms of past events and future possibilities. This gives the portrait approach a different emphasis from others which might be called life-history approaches, though they do share some strong similarities. Kelchtermans (1993, pp. 443–56), for instance, suggests that they all tell subjective stories located within particular contexts, which are affected by these contexts, and that the person constructing the story changes as the story itself develops. Nevertheless, portrait methodology differs significantly in terms of focus. Bryman (2001, p. 316) suggests that the life-history method 'invites the subject to look back in detail across his or her entire life course' and displays 'a clear commitment to the processual approach of social life, showing how events unfold and interrelate in people's lives'. Our approach, however, was far more concerned with portraying an individual at a given moment in time, with respect to the job they did and how they did it, the challenges they faced and how well they felt they were currently tackling these issues.

Our variant of portrait methodology was then originally viewed as cross-sectional in nature, as an attempt to capture the views and feelings of an individual at a particular moment in time. We were, however, to find that it could be used for longitudinal purposes as well. As we re-interviewed a number of educational leaders, these interviews and portraits began, over a period of time, to form a richer picture of that individual, which added depth to personal reflection, as individuals at the second interview often commented upon how they had re-read the first portrait before the second one, only to be surprised at how much they had forgotten, and how much they had changed during this period.

A **third distinctive feature** of this variation lies in that it attempts a clear separation of voice between the researcher and the researched. This makes it quite different from Lawrence-Lightfoot's approach, for example, who deliberately wove the investigator's voice into her portraits. When this is done, as Hackman (2002, p. 53) suggests, 'the line of demarcation between researcher and researched … does become a bit more hazy'. This is probably the reason for English's criticism (2000, p. 21) when he argues that by privileging the view of the portraitist, there is 'no external independent referent for ascertaining the truth-telling capacity of the portraitist'. In the variant we developed, such interweaving and privileging of access was never felt useful nor necessary: while a portrait 'story' was written by the researcher, we tried to be as faithful as possible to the perceived meaning of the interviewee. To this end, respondent validation was always used, and so both portrait and transcript were sent back to the interviewee for their comments. By so doing, interviewees were then able to reflect upon the portrait construction, and disagree with it if they felt it was not a fair representation. Very few have had anything to say in this respect, and normally comments made concern little more than factual, spelling or typographical errors.

A **final distinguishing feature** of our variant is that though the use of a portrait approach is not unique in educational leadership research, its emerging use as a professional development tool almost certainly is. As will be described later in the book, we have also developed it to be a reflective tool for educational leaders to use for their own personal and organizational benefit. As we shall see, it then not only examines the current sustainability of an educational leader; it may also contribute to such sustainability as well.

Constructing the methodology

The research then was first piloted and conducted in England in the early 2000s, and a first cohort of twelve primary principals was selected, in part based on geographical proximity to the UK researcher's university, but with the intention to have represented in the portraits both experienced and inexperienced head teachers; males and females; principals who worked in 'comfortable' and 'difficult' schools, and those from denominational and non-denominational schools. When the opportunity arose to conduct research in Hong Kong, the same approach was taken there, and eventually an initial cohort of twenty-four English and twenty-four Hong Kong primary and secondary principals were interviewed. In England, only the English member of the team conducted the primary school interviews, while the majority of the secondary interviews were conducted with two Hong Kong academics also attending. In Hong Kong itself, given that the principals were all Cantonese, the offer was made for the interviews to be held in Cantonese. On very few occasions this was accepted, but in most the principals were happy to be interviewed in English, and a novel approach was then taken, with the English interviewer leading the interviews in English, but with the invitation for the interviewees to talk in Cantonese should they find it easier to express themselves in that way. This carried a number of potential challenges. One was that having what amounted to a small group of interviewers could prove intimidating to an interviewee. A second was that there might be misunderstanding at both linguistic and cultural levels. A third was that the lead (English) interviewer might not have known that he did not know something, and so failed to raise it. All of these issues were discussed beforehand, and a number of strategies were adopted to overcome these problems.

- A first was the very careful piloting of interview questions with both academics and principals.

- A second was the provision to interviewees of the questions beforehand in both English and Cantonese.

- A third was the opportunity for the Cantonese interviewers to interject at any time if they felt something had been misunderstood – which did happen on occasions.

- A fourth strategy was to leave plenty of time at the end for both interviewee and Cantonese interviewers to raise any issues or difficulties.

- A final strategy was that immediately after each interview, a sustained discussion took place between the interviewers about whether the lead interviewer had misunderstood answers or omitted important questions through ignorance of language, culture or context.

The result of taking such care was that the approach worked remarkably well, with a number of interviews ending up as bilingual conversations between three to four people, a principal and two to three interviewers. The degree of success here had not been expected, but was extremely enjoyable, open and informative.

In determining the kinds of interview questions asked, published academic literature, official documentation and personal experience were used, as well as short interviews with principals, concerning the key questions they felt would be important as an initial scoping tool. The result was that a number of important external issues were raised, particularly concerning the effects of legislation over the previous two decades, the inspection procedures used by government, the effects of marketization, parental choice and competition, and whether time pressures and lack of energy were issues for them. However, in addition, because views at pilot interviews had suggested that personal relationships could be as problematic as externally generated issues, questions were asked allowing considerable flexibility in identifying personal 'issues' or 'problems'. The semi-structured format allowed detailed exploration of issues, and transcriptions of these interviews were then used to produce a person's portrait.

Producing a written portrait

A number of stages were involved in a portrait's production. Initially, head teachers or principals were contacted, the purpose of the research explained, as was the promise to make all portraits anonymous, and of their total control over content throughout the research process. Permission to tape interviews was always asked, and was always granted. They were also told that they could delete or change any of the content up to the moment of publication. This, it is believed, helped generate trust and confidence in the interviewers and the process. The questions were either posted or emailed well in advance of the interview. While we realized that this might lead to the preparation of 'fabricated' responses beforehand, this was done in part to generate trust, and also to allow interviewees the time to reflect on these questions. As demonstrated elsewhere in this book, such trust was repaid and has reaped rich dividends.

The interview was always conducted at the interviewee's school. Full explanation of the procedure was once more given prior to the interview, and the interviewee was asked if he/she had anything to ask. When this was completed, the recorder was turned on, and the interview conducted. A verbatim transcript of the interview was subsequently made, and the accuracy of the transcript checked by reading it at the same time as the tape of the transcript was listened to. Issues discussed were written in the margin, while key responses to the issues were highlighted.

The portrait writer then placed the transcript to one side and, based upon listening to the tape and reading the transcript, began portrait construction by drawing up a preliminary set of what were termed 'aerial codes' – reflections on what were perceived by the interviewer as the respondents' main concerns, their views on their ability to deal with these and the strategies they used. These preliminary codes then framed the beginning of the first draft of the portrait, being used as section headings for the description. For each of these sections, the transcript was then checked for such discussion, and a summary written of the interviewee's position on these issues, with extensive use of their own words present in most sentences of the portrait (see Chapters 4 and 6 for examples). However, as the transcription was checked, and as the sections were written, there were sometimes felt to be other better ways of describing the overall picture, and so some of the initial code descriptions were amended, as occasionally were the number of codes.

When the portrait was eventually completed, the portrait and transcript were sent to the interviewee for their thoughts and comments, and an invitation was made for further discussion. Some head teachers/principals provided written comments on their portrait; others were happy to discuss these by phone; others invited the researcher back for lengthier discussion. Later in the process, as we shall see, re-interviewing became standard practice in order for the team to investigate the effects that the transcript and portrait had had on the interviewee. Very few changes were made on the basis of such feedback, and as noted earlier were nearly always concerned with matters of expression, or occasionally, misperceptions of an interviewee's comment. If this happened, the portrait was amended and then sent back to the interviewee for their approval.

The range of portrait uses so far

One of the pleasant surprises of using this approach has been the discovery of its considerable adaptability. So far, it has been used in five different ways:

(i)   To investigate the thoughts and feelings of twenty-four UK primary and secondary head teachers, and twenty-four primary and secondary Hong Kong principals, on the nature and extent of the challenges that they faced in their role. In a small number of cases, individuals were re-interviewed a second time and further portraits written. Material from this project is used in Chapters 6 and 9.

(ii) To understand the sustainability challenges to and support for two sets of leaders, one in the UK, the other in Hong Kong, caused by the organizational cultures within which they worked. In total, seventeen portraits were written for this project. This is covered in Chapter 7.

(iii) As a developmental exercise for staff at the Hong Kong Institute of Education, members of staff and the authors of this book interviewed and wrote portraits for nine principals.

(iv) To investigate how individual leaders go about developing an education for sustainable development. Ten people were interviewed, of which two portraits are presented in Chapter 4, which demonstrate how highly effective leadership can be enacted through very different approaches.

(v) To determine the impact upon these leaders from the reading and reflection on their own portraits. Twelve individual impressions of their own portraits were then gathered. This initiative is reported in Chapter 11.

In total, then, this approach has been used with nearly 100 head teachers and principals, most times to gain a cross-sectional portrait, on a few occasions to gain a longitudinal picture.

(vi) Finally, a small number of doctoral candidates have successfully adopted this approach (Collins, 2011; Fabrizi, 2013; O'Dea, 2018). Collins adopted it to investigate the reasons why students left a college in Ireland during or at the end of their first year; Fabrizi used it to investigate whether personality was an important factor in US teachers using fantasy literature to teach critical literacy; and O'Dea used it as both a cross-sectional and longitudinal tool to investigate the personal changes individual Chinese students underwent in a year's study at an English University.

Benefits of this approach

There seem to be at least three benefits from the use of the methodology.

(i) It focuses specifically on the individuals, rather than on their performance in the role.

This is important, as interviewees quite often remarked how activities like their formal mentoring, or the visit of school improvement partners were normally used as one element in the measurement of their performance in the role, and only tangentially focused on providing them with support as individuals in a leadership role. Indeed, none of the individuals interviewed could think of professional provision which precisely focused on them in the way this approach did:

When the SIP (School Improvement Partner) comes in, it will be about school issues, it won't be about me.

What people have got to realise is that this is personal development ...
and that is so important ... and yet is overlooked by a lot of people.

It then seems very important not just to reflect on what is done, but to understand the person who does it, and why they do it. This is because underlying motivations, values and concerns, and previous memories and experiences, as well as deeper lying aspects of personality all tend to mediate the pressures, challenges and opportunities that are faced. If this is not understood – both by others and by the actors themselves – then the ability to develop better personal strategies, performances and coping mechanisms is not developed. The portrait approach then allows an individual, and a knowledgeable other who does not have a vested interest in assessing their performance against external standards, to discuss such things in considerable depth. Then, if additional insights are produced, further discussion might then take place on such needs – not just professional needs, but emotional and spiritual ones as well. Through this approach, then, other, perhaps more important issues than those of performance can be identified and responded to.

(ii)   Portraits provide individuals with feedback on how others see them.

Having another person's view can provide an individual with an independent source of feedback on how others see them. This does not just provide potentially valuable self-knowledge; it can also be invaluable to anybody whose job it is to present a public image which may not always match what is felt inside. The portrait then presents an image of themselves, which they may not see, or which they may not realize is 'leaking out'. Thus a tendency within an interview for a respondent to return to the same issue may well lead the interviewer to point this out in both interview and in portrait, and for the interviewee, perhaps for the first time to notice this, and then to reflect on whether this indicates a concern greater than they had formerly realized. In this way, the portrait approach can provide a trusted outsider's view of personal concerns upon which the interviewee can reflect.

(iii)   The process allows the individual to talk without feeling that
        they are being evaluated on what they say, and thereby facilitates
        greater honesty.

As a number of interviewees remarked, the role of 'a trusted outsider' is pivotal to the success of this method:

The critical thing is the relationship and whether I trust them [the interviewer].
   It's got to be somebody that you trust. In many ways I've let my guard down during this [the portrait interview], *because you don't stop performing when your SIP walks in, you crank it up a notch, you know*

what they are going to expect you to be, and you've got to be in character. It's the same with an Ofsted inspection.

Now, as already noted, in many countries currently, much professional reflection is facilitated with a strong focus on performance for school improvement, and this is normally conducted by individuals who are appointed for that purpose. While school and individual performance is clearly very important, a focus which excludes other issues important to the individual can lead to their lowered morale. In addition, and as a number of interviewees remarked, they were always likely to be on their guard where hierarchy and authority were involved in interviewee situations, always likely to be careful about what they said:

> *They* [Ofsted inspectors or members of an LEA] *will be making some kind of judgement on you and* [therefore] *what you say, you say favourably, to try and ensure that the judgement will always be favourable. I know you will make your judgement, but with respect, it doesn't influence my career. Potentially, the judgments made by Ofsted and the local authority do* [matter] *... and therefore you are guarded.*
>
> *I don't have to distrust you because I don't think you would have other purposes in getting something from me.*
>
> *I know* [with this interview] *that is not going to end up on ME1* [a local authority form]. *It's not going to be reported to Ofsted, it's not going to be reported to anyone else ... it's not going to be something for which I'm going to be held to account.*

In most low-trust environments, individuals will be concerned that their comments will be taken down and used against them. The portrait interviews, however, were conducted by individuals who sometimes were known to and trusted by the interviewees. When the interviewees didn't know the interviewers, the interviewees were normally given the names of other head teachers or principals who had been previously interviewed whom they could contact, to talk about the process, and about the nature and purpose of the individuals conducting the interviews. In addition, because promises of confidentiality and anonymity were rigidly adhered to, we felt our approach was more likely to inspire the degree of trust necessary to enable the interviewee to feel they could speak with freedom. Our results bear this out.

Leadership and confidentiality

Why, however, should educational leaders, fulfilling their role to the best of their ability, need confidential sessions with others? Why would they not wish to have all their thoughts out in the public domain? One reason is that the best decisions are normally made when space is given for 'mulling over' a problem, where alternatives are raised, discussed and sometimes dismissed, and where sufficient time is given for the right decision to be made. If however, problems are identified as 'tame' when in fact they have more of a 'wicked' nature about them, and when they are framed too quickly, solutions may be produced which will not work because they have addressed poorly described problems. Indeed, when solutions or responses are identified too rapidly, and decisions made too hastily, problems may actually be exacerbated. Where the nature of a problem *is* adequately captured, mulling over a range of possible solutions is almost always going to be beneficial, as it provides individuals with the thinking space, preferably with trusted others, to develop more nuanced understandings, and thus facilitates the ability to think creatively, and generate more productive solutions.

The position of the educational leader then can be an isolated one, increasingly subject to what may appear to them as 360-degree-wide surveillance and evaluation of their performance. Such surveillance can lower morale and stifle creativity, lead to caution and conservativism in action, and pressures may then build up which contribute to problems of recruitment and retention to leadership roles. In such a world, it is important for both practical and ethical reasons to create a process in which educational leaders feel that they can talk about what concerns them most, without feeling that what they say will be noted down and used in evidence against them at some later date. The portrait approach provides such intellectual, emotional, spiritual and professional space. It champions the need for leadership privacy and places the notion of trust centre stage. It celebrates the idea that the core of educational activity and achievement is not achieved through abstract visions, strategies or processes, but through people. It provides a space where individuals can reflect upon themselves and their unique contributions to the educational process.

All of these benefits may help to reduce the stress upon educational leaders, because concerns over leadership recruitment and retention seem in part linked to increased rates of pressure on those in the role. An important use of the portrait approach is then as a means of providing individuals with the non-judgemental space to reflect upon themselves and their performance, and to develop supportive networks of peers who can help to sustain them. This approach then could be an important strategy in the remediation of current issues of recruitment and retention with respect to leadership positions.

Conclusion

This chapter has then outlined why and how our portrait approach was developed, and what forms it has taken. It has also provided evidence of some of its perceived benefits to those interviewed. In particular, it has begun to show that it is possible to better understand how leaders in different cultures feel about their role, and what they think would make it more sustainable.

The next two chapters then provide examples of this 'portrait' approach and, in doing so, examine further issues of individual sustainability. Both emphasize the highly personal and individual nature of the leadership role. The first of the chapters provides portraits of two individuals, both highly rated in official circles, but who have managed high-quality practice in very different, distinctive and personal ways. The second of the chapters provides two more portraits of individuals, both anonymized, who were new in the role and facing challenges that required real resilience. They came from very different contexts and cultures, but required a similar toughness in their make-up. Both chapters then demonstrate how measures for greater sustainability need to be tailored to an individual's personality and situation. It is to the first that we now turn.

PART ONE

The Micro-Context of Sustainability

CHAPTER FOUR

Individuality and Leadership Sustainability

Chapter outline

Introduction

The reality of leadership is one of individuals working with others within unique combinations of particular levels of contexts. Yet too often, the individual and contextualized nature of leadership can be seen as a hindrance to the ambitions of higher level policies, and existing and prospective leaders are then seen as needing to be trained in desired competencies in order to 'smooth' out such differences so that similar leadership responses can be assured time after time. Yet this is not only a radically impoverished view of humanity, it is also a highly limited and insufficient view of how to achieve leadership excellence. In an age of new and challenging demands at all levels of policy, the need for a variety of approaches to deal with new contextual challenges could not be more urgent. This chapter then uses leadership portraits of two very different individuals to demonstrate how their very dissimilar approaches can both produce results recognized as leading exemplars. These portraits also send out the important message that outstanding leadership needs to be seen as, in part, a function of individual personalities, driven by moral purpose. This not only suggests a tension between the uniqueness of leadership and standardized approaches to headship; it also raises questions about policies for developing models of sustainable leadership.

Tensions in policy imperatives for leadership

Some of these concerns have been recognized in recent years. While Gunter (2016) suggests that many leadership approaches are still heavily based upon transformative approaches, official pronunciations are now more thoughtful, moving away from visions of single transformative individuals leading workforces in the delivery of national standards through trained sets of competencies, towards more contextualized and value-driven approaches.

Not that targets, benchmarks and punitive inspections have disappeared; official views of the nature of educational leadership can often seem an uneasy blend of different concerns. The micro-assessment of individual performance and obligations placed on leaders to deliver on standards closely aligned to policies of economic growth sit almost grudgingly next to recognition of the moral, contextualized and distributed nature of leadership. Gronn's (2003) description of 'designer leadership' – individuals trained in desired competencies, and then inspected and rewarded or punished on these – needs contrasting with the earlier assertion by Leithwood et al. (1999) that 'outstanding leadership is exquisitely sensitive to context'. In the same way, heavily steered versions of leadership, where targets and accountability seem to constitute the core of leadership, need contrasting with deeper recognition of the leadership role by books with titles like *The Moral Imperative of School Leadership* (Fullan, 2004) and by publication of official texts like that of Porritt et al. (2009) with a section beginning (p. 12) *Leading from Moral Purpose,* and with a diagram of leadership practice (p. 25) with 'moral purpose' as the quality at the very centre.

So how should effective leadership be developed? What model of leadership should be adopted? In 2007, the English NCSL (Jackson, 2007) did take a position on the kind of leader required, and espoused a 'distributed' model as the best way forward. However, one might ask whether the adoption of any particular model of leadership is the most important consideration, and whether this needs to be determined more by the presenting problem, the personalities and the particular context. This question is then examined through two portraits of English head teachers, and how they have approached the development in their schools of an Education for Sustainable Development (ESD). It is important to note two things here. The first is that this is the only chapter, and these the only examples, where the real names of the two leaders are used. This is because these individuals were confident of their approaches, and were happy to be known for them. Their real names then had been used in a previous article about these two individuals (Bottery, Wright and James, 2012). The other thing to note is that this chapter is not about ESD per se, but about the individuality of their very different approaches to ESD. Both have strong personalities, both have been nationally recognized for their work in this field; both have gained part-time doctorates while successfully fulfilling the role of head teacher (Dixon, 2009; Robinson, 2009); and both express clear views about ESD and its implementation. Yet they are very different individuals, with very different approaches to the subject. This chapter then provides contrasting portraits, where the interviewee's words are used wherever possible, and are signalled by italicized words and phrases in sentences. The chapter provides strong evidence that each has been successful in developing this area, and suggests the need for a policy approach to leadership development which recognizes, celebrates and supports the more individualistic, contextual and artistic nature of the role.

The David Dixon portrait

David described himself as 'pretty self sufficient', a man managing the practicalities of running a school, moving the school to a committed position on ESD, who saw the need for an academic and theoretical underpinning for such commitment, going beyond what he termed 'received wisdom'. At the time of interview, he had just completed a doctorate in the area, which had led to a fairly radical stance on what schools, education and society needed to do to address environmental sustainability issues.

Background and the path to headship

David's origins were largely in 'rural environments', and when it came to training as a teacher, it seemed natural to him to take environmental education as his main subject. He got his first job in 1979 in a middle school, one 'which had a strong emphasis on environmental studies'; from here, David 'aspired to be a subject leader' in the area, achieving this in 1985. At first he thought it was viewed as an important element of the curriculum, but then with the National Curriculum he thought that 'everything went back into subject boxes', and he felt it 'somehow jumped off the radar'. However, he still thought it 'made sense to teach in a cross-curricular way', and so 'I tried to keep most elements of it'. Even then there was a sense of being a man apart: 'I pursued it as a class teacher, but I found it was quite difficult to convince other teachers to adopt that approach, and part of that is still true today.' Now, as then, he feels that 'knowledge of environmental education and lifecycle education on the biology side is very scant in primary education ... but also the social side of it as well, the way that society operates in relation to the natural world'. Then and when interviewed, he felt it remained 'on the periphery'. He was promoted to deputy head teacher, and stayed at that level for six years, 'and then I became a head teacher'. At the time of interview, he had been a head teacher for fourteen years.

Setting up a programme of ESD

The school David inherited 'wasn't eco-friendly at all'. It was located in an area of council housing – which was 'no.3 in child poverty' in the local authority, a curious blend of the very old and the very new. It was 'based in an old army camp', and that was still easy to see, even if one thing David started to do 'was think about knocking the building about because it was so old and horrible'. A strong reason for doing this was that 'this made an impact in terms of how people started to perceive the school'. There were other kinds of problems that had to be faced: 'the learning environment was very poor' and he thought that if Ofsted (the English national school inspection body) had been doing inspections at that time, 'it would have been in special measures'. It wasn't just the learning environment that was a problem: 'the behaviour of the children was appalling, the curriculum wasn't working, so it was really a start from scratch job'. David was concerned to make 'the curriculum more motivational', and he thought that 'a cross-curricular approach' was the best way to achieve this. There is clearly a link here with sustainable development education, but he felt that there were two major problems he faced in making this link stronger. One was that some of his teachers were hampering the integration of various elements. These were individuals 'who don't particularly understand any of those elements very well'. It was important therefore 'to make it more understandable', and that was best accomplished, he suggested, by concentrating on 'a manageable chunk that people will understand ... it is trying to do a part that people will understand at a very practical level'.

The second problem was the initial 'very poor behaviour of the children', and while a 'rigid behavioural management scheme' was put in place, it was also felt necessary to 'make the curriculum more relevant to the children', and this was where 'the cross-curricular, hands-on experiential learning started to be introduced'. In terms of ESD, David concentrated at first on 'easy wins' and 'low hanging fruit': after introducing recycling bins, 'special events started to come in, green days, low energy days ... slowly introducing more of this into the curriculum'.

But David felt there remained ongoing problems. Because 'it's a big challenging school ... when we advertise for posts, we get very poor responses'. The result was that 'we can't select exclusively on how eco-enthusiastic somebody is'. Of course, 'people looking at our website know what our ethos is ... but we do have to do extra work with people who join the school, and particularly with younger teachers who are probably less aware on some of the issues'. The doctoral study backed this perception up: David found that it was largely 'a generational thing – the younger teachers are Thatcher's children – they are more self-centred. It's a different mind-set.' Part of his job then was to get 'some of these new teachers to look at *some of their own values, because I think unless you start to live a more sustainable life yourself, you can't go into a classroom and embed it in the curriculum very successfully'.*

The importance of ESD in the larger scheme of things

But if there was a lack of awareness of the ESD agenda at the school level, David did not feel that it stopped there. The change from link inspectors to SIPs (School Improvement Partners) had, for David, narrowed their role from an advisory to a monitoring one: '*I think the new SIPs have a smaller remit than the old link inspectors. When we had link inspectors ... there was more time and space to discuss some of these issues. But now there is not.*' The result was that '*the SIP and I have never had any discussions about this ... It has always been the case of just looking at your targets for improving attainment ... unless you can do it in the context of "how is it going to raise attainment?"*' The result had been that '*unless you can maintain your attainment at a certain level which is deemed to be acceptable, then if you start talking about this agenda you are sort of slapped down and reminded that you have got to get these other targets up*'.

David felt that this governmental concern with targets and attainment was very important in explaining why there was limited official backing for ESD: '*As yet, research is not showing a definitive link between an ESD approach and a raised attainment ... . This is why I think they are standing back and not making this statutory.*' However David was of the opinion that things might be changing: '*the OFSTED research that has been done is suggesting that there is a link ... . They have looked at schools with this sort of agenda and found that they tend to be better in terms of attainment.*' Nevertheless, David remained to be convinced of so direct an effect: '*who is to say which way this is causal ... . I think a lot of schools tend to be in the leafy suburbs, so you have got a lot of things that make an impact that aren't directly attributable to an eco-agenda.*'

The result then seemed to be that government priorities and its ministers were less than supportive of this agenda, unless it could be clearly demonstrated that the pursuit of ESD raised attainment. But even when it was given support, David was concerned about what was on offer. For a start he felt that '*there was no working definition like there is for other areas of the education system ... and it is easy to have tokenism ... you can have a green flag school, but it may not be a particularly sustainable school*'. He described current government, NCSL and Ofsted approaches as '*giving a sort of watered down version of what a sustainable school might be*'. Another problem for David was that most teachers and head teachers didn't really have a grounding in the knowledge base of this area from the physical and social sciences, though '*the [headteachers] who you could describe as the deeper green definitely do ... they understand how the planet basically works*'. Finally, David believed that to fully appreciate the problems humanity is facing one needed what he called '*a sort of eco-postmodern* stance': this needed to be '*critical of the modern in terms of the economic neo-liberal model*'. He felt then that there was a need to '*stand back and look at it in a critical way and literally look at radical alternatives*'. This meant being '*very sceptical of received wisdom, to question the way we have our economic system*'. Yet he saw very limited evidence of this perspective, only a rather diluted government version, '*through NCSL and OFSTED ... so you really have to put your head above the parapet to take things further, or to question policy*'. David recognized that '*that seems a bit subversive or outside the remit of what a school should be doing*', but felt that '*there are clearly issues that need addressing*'.

Unsurprisingly, given the '*watered-down*' approach he thought was being recommended, David also believed that '*the general CPD system and network really hasn't got this as a main agenda item ... you're not in schools encouraged to think about what should be the values of education ... there doesn't seem to be a lot of discussion of that, it seems to be all utilitarian, how we are going to implement things*'. The result was then unsurprising: '*It's very difficult to find out about these things in sufficient depth*.' This, for David, was a major motivation for reading for a doctorate.

The doctorate and its findings

There were other reasons that David gave for embarking upon a doctorate, however. The first – '*a bit of sado-masochism I suppose*' – may well be '*applicable to many doctoral students*'. The second – that '*I've always been interested in the theoretical sides of education ... because it helps to give you a fresh perspective on things*', is also likely to be fairly common among those who feel that '*you get very bogged down with the day-to-day stuff and don't always have the time to question it*'. But there was also a highly personal element here: '*It's going back to childhood experiences: I failed my 11+ and ended up going to quite a rough secondary modern ... it was only when I got to the end of teacher training that I thought of myself as being as good as others in terms of academic achievement, so it has given me the incentive to try and improve myself academically.*'

Finally, there was a '*practical angle*' as well: '*I always thought I never wanted to "soldier on" as a head to 60-65*', and doing a doctorate '*might give me some other career options*'.

The doctorate was centrally concerned with developing a new leadership model for ESD which asked whether it was '*valid to give someone a green label when we don't know what this means*'. To this end, David looked at '*definitions of greenness*', and then started to look at issues of '*green wash, green tokenism, how certain groups wanted to control what the definition of "greenism" is. And eventually it took me to green leadership ... and from there looking at the NCSL leadership approach towards sustainability ...*'

and exploring whether green leaders' used distributed leadership as the major way of making this idea a reality in their schools.

David ended up looking at *'eight leaders of green flag eco-schools ... it looked into their childhood and training and professional influences, to see if there were any commonalities which led to this line of thinking'*. One thing David thought was *'not insignificant'* was that *'six of them were from church schools'*, which he thought might be explained by their *'caring ethos'*. But beyond that, there seemed to be two different kinds of people in his sample who had gone for green flag status, what might be called the Utilitarian and the Committed. The Utilitarians consisted of those who saw ESD as a useful aspect of the curriculum, which could improve easily measured standards. But the Committed were *'a bit like myself, had a lot of childhood experiences, that led them down this road'* – they seem to have commitment which was *'really deep-seated'*; and they also seemed *'to be the type of leaders who lived their life in a sustainable way'*.

Interestingly, David thought that *'most of them did seem to share one common theme: they seemed to be very Machiavellian'*, by which David was referring to what he believed was a reality of much headship: that *'it is the head who is ultimately accountable'*, and David's belief was that *'if you are too distributed ... you may end up with people doing things which may ultimately make you suffer as a head'*. Moreover, he suggested, *'it seemed that the heads I was looking at (and I include myself in this) didn't follow distributed leadership: they might use it as a technique in order to deliver the ESD approach ... but their value system was based on the belief that we needed to do something to combat the ecological crisis'*. In other words, these heads – and again David included himself – had a personal *'moral framework they were working from'*, which they felt at times had to override a fully implemented distributed leadership model. This was why David said that he doubted the sense of *'the incessant promotion of distributed leadership'*: it had its place, but he felt that there were other (and sometimes more important) considerations and values that a leader had to address. For him, the driving force was very clear: *'We need to do something to combat the ecological crisis.'*

This was an interesting position for David to take, and it raises important questions. In particular, it seems to support a view that personal or distributed leadership may not depend upon a philosophical belief as much as a pragmatic one – that if you really need to achieve something, and the measures aren't in place, you may feel it is part of your role as a leader to lead on this issue. This may not be comfortable for some, but it may reflect the need to deal with a wicked rather than tame reality.

The Sue Robinson portrait

We have just seen that a critical element of David's approach to the leadership of ESD was the belief that you need to be an expert in the subject.

Thus, to lead and develop ESD would need a grounding in the natural and social sciences of economic, social and environmental sustainability. David's portrait describes a head teacher with just these qualities – he gained a doctorate in this area, and through personal values, staff selection, organizational acumen and the force of his personality, he had made this the distinguishing feature of his school. His school, like Sue's, was visited both by researchers and government officials, who wanted to know how these two head teachers performed so well. Both were individuals with a core moral purpose in their conception of the job. Both have gained doctorates part-time, but where David's was a study of 'green' leadership, Sue's was a study of the development of headship in a context of constant change and increased steerage of the profession. One of the main recommendations of her doctorate was of the need for governments to allow the greater exercise of personal and professional judgement by leaders in responding to local contexts. And while Sue recognized the importance of ESD, she had other priorities and was comfortable for others in the school to lead on it. Moreover, while David had strong reservations about the role of distributed leadership in driving this agenda, Sue made a strong case for its necessity if the ESD agenda was to be sustainable beyond her headship. This portrait therefore needs to cover her general approach before it talks about sustainability, because Sue's approach to ESD is largely a consequence of her vision of leadership.

Sue's background

Sue was a problem child: '*I wasn't a popular child in school, teachers never liked me, probably because I never shut up*.' She was '*privately educated*', but '*not terribly well behaved ... I was bored witless when I was at school*'. She '*left school at 15 ... dropped out of some A levels prior to university and never went*'. So as a child she was outspoken, easily bored and, one suspects, didn't like being told what to do without very good reason. If the girl is mother to the woman, then Sue seems a very good example, as the same traits seemed very much part of what she was at interview. But there were other traits which need describing: she was unconventional and surprising, and when interviewed, torrents of passionate words poured out of her mouth, and what she said much of the time was provocative and courageous, in that she dared to do and say many things that other head teachers would probably never dare utter. She declared that as a head teacher '*you can do what you like, you have been able to do what you want in the curriculum for years*'. She then went on to state flatly that '*I don't think I am remotely courageous*', that she was in fact '*incredibly lucky*', because she had had the good fortune of being surrounded by lots of capable people: '*I think people are actually a lot better than people usually give them credit for*'. She talked of the role of head teacher as really very simple, that at bottom all you have to do is trust people: '*The people I have trusted have all come through*'. And yet, as the interview proceeded, one realized that the strategy might be relatively simple to describe, but its cultivation and its assessment were based on a continuous process of talking, listening and consulting. She talked of how '*I am around the school like a rash, I am here at 7.00 am and I don't go until 6.00 pm ... but I walk round it, I go in and out of the classrooms ... . I talk to the staff, and the most important conversations are sitting at the desk at the end of the day ... it is here that you learn about school*'.

So Sue's approach may be relatively simple to describe – management through people – but its realization was anything but.

When Sue eventually decided to go into education, it was, she said, '*because my friend went into education*'. The choice as she described it was stark: '*It was either that or mucking out horses, and I decided it would ruin my nail polish.*' Nail polish or not, she found she had a gift for teaching – and that she cared about what happened to the children she taught: '*I actually met this child ... and he couldn't read. I was listening to him read, and he said, "I can't read" ... . I said you can read actually, but the words are all in your head, but you haven't actually chosen to say them yet*', and she showed him how; and with some justifiable pride told me how '*he is now a gynaecologist at a hospital*'.

Running the school

Sue is an enthusiast, not just about education, but about life generally, and certainly about her doctoral study. She talked of how '*I couldn't get enough of the reading ... it was like a light bulb*'. But enthusiasm didn't seem to get in the way of appreciating and utilizing others' talents: in fact it seems fuelled by it. She was clearly eclectic, looking for talent and help anywhere and everywhere, and cultivating it when she found it. When Sue described her school, the eruption of words and detail, along with protestations of how simple and straightforward it all was, could lead the outsider to think that there is something slightly mad or magical here. Certainly it is a highly personal approach, and it is perhaps unsurprising that she said that her favourite quote was that '*using standards and competences to describe leadership is like using a quantity surveyor rather than an artist to capture the grandeur of St. Pauls*'. But to think that this meant that her approach was a product of feeling and whimsy would be seriously misleading: there was a cleverly conceived and articulated plan here, which was organic rather than mechanical in nature, and it seemed central to how Sue and her school dealt with the issues of sustainability.

A critical aspect of Sue's leadership, like David's, concerned values, and their infusion into the school: '*I think what I set, from a head's point of view, is the school's values.*' And for Sue, probably '*our core value has to be respecting other people ... . And if you are doing that and caring for each other, and you are looking at being respectful, you have to be the same with the planet, because that is what our children are going to live in.'* A first link to sustainable values is then made – rather like Peter Singer's (1976) notion of an expanding circle of moral concern; in Sue's eyes, respecting and caring for other people was the inner part of a moral circle which should expand outward and lead to a respect and care for the planet as well.

But if part of the first phase was in identifying and developing what should be encompassed by moral concern, an equally important part was in creating a process which develops through other people: *'I think the key element is allowing your school to evolve through trust and relationships and distributed leadership.'* However, it's one thing to espouse the values; it's quite another to ensure that such values are embraced by the whole school. This is why Sue told me that *'it's not me, because lunch time supervisors will do it, our school business manager will do it, other children who come here will do it, it has to be shared'*, and the triumph for Sue came when the children said, for instance with respect to bullying, *'We don't do that here, that's not part of what we do.'*

But Sue could be disconcerting: uttering a statement like *'I think all you need are values, you don't need anything else, and you let everything else work itself out'* could sound like an open invitation to a government inspection team to put the school into special measures, but then she immediately made it clear that this wasn't all that was needed, *'Because you question all the time, and you say is this in the best interest of the children? Is this going to help make them good citizens? Is this going to help them access the future?'* Nor must one forget that she was in school early, home late, and always round the school *'like a rash ...'*, so while she thought that *'the beauty of primary education that it has that flexibility'*, the job, it is evident, still required huge amounts of continual looking, questioning and probing at what was being done.

So the values championed by Sue, when she arrived, were gradually embraced by the others at the school. They formed the backdrop to everything else. And Sue was clear that while she could have many ideas, she couldn't have them all, and for that she needed a talented staff. For her a core function of the head teacher then was being a *'strategic school leader, because you can't possibly know everything there is to know about everything'*. Again, disconcertingly, she could give the impression at times that this was all a matter of luck. She said that *'if you trust people, 90% of the time they will come through for you'*. But trust for her entailed checking that trust given was trust used appropriately. And it was clear that she had teeth as well, which were used when deemed necessary. Her enthusiasm was then backed up by massive hard work, as well as by a lack of toleration for those who didn't make the effort. This is also why she believed that *'you do need Ofsted ... . I've worked in a lot of schools, and ... you go in [to some] and cry, because you think how could you be allowed to do this to children?'*

The result of such an approach, for Sue, was that if you have a talented, committed and hardworking staff who you can trust, then (and again a little disconcertingly) '*you don't need a literacy or numeracy strategy, and you don't need a particular curriculum: what you need is children to have the skills ...* and the skills are *if they can problem solve, if they're creative and they enjoy it, and then they want to do it, that makes the curriculum*'.

So an ability to generate a set of core shared values was allied to a trust in others' abilities and commitment to creating a stimulating and complex curriculum; and these were backed up by her talking, visiting and watching, and watching and talking again. But there is still more to Sue's approach than that. She believed that if everyone shares the same core values, and has the same commitment, then '*trust works because people don't want to let you down*', and this means that other people will want to do some of the work of oversight and observing and talking as well. This is part of how Sue described what happened when she said that the school was '*actually run by a committee ... we have constantly got teacher voice, pupil voice, parent voice, and last week we had governors in. So it's this multi-layered approach all the way*', and when she said '*I think that is the only way that it works*', one begins to understand what distributed leadership meant for her.

Yet Sue's portrait has an extra layer of complexity which needs capturing, because, despite the talk of sharing and trusting, and distributing leadership, she was convinced that as a head teacher *you have to be 'charismatic'*, because, she thought '*the key in leadership is intentional influence*'. One then seems to end with apparent paradox – the advocacy of charismatic distributed leadership! Surely, one might argue, the roots of charisma and distribution are at odds, with the one saying 'follow me' and the other saying 'take the lead'? Sue thought this was not actually the case, and argued that the combination worked when charisma inspired confidence, trust (and being trusted), cooperation and collaboration in others, and which didn't stifle and overwhelm personal initiative, but actually encouraged it. So for Sue, a charismatic head needed to be able to motivate and encourage and, crucially, empower, because a strategy of '*Go in, follow me, I will solve your problems, is not sustainable, because when you are not there ...* '. For Sue, then sustainability was a critical issue, and she believed that her style of leadership encouraged it.

The meanings of sustainability

For Sue, sustainability '*is a catchall term*'. She used it in at least three different ways. It could be primarily about '*the curriculum and recycling and making sure the school is as green as it can be*'. And to really work, this couldn't be an isolated enthusiasm: it's '*a lot more than just learning to turn the lights off ... doing eight weeks of recycling*'. If it was going to be more about '*ensuring the sustainability of the planet, and green issues, then it had to be ... embedded all the way through, an integral part of the school*'.

But she also saw sustainability as a much broader concern: it was *'the sustainability of whatever you are doing – the sustainability of the SEN agenda, or sustainability of Children's Centres, or sustainability of distributed models of leadership'*. In this sense, the green agenda was one part of a larger objective, a process of *'looking at those elements that are necessary and allowing them to evolve organically'*, through debate, discussion, observation, talking, using different talents, etc. So when Sue said that the global green environmental agenda *'doesn't wake me up personally at night'*, it didn't mean that she wasn't interested: *'I can understand the intellectual argument ... . I think it is being realized that something has to be done about it'*, and her core values of respect and care, as we have seen, expanded to embrace global agendas. And it did mean that because she felt her most important concern at the school at the time of interview was that of addressing the needs of a *'very diverse community'*, this meant that her personal focus had to be on the *'personal, social and health agenda'*, and of the sustainability of that agenda.

Her focus here was balanced by the fact that she had set up a system whereby others at the school were empowered and trusted – and felt sufficiently trusted to bring up a concern about a green agenda and to pursue this. Sue candidly admitted that *'to a certain extent it's come on my radar because it has been brought to my attention, rather than that I have gone out and found it ... a lot of [ESD] sustainability started because people have an interest in it'*. So its identification as an important concern for the school didn't have to come from her, and nor was the *'curriculum imposed top down from the senior leadership team ... . it is not a question of someone sitting down and saying OK, we will make sustainability a part of our school ... it is everyone coming in with different ideas about it, and at different levels'*. One then begins to understand what she meant when she said *'it comes back down to people and relationships again you see'*.

A portrait embodying the paradox of charismatic distributed leadership probably needs to finish with another. Sue advocated the encouragement of personal and contextual solution of problems within a government framework where currently *'the biggest problem is micro-management'*, where government didn't allow individual leaders to use their professional judgements sufficiently. Her solution was quietly subversive: *'The leaders who succeed are the leaders who can manage the agenda ... and manage it in a way that they know is best for their children.'* So is this the best way to further the ESD agenda? Surprisingly perhaps, Sue believed that *'the government has to push it more, and I hate to say this but it has to push it through the control agenda, it has to push it through Ofsted'*. In a world where there may not be the time to develop a requisite number of charismatically distributive heads to sufficiently promote a vigorous system-wide ESD agenda, there may then need to be paradoxes not just at the personal and organizational level, but at the system level as well.

Conclusion

David and Sue became successful educational leaders largely because of who they were. Both rejected a competencies and standards-based approach to leadership, and instead chose – with some courage – to pursue their personal moral visions of education. A little paradoxically, they became nationally recognized because they rejected national policy recommendations for leadership; and they did this in very different ways. While dissimilar, they both took strong positions, they both possessed transformative abilities, and they both appreciated that the nature of the world, and of leadership itself, is more complex, non-linear and wicked than much discussion on the subject suggests.

The strength through difference of both David and Sue is extremely important. They were successful at least in part *because* they did not follow a prescribed agenda: they had the courage to develop their schools from the moral position they took, and the context they felt they were dealing with, rather than simply accommodating to a set of standards and competencies. David's moral position was a fusion of a global environmental vision and a concern for the children in his charge, leading to a passion to convey and make part of the consciousness of those around him a greater sensibility of global issues of sustainable development. His analysis suggested to him that his school context needed him to be the leader in a rather traditional sense – the expert, the *head teacher* who leads from the front. Sue began from a different vision: her moral position, essentially concerned with the growth and empowerment of individuals, meant that sustainability, as many other agendas in the school, was driven through the encouragement and promotion of different individuals' interests in the context of the school and its particular challenges. This resulted in different visions of sustainability: David's was focused on the environment, and through that on the wicked interconnections between environmental, social and economic issues; Sue's was more focused on local social sustainability, developing into a perceived need to have wider sustainability in all endeavours, of which environmental, social and economic concerns were one part. Sue's analysis led her to believe that her context required her to be a leader, both charismatic and distributed. This doesn't favour one version over the other, but does suggest that personality, context and particular challenges may require different forms of leadership, each with its own strengths, underpinned and driven by personal moral commitments. The essence of much good leadership may then lie precisely in the exercise of a personal moral responsibility, which cannot be reduced to – nor dictated by – any particular set of skills and competencies.

This is further emphasized by the complexity, paradox and irony they both saw in their role and in the wider world, which contradict any simple vision of headship and leadership functioning. Both had wide visions of the role of education. Sue's vision, an almost Asian vision, which was also captured in the argument of her doctorate, was located within a political and economic picture of societal and global flux, of constant change and demands upon education practitioners, with educational leaders needing to move beyond a traditional role, to work across and through other institutions as well as their own in describing the nature of new problems, and in creating new solutions. It is an 'ecological' vision of joined-up systems thinking, of recognizing the role of the organic, the complex and the wicked in much thinking and practice, which is very different from more traditional standard models of practice. This resonates strongly with the kinds of 'ironic situations' (Hoyle and Wallace (2006)) which many educational leaders find themselves in, because of the very nature of their role, but which tend to receive limited official recognition. It is probably this lack of recognition of the wicked nature of reality which led Sue to her occasional subversive utterances about tame governmental policies. David's vision also had a wicked perspective, but was more environmentally focused, viewing current political and economic practice as fundamentally damaging to the ecosphere, and sharing the belief with Sue that too few people see the complex inter-linkages embedded in current systems. It is not surprising then that David expressed similar concerns about tame government policies and visions, and felt impelled to be similarly wickedly critical. Once again, one sees two different personalities, coming from different positions, but who had arrived at similar wicked epistemologies, and therefore similar understandings of the kind of changes that needed to be made.

These portraits then suggest that for leadership to be successful and sustainable, centrally defined standards and prescriptions need to be interpreted in a manner which allows them to dovetail not only with the context within which an individual practices, but also with that individual's approach and moral drive. Like the throwing of a bird, the fusion of these can never be entirely predictable, entirely linear, because it is of the nature of such interactions that the unexpected will likely happen. Leaders then must have something of the ethical dialectician about them (Bottery, 2004); leaders who have internal moral compasses, yet who are also aware of the complexities of the external world, and of their own personal and epistemological limitations. They need to know that they must listen to others, and adopt a 'provisionalist' attitude to the world, but one which increasingly embraces a future orientation, an ecological awareness, and the greater embrace of notions of global public good and cooperation, as opposed to national or private self-interest and competition. David's and Sue's academic work and their practice both make it clear that the interconnected nature of global, national and local pressures on education will not be fully understood or appreciated by tame, linear or uniform solutions. Rather a greater embrace of the complex, the ambiguous and the non-standard is needed. Both leaders appreciated this, and both had the moral courage to formulate better problems and make better responses than officially sanctioned ones. A tame mediocrity of leadership caused by cultures of standards and conformity is likely to lead to only greater wicked problems. The best way of rising above mediocrity may well lie in the exploration of different approaches to developing leadership within the same legislative and cultural context, and in the process, of producing leading examples of sustainable leadership.

These two leaders then exhibited a moral courage to choose distinctive paths, which had almost certainly led to the national recognition of their practice. Yet moral courage is needed in many other, less exalted, situations as well. Sometimes it is the courage that must accompany a head teacher or principal, new in the role, where the lack of personal experience in the role makes challenges particularly daunting. The next chapter then provides portraits of two such leaders, the threats to their sustainability they had to face in very different contexts, and the resilience they needed to draw on.

CHAPTER FIVE

Leadership, Challenges and Resilience in Two Cultures

Introduction

Previous chapters have described how individual sustainability can be threatened or enhanced by forces located at different contextual levels. They have also suggested that the culture within which leadership is practised can generate very different values and mind-sets, leading to very different approaches. Yet cultures are not impermeable, and the practice and values of one may well be seen in another. This chapter provides portraits of two anonymized school leaders from different cultures, one from the UK and one from Hong Kong. These portraits demonstrate how leadership challenges are most times a function of not one but a number of different contexts. The first portrait describes how a professionally critical national policy context led to a local authority placing unreasonable demands upon a new school leader in that authority; the second describes an unusual organizational arrangement of 'AM' and 'PM' schools on the same geographic site, and how the power relationship between the leaders of these two schools led to the undermining of the changes the newer principal was trying to introduce. Both portraits demonstrate the importance of *individual* leadership, of how single case studies can be of considerable significance in a research world more enamoured of large quantitative overviews. This chapter then shows how cultural practices can provide larger contexts for individual practice, but also how very similar human responses can transcend these contexts. The two portraits describe very different personalities in very different contexts, yet each is faced by challenges which seem readily understandable in and beyond either culture, as are the individuals' reactions.

The 'Harry C.' portrait

Harry was an English headteacher, interviewed on a cold and windy day in December, in his office at his school. At the time, he was suffering from a very bad cold, as well as the fatigue that can come at the end of a very busy term, and at the end of a first year in post as head teacher. Such fatigue also came, as we shall see, from other pressures to do with the nature of the school and the SATs results currently being recorded. After the provision of appropriate cups of coffee, the interview was conducted and taped. It was subsequently transcribed, and listened to twice more, before the portrait was written, and sent back to Harry for his approval. The portrait is reproduced immediately below.

Harry's challenges

This was Harry's first headship, and he had been in post for just one year *'almost to the day'*. He laughed ironically when responding to my question as to whether it seemed longer than that, by simply commenting that *'it does seem long, believe me'*. There were many things, he thought, that you can learn about headship from books and from others, but there were many other things simply not covered. By way of illustration, he told me of the child who took his SATs papers *'in splendid isolation in the loo'*. Why, I asked, did he take them there – because it was the only quiet place available? Harry's response was short, and accompanied by a shake of the head and the same ironic smile: *'wouldn't come out'*. Such a situation, he thought, was *'not something that you ever get taught to deal with'*. So, for Harry, his first year in charge had been one where *'everything's been a first'*. What do you do in such a situation? One strategy was to ask yourself: *'How have I seen other people deal with this?'* But that in itself he thought was insufficient, for each person has their own unique way of dealing with things, and each school has its own history, its own context. So it was essential to also ask: *'What's the history of this school, and how [would experienced others] deal with this?'* Nevertheless, this was still insufficient, for Harry believed that it was vitally important to ask of oneself: *'What's my own personal philosophy and belief?'* Only then was it possible to begin the process of *'trying to match it all up'*, and even then *'you don't always get it right'*.

So what did Harry's personal philosophy consist of? For him, '*the bottom line is, I came into this profession to help the children to improve their lot*'. More than that, though, '*They get one chance in education, and I think if we mess it up for them, we've got a lot to answer for.*' In such circumstances, then, '*my belief is that we provide absolutely the best we can, give them every opportunity we can*'. However, there had to be another ingredient: '*At the same time we [must] try to make it as enjoyable as we can, because nobody likes to go to work and be unhappy.*' And such an education should not be a purely academic one: '*I think everyone needs to have the opportunity to prove that they are academic, but if they are not ... they then need to find something that they can be a success at.*'

Harry may have only been in the job for one year, but he nevertheless believed that his opinion and values mattered. While influential, other's views – such as the local education authority (the LEA), the national inspectoral body Ofsted, or the government of the day – were undoubtedly important for the school –and legitimately so – '*their view of things is too wide. They are looking at too big a picture.*' Unlike them, who had to '*consider every school in the country*', Harry thought his focus had to be on '*these pupils in this school*', the result of this being that '*I can narrow it down a lot more than they can*'.

Part of such refinement through knowledge of the context, had led Harry to believe that, for this particular school, '*the key issue to improving children's life chances*' had to be the development of the home–school relationship. Yet currently this was '*a huge problem ... . we don't have people who come in and help, we don't have the level of parental support for homework, and things that we would like, and if we could turn that around, that would have a bigger impact on standards, and raise our results more than all the other projects*'. Such belief in the importance of developing this relationship was underlined when, towards the end of the interview, I asked Harry what he would do were he given a sabbatical away from his day-to-day job; he answered that it would be to research the question: '*What is it that would bring parents into school? What is going to turn their attitude towards education from complete indifference or very negative, into something positive? What is it that would switch parents on?*' For what he in effect wanted to do was to '*change the culture around the school*', and he felt he was doing little more at the moment than '*a quick fix*'. And this, he thought was because of poor SATs results, and therefore the very real possibility of an early Ofsted, inspection.[1] He was then being pressured by a number of sources to prioritize areas other than those which he felt

---

[1]Ofsted has gone through many changes in its style of inspection. At the time of Harry's interview, it operated on an inspection basis of every 2–3 years, but with more immediate interventions when poor results were reported from a school. At the time of writing this chapter, it operates on a day's notice, and is moving towards a no-notice system.

were the most important. The result was that, for Harry, while some of his problems stemmed from his lack of experience, quite a few stemmed from his inheritances at the school.

The school context

Nevertheless, Harry still felt that there were some undoubted positives about the school. One was that current pupil numbers were relatively stable, and 'over a period of four years, we're predicting numbers of pupils on-roll to drop by [only] five'. As we learnt from other interviews in both contexts, declining rolls placed special pressures upon head teachers and principals, pressures like the threat of staff reductions, the increased need to retain existing children and recruit new ones, and the real possibility of complete school closure. Another positive for Harry was that, in the following few years, a regeneration housing project in the city was likely to lead to beneficial changes to the local area, as it was likely not only to maintain school numbers, but perhaps even improve them. Harry had also inherited a very committed staff who really knew the area and its problems. Finally, he was particularly enthusiastic about the fact that most visitors commented on 'how calm and how caring the school is when you come into it'. For Harry, these positives were very important – 'a really good strong secure base to be building from'.

Harry then felt that these were all very encouraging. Yet there still seemed little doubt that he had inherited a very challenging situation. The school was located 'in one of the most deprived wards in the country. We are ranked number 1 out of 23 on the deprivation index for [the city], for electoral wards, and nationally, out of 7932 electoral wards, we are ranked 15th'. The school also faced 'high levels of pupil mobility', which in the previous year had stood at 48.3 per cent, 'the third highest in the city'. When virtually half of a student body move within any one year, planning and continuity in teaching become extremely difficult. The area was also marked at that time by large amounts of housing that was 'private rented, short-term let'. It was perhaps unsurprising then, that the school had a high number of 'free school meals', as well as a substantial number of 'extremely challenging' children with special educational needs. Indeed, ' almost 50% of the cohort were on the special needs register, and about 15% from this special needs register [was] for behaviour, and that behaviour was quite extreme for 2 or 3 of them' – and hence the situation of the child doing his SATs test in the loo. In addition, Harry added, 'for the city in particular, we have high levels of English as an additional language'. And while this was 'only' around 15 per cent, it was still 'seven times the city average'. Finally, the members of staff were working within 'a building that is particularly cramped, hasn't been decorated for 20 years'. Certainly, the impression gained upon entering the school was an overlay of bright materials and ideas trying to disguise a poor basic build.

However, perhaps the major pressure on Harry stemmed from his inheritance of poor SATs results for the school, and the lack of significant improvement since then. This situation had to be understood within the context of a city which had a poor academic reputation nationally, and whose LEA was about to undergo an Ofsted inspection itself, having had a very critical previous one. Ofsted held fears for many. For Harry, it was *'because people feel that careers are made or broken on the strength of a group of people for a few days in your school looking round … what they write can be extremely damning to you'*. But it was not just the public disgrace: *'Even if it doesn't affect your career, it can affect you psychologically. You can feel almost a failure. I mean, if we as teachers wrote a report about a child and said nothing positive whatsoever …'*

It is important to mention here that there was severe pressure from central government upon this LEA, in a scenario of an overall declining schools population, to identify a number of primary schools for closure. In such a situation, there was understandably heavy pressure on Harry from the LEA to produce SATs results which prevented the triggering of a further Ofsted inspection, which might add further pressure on the LEA. So while numbers were relatively stable, the poor results were, to Harry's mind at least, *'one of the main reasons we are on the long list [for school closure]'*.

The consequences of an Ofsted focus

'If you have a series of bad results, which unfortunately we have, then … you're likely to get Ofsted again.' As mentioned above, this was not just a concern for the school; the LEA was also under intense scrutiny, and there was therefore considerable pressure on Harry to change this situation. The result, Harry felt, had been that *'the focus of what we are doing has been skewed enormously towards preparing for SATs'*, and this was problematic for him in all sorts of ways. For a start, he had inherited a staff who *'don't agree with SATs at all'*, and so there was real resistance when he had to make this the school's priority, and say to staff *'this year we've got to do Maths, English, Science, Maths, English, Science, to get our results up to avoid the consequences'*. Not only did the staff dislike *'the notion of training for the SATs … they also didn't like that it detracts from the other subjects on the curriculum'*. Such an intense school focus also went against Harry's personal philosophy of the need for a broad education, as well as running against his fundamental belief that the school should be principally concerned with developing greater parental involvement. Yet, having said that, Harry's views on SATs were shades of grey, rather than ones of black and white. He did believe, for instance, that *'there is an academic ability attached with [them] … there is that knowledge element, there is that skill element'*. In addition, he also felt that it was the school's job *'to make sure that children leave … with the best possible chance of success, and to be able to hold their heads*

up alongside any other child in the city'. So in terms of the ratification of academic ability, in terms of raising the children's self-esteem and in terms of '*the kudos of getting level 4*', Harry candidly felt that '*at the moment we've let some of our pupils down*'. He was clearly conflicted over this.

In addition to such tensions and pressure, the LEA was putting massive pressure on him to take note of not one but several improvement plans they had devised for the school. So Harry was faced by the fact that '*we've got our school improvement plan, but we've also got an LEA support plan, and we are in a programme called the Intensifying Support Programme*'. They all had the same objectives: '*all focus on attendance, behaviour, and standards in core subjects*', and all had just one objective, for '*everything is just geared towards making sure that we are doing everything we can to avoid ... Mr. OFSTED knocking on our door.*' Now Harry was happy to acknowledge that there were '*huge elements of what they [the LEA] are doing that have been supportive*'; nevertheless, the overall result was beginning to amount to '*a nightmare*', for now Harry saw his biggest problem as not one of parental issues, market issues or even of Ofsted issues, but '*the attention that I've received from the authority because of poor results*'. Thus he had had '*11 people consulting and advising me over the last term ... [and] every time you get an advisor or a consultant ... they write a report: a Service Visiting Report*'. Harry had already had 22 of these in that particular term – '*and I know that I'm owed about 8 or 10 that haven't yet come through*'. Moreover, included in each report, at the bottom, was a section designating the '*action required by the school*'. So when one considers the impact of the meetings, the three separate improvement programmes, the eleven people consulting and advising, and twenty-two reports requiring action, and with more of the same still to come, it was unsurprising that Harry should feel fatigued, that he was under the weather, and should feel that '*I've spent half the term talking about what I'm going to do, and the other half of this term preparing for the meetings where I'm talking about what I'm going to do, and absolutely not enough time at all to do what I'm supposed to do*'.

In such a situation, Harry felt he needed to manage the LEA advisors as much as they were trying to manage him. A first step in this had been for him to begin to consolidate the three programmes into just one. In addition, Harry has ensured that when people came in with advice, '*I've kept them focussed on what I consider to be the major issues, rather than them trying to say: oh well, I think you should do something on this.*' Finally, he felt that he needed to ensure that they understood the sheer volume of advice confronting him. At a recent review meeting, for example, he had laid out all the different sets of plans on a table, '*so that when they came in, I said "I'm not trying to make a point, but which one are we talking about?"*' He related, with the same ironic laugh, how '*they took that point*'. Whether this would reduce the quantity, and mean that advisors would attempt to coordinate advice, rather than responding to the pressures being placed upon *them* by simply sending more material down the line to Harry, still remained to be seen. What was clear was that the current actions intended to help Harry only served to increase the pressures on him, and reduce the time he had to deal with advisory agendas and advice. The fact that he continued to believe that the really important issues for the school lay elsewhere didn't seem to have been picked up on others' radar.

So the school focus boiled down to addressing anything and everything that 'keeps OFSTED from the door. *I mean, our policy for things like attendance and punctuality is geared to being able to prove to OFSTED that we are doing everything we can ... because low attendance figures can trigger an OFSTED'*. Essentially, then the policy was one of '*trying to make sure that, one: we avoid it until it's our turn in the cycle, and we don't bring it forward, and two: that when they do come, whether it's early or when we expect it in the cycle, that they are satisfied with what they see'*.

Harry was well aware of what Ofsted would be looking for – which amounted to evidence to back-up decisions being made – and he simply didn't feel that currently the school had it. The focus then was determined for him, with '*most of the decisions I make [being] geared towards thinking "what would OFSTED look for"? What would they deem acceptable? ... Every decision is based on: "is this acceptable to OFSTED?"'* It was not surprising then when Harry said that '*for the next couple of years it will be my driving force ... because there isn't the back-up evidence that I know will satisfy them ... . I don't have the banks of evidence, I can't open my cupboard and say there is my monitoring file, there is my policy audit file, and so on.'*

It is important to note that Harry had been deputy head teacher at a school where there were such '*banks of evidence*', which were maintained '*at an appropriate level*', and he strongly believed that had things happened differently, and had he been appointed head teacher there instead of here, his situation and his approach to the job would have been very different from his current one, for there '*I could have put my energy into developing the things that genuinely are the right things to do'*.

Markets, parents and staff

Given this pressure to meet Ofsted demands, it was unsurprising that other agendas were interpreted in the light of such concerns. Markets were one such issue. Harry thought that there were at least two markets at play in schools generally, and at his school in particular. One was concerned with parents, their opinions and their involvement in the school. Within the term 'market', Harry included not only parental influence upon school decision-making, through the power to move their children to other schools, but also the strong educational need to involve parents in the school for the benefit of their children. Now it has already been noted that numbers were relatively stable, and were predicted to be so for some time to come, and this in one sense reduced market pressure, but high pupil turnover counterbalanced such benefits. Harry was also very conscious of the importance of parental opinion, and of how instances of poor behaviour could be the basis for parental disaffection. He admitted that there 'were *parents who come along to admit their children to the school, and there are times when I don't want to admit, because I know that other parents will want to then remove their children ... but I get my hand forced there, because if they're in my catchment area, and I have places, I can't say no*'. This desire to be selective also applied to exclusions: there was, on occasion, the temptation to push for an exclusion because it would '*send a message to parents that we are dealing with this ... that we are not letting it slide by*', for there was little doubt in Harry's mind that '*that's the bit that they see as being just, because it's more public*'.

Harry then believed that 'the market' referred to parental involvement and attitudes to the school, and he ultimately saw the school as '*not about Ofsted, but about children and their families. We are here*', he believed, '*to serve the people of this community, and provide an education for their children*'. And yet he felt that '*we are not making progress with the parents ... we are making lots of progress in terms of Ofsted ... but what I won't have is a set of parents who understand what's going on in the school, who support what's going on in the school, and come into the school*'. The ultimate tension for Harry then was probably that while '*I'm not here to satisfy some man with a clipboard ... yet that drives me more than the needs of this community*'. For Harry, that was '*a terrible admission, but I think it's true*'.

Yet if parents were one market, the other was '*the pool of staff that I attract to the school*'. Harry was clear about the effects of such a market, and believed that '*it's a market which I'd better be in, to get who I want*'. This was, he believed, now a much more informed market, for '*as teachers are applying for jobs, they do go onto the website and they do read Ofsted reports*'. The result, thought Harry, was that Ofsted was now becoming a kind of *Which* report on schools, and so, consequently, '*if you do get a bad Ofsted report and then you advertise a job, people look at the Ofsted report and think: not going there*'. The result, he feared, was a vicious circle: '*You won't be able to get the quality staff you need in order to lift the school from the position it's in.*' So far, he felt he'd been lucky: he'd made two new (and, he felt, good) appointments for the school, but one had resulted from a personal knowledge of the school, and the other from recommendation from someone who knew the school. Such personal experience and word-of-mouth recommendations were very useful, but what concerned Harry was that there might be '*many other people out there looking for jobs, because it was a promotion post*', but who didn't have such knowledge, and simply didn't bother to apply.

Pressures from Ofsted, the LEA and parental attitudes

It is perhaps unsurprising, then, that 'the market' wasn't as big a part of Harry's subconscious as Ofsted was. It was also not surprising that Harry should '*feel terrible that market forces aren't a bigger part of my subconscious*'. So this was Harry's current dilemma: '*We are forced down this route of raising standards through paperwork, you know: make sure your planning's right, make sure your assessment's right, make sure you're doing this, make sure you've got this on the wall, make sure you've got that on the wall.*' But the problem for Harry was that '*we are not changing the culture and the attitude towards learning*'. The end result seemed to be that while '*we are actually making the staff work harder*', when the idea should be that '*you don't work harder, you work smarter*'; and Harry didn't feel they were. So he felt that while

> we are making lots of progress in terms of things like Ofsted, we are not making progress with the parents ... I want to get parents into the school more, and there are lots of projects I've talked about with various staff, but we simply haven't got time. We want to have ... family training days, curriculum days, get people in ... [yet] my staff meetings for next term are booked up and into the summer term already, with ... this business of working towards any potential Ofsted inspection.

Ultimately, then, Harry felt there was a price to be paid for such focus, for '*what I won't have is a set of parents who understand what's going on in the school, who support what's going on in the school, and come in to the school*'. And the reason was simple: '*The focus has been elsewhere, nobody has put any time or energy into it, so we are not making any progress.*'

Harry was then faced by a number of pressures: his inexperience as a head, the demands of a new school and its culture, poor results, pressure from the LEA, the threat of an Ofsted visit and its possible consequences, as well as his own personal pressure to really get to grips with the lack of parental involvement in the school. Yet, despite all the demands associated with Christmas, and working with a heavy cold, there was also a determination to succeed. Harry had his values and his vision, and he was still resolute in attempting to solve present difficulties and realize his ambitions for the school. Remarkably, the same resolution is to be seen in the next portrait, that of Emily W.

The 'Emily W.' portrait

Emily's interview took place at her school in a fairly run-down part of Hong Kong. For a Western interviewer used to many primary schools having space and fields, to drive into a busy shopping district, and then to have a large metal gate opened by a parent helper onto a school with a small concrete playground overshadowed by high-rise flats, was a little unusual. For the other interviewers it was of course normal and unremarkable. Emily's room was snug and comfortable, with enough room for three interviewers and the principal. Once our china cups of hot water had been delivered, we were ready for the interview.

The English interviewer had been told (and had read) of Chinese cultural characteristics such as saving and losing 'face', of a reticence to divulge the personal and the problematic, and of the real issues and difficulties of conducting an interview in an interviewee's second language. However, and rather surprisingly, Emily chose not only to give the interview almost completely in English, but also to provide opinions which were forthright, critical and personal. It became very clear very quickly that the local context was critical to an understanding of Emily's challenges.

The importance of context

For a number of reasons, at the time of interview, there was still a quantity of school buildings in Hong Kong which in effect housed two different schools: a morning (or AM) set of pupils, and an afternoon (or PM) set of pupils. These 'schools' had separate principals and separate teachers. One might have thought that few problems would arise from such an arrangement, except perhaps issues of daily transition, of storage of materials, and of other factors stemming from such site sharing. This, however, does not really describe the situation. It was instead usual for the AM and PM principals to share a similar curriculum, and general planning of the school. Indeed, it was actually nearer the case to view the situation at Emily's school as there was only one school, but with two principals appointed to run it. In such situations, how was authority determined? Emily, whether she liked it or not, knew that she occupied the less powerful principal's position. This is in large part explained by the fact that the previous AM principal had left, and Emily, at that time teaching in another school, had applied for the job, 'but had "failed to become the AM principal"'. And who became the AM principal? 'Actually, the AM principal is the previous PM principal ... and then they had a vacancy here for the PM principal.' So this was now the post that Emily occupied, and at the time of interview, Emily had only been the PM principal for a short period of time – 'a greenhorn' as she called herself. Given this, and the fact that the other candidate got the post that Emily originally applied for, it was perhaps unsurprising that Emily was clear about the leadership hierarchy: as she said, 'They promoted the PM principal to be the AM principal' (Emily's words, our emphasis).

As if this was not difficult enough, Emily also encountered three other problems which might have finished off a less resolute individual.

First, she found herself in the situation where, because of the widespread problem of declining primary numbers in Hong Kong, her own PM school was going to be closed for the following academic year, and the AM and PM schools would be merged into a whole day school. At the moment, said Emily, '*we don't know who will become the full time principal*'. And yet Emily was no fool: she knew that she had failed to beat the other candidate for the AM school position, and would almost certainly be facing the same person again for the combined school position.

Second, and to add to her problems, because the AM principal had been the PM principal only a little time ago, when Emily wanted the teachers to do something different from what they had been used to, '*they will tell Y, and then Y will stop me from that doing so*'. Indeed, the hierarchy was so pronounced, that the AM principal did not feel the need to justify her decisions: '*[Y] just says I want it to be like that, I don't need to explain to you because I am the principal*'.

The problems didn't stop there. It is conceivable that someone could endure being treated as a deputy principal instead of a full principal, and not being fully consulted, if the school situation was a healthy one. But Emily did not believe this to be the case. '*My school*' she said, very early in the interview, '*is just like a Jurassic park*'. After my eyebrows had come down from the ceiling, we began to explore why this was the case. This then forms the third challenge for Emily, and it deserves a section of its own.

Other internal problems

Emily then found that she occupied an inferior position, but that even there she was undermined. The real problem, as Emily saw it, was that the school was in urgent need of reform and yet few others seemed to realize this: '*The teachers are quite used to the old system ... there is not any system here, no discipline, no system, and they cannot see the problems.*' Emily's primary concern was '*the teaching and learning area, because I think everything starts with that*', and yet '*I found most of the teachers here are not so conscientious and diligent about their work*'. She had, for instance '*checked their marking of exercise books*', and she thought it '*quite outrageous to find how bad they can be to deal with the daily routine*', and felt that part of the problem was because '*the teachers are very enclosed by their present environment ... . I mean, they feel safe to have a job before and they not need to think of any improvement.*'

However, Emily was also clear in her own mind that '*the main factor [is that] the previous organization did not keep an eye on them, or they just don't care about how the teachers do in the classroom*'. Indeed, she felt that not only had the previous regime let the teaching quality slip, but it also didn't include the teachers in any decision-making, which probably contributed to the problem: '*I want to adopt some policies to be fair, open and transparent enough to let all the teachers know what is going on, but I think the previous practice is not like that, they* [the principal] *keep everything secret to themselves, and they don't reveal the truth to the teachers that often.'* There then existed, Emily believed, a regime employing a fairly deadly combination of not including teachers in decision-making, while at the same time '*nobody says you are doing a lousy job and nobody cares at all'*.

It is important to note that the kind of students that the school admitted probably added to Emily's concerns: '*About 80% of our students are new immigrants coming from mainland China, and we've got a lot of family problems.'* However, Emily also pointed out that '*I don't think they should have problems because they come from the mainland China ... . I mean the location of the school will have some impact on that...from the school I taught before ... there are new immigrants from Mainland China too, but they are very good students, they've got fabulous performance and their parents are very good.'* However, this school seemed to have a very different kind of intake: '*There are many cases such as child abuse, family violence, and some of the parents don't have time to take care of their kids.'* The result, Emily felt, was that '*the teachers here will think all of the students are just losers, because they believe they can't learn, because their standard is very low ... they just give them up'*. Yet if she felt that the teachers didn't have a high regard for the children, she also felt that this feeling was reciprocated. When asked why the parents chose this particular school, she felt it had little to do with its quality or its distinctive message, but simply *because* '*this school is not a good one ... because they can get in easily'*.

Context steering other perceptions

Given Emily's views on the context she worked within, it was perhaps unsurprising that most of the other questions were interpreted in the light of this context. For example, when she was asked whether time was a major issue for her, while the intention of the question was to explore whether she managed to fit all of her various demands into a very intensive workload, and what were the major pressures within this workload, Emily interpreted it in a very differently. First, she thought that time was a problem because '*if I want to modify this school, I may not have enough time because I may just be the principal for the rest of the half year and certainly know that won't be enough'*. Her perspective was six monthly rather than daily or annually. When I asked her to think of the question on a day-to-day basis, the answer was understandable: there wasn't enough time because of '*so many problems, so many things I need to do'*.

However, time was important to Emily in a different way, and more to do with *timing*. As already noted, the former PM principal had been appointed to the AM position to start the new academic year, and the sponsoring body then found itself in a position, with little time of needing to appoint a new PM principal. Emily had therefore only been invited to be the PM principal at the last minute. The result of this was that '*I don't have much time to know more about this school before I came here.*' and perhaps more importantly, systems were already in place for the coming year, so that '*after I came here … I just could not change when I found they have problems, because it is already set and already made known to everybody*'.

There was a similar contextualized response to questions of energy. The original question was designed to elicit perceptions on whether external or internal issues had the more significant effect on energy levels. Emily interpreted the question in terms of wasted energy: because her hands were so tied, any energy expended on transforming issues, which had an impact on the AM sessions, would be wasted energy – and that meant nearly everything. This was in part, she felt, because of the dominance and attitude of the current AM principal, but she was aware that there were problems solely in the PM school. However, she was aware that real change needed the energy and enthusiasm of more than just the principal, for she knew that '*I need a group of people to be cooperative with me, to work with me; I could not make this school a better one by myself*'.

Even questions of legislation were interpreted through the frame of Emily's current predicament. When asked whether there were any decisions that she felt were right, but which would be difficult to carry out because of the consequences of violating educational legislation, the question's original intention had been to see whether Emily thought there were educational issues or aims (such as greater creativity and greater autonomy) which might be hampered by directive and centralizing legislation. Emily's answer was to suggest that there was a major problem in her ability to sack teachers, '*because it is not so easy to sack a teacher in Hong Kong*'. Now she acknowledged that such difficulty '*is good in one way because it can protect the rights of teachers*'. However, given her situation, it is perhaps understandable that she should say, '*It is so bad in the other way if you find some of the teachers are incapable of doing what they should do, and you just can't do anything to stop them … you will need to undergo a very complicated process, and ultimately you cannot sack them.*'

Emily even related the issue of inspection to the situation that she believed she currently faced. She mentioned a previous '*quality assurance inspection*', at which the school '*got very poor results*'. She said that the school supervisor had informed her that largely on the basis of that report, '*There are a lot of changes, a lot of good changes in this school already*'. Yet once again, Emily was unequivocal: '*If that is a good change, then it is not good enough!*' Indeed, Emily felt that most of the staff were so casual in their approach that '*they don't know at all about the external inspections, so they would not care about which area would be inspected*'.

It was already clear from the fact that the AM and PM sessions were going to merge, that there were problems with numbers. Part of the reason for this was a declining birth rate in Hong Kong; but as other interviews showed, some principals believed that it was possible to halt a slide in numbers by establishing a good reputation through providing a good-quality education and good academic results. Reputation then was seen as critical, and market issues were a constant concern for many (and see Chapter 9 for more on this). Emily was no different: she believed that the market was a very serious issue for the school '*because it is totally out of our control ... the other aspects, the legislation, the inspection, or time or effort, there are always ways to resolve them, but not the market*'. However, and continuing the same critical theme, Emily feared that school performance was already so poor in the eyes of parents that '*I could not do anything to damage the market consequences any further!*' This however was not a counsel of despair: as with all the other issues, Emily was very clear on what she would do if her hands were not tied in the way they were. Thus, she thought that '*you would need to adopt a special kind of strategy to make the students learn better, because you would need to cater for their needs, and if the parents feel that your school is taking care of the students quite well, they will put their children to our school*'. This seemed a very positive educational vision, one of solving market problems and declining numbers through establishing a reputation for good-quality education. All the more frustrating then that she did not feel this was something she could currently achieve.

Emily's awareness of external issues

So while Emily understandably concentrated upon internal issues, her appreciation of market issues demonstrated that she was not unaware of external pressures upon the school. Her approach displayed what seemed a balanced criticality. Thus, while she was not opposed to curriculum reform, for instance, '*I just don't agree with the way they ... implement the changes to the schools ... how come they can expect teachers to take up so many new roles in a short period of time to deal with all those changes ... to plan a new curriculum framework is not a simple task.*' The preferred method, she said, seemed to be to provide each school with '*a Curriculum Designer (CD) – a new post for 5 years*'. However, she thought that this teacher '*will need to start doing the changes while he is still learning how to do it*'. These CDs, then, would need to have in-service training to help them understand the new reforms and their implementation, but Emily thought this would be '*a very poor system to deal with such a drastic reform*'. Such in-service training, for example, '*is not compulsory for the principal*', and in her own school, '*My principal does not know about the curriculum reform at all, and just relies on that CD to do it, but if you don't know about curriculum reform, how could you ensure that the CD would do a good job, right?*'

Emily was also concerned about the general lack of consultation. Thus, she believed that these changes were '*introduced by the EMB* [the Hong Kong Education Department], *not originated from school ... and before they introduce that reform, nobody knows what they are going to do'*. Moreover, when asked whether she had been consulted on the reforms, she stated that *'they did not have that process'*. Indeed, it seemed that she doubted whether a consultation process would make much difference: *'Even if you say it, even if you tell them how you think, they will just neglect it, because they believe they are doing the right things.'* Further, when asked whether she thought that the lack of consultation regarding her opinions might be due to the fact that she was a very new principal, she doubted whether experienced principals would be able to provide much insight: *'They may not see the problems at all ... they may just rely on the CDs.'*

Emily then had a forthright personality, who believed in the central importance of the principal's role in developing the school, yet who recognized the need for team support; who believed in her own ability, were she to have her hands 'untied', and if she were given the time to turn things round. The portrait may suggest that Emily was a hyper-critical individual, but this was not the impression of those conducting the interview. What came across was a sense of frustration occasioned by Emily having a vision of what needed to be done, and yet apparently prevented from achieving this. There then seem clear parallels between Emily and Harry C.

Conclusion

Harry's and Emily's practice were nested in very different cultures, in very different kinds of schools, facing very different challenges. One was working in a gritty, inner-city school in Northern England, focusing on Ofsted and LEA demands; the other was working in a PM school in an area of declining rolls in Hong Kong, feeling deprived of any real power by the presence of a dominant AM principal and a staff acquiescent to her. Yet through their uniqueness, these two portraits do a number of surprising things.

A first is that while cultures apart, it is possible to recognize their common humanity. They show similar reactions to the situations they face – frustration is there, just as on occasions is exasperation; yet so also is a similarly resilient attitude. Both interview and portrait suggest that they intended continuing to do the best for their schools and their children regardless of the constraints and pressures they faced. These portraits also suggest that it is possible to understand what others, very different culturally, are feeling and doing. The struggles of these two individuals may paradoxically provide a measure of hope that humanity can cooperate in solving the more global challenges it currently faces.

However, secondly, if this chapter has demonstrated that individuals from different cultures share a similar resilience, it should be pointed out that not all interviewees showed this. There were individual differences within and between societies. Some in apparently better situations, through age or diminution of ability to implement their missions, showed much less resilience than Harry and Emily (see Chapter 9 again on this). One therefore has to be careful: encounters between contexts, and personalities nested in these contexts are invariably unique – and are always changing.

So once more, if policy is to have successful implementation, we need to appreciate the particular circumstances of each example of school leadership. This is a function of not one but a number of contexts at micro-, meso- and macro-levels. Where policy is unthinking and the personal and the local are ignored, or they are seen as impediments to the visions of those elsewhere, then policy success is likely to be low. Hoyle and Wallace (2006) have argued that successful policies are those which appreciate the local, and that 'successful' professionals are those who are aware of the ambiguities, dilemmas and ironies generated by the potentially conflicting demands of policies, organizations and people, and who are still able to display the personal characteristics needed to deal with such realities. These involve, we suggest, an understanding of the need to mediate between legislation and the local context, and for a pragmatic and piecemeal approach towards implementation. This then suggests the need for individuals – in collaboration with others working in the same context – to 'construct' an implementation which reflects their particular circumstances, (the 'bricoleur' leadership which Grint (2008) talked about) just as it suggests an approach by policy-makers which appreciates this reality and allows sufficient flexibility for this to be possible.

The result then is a very different picture of professional practice from a hierarchical, rationalist, planned and controlling one. It is instead a picture characterized by personality, context and pragmatic implementation. While it does not ignore the need for central pressure and direction, it also suggests the need for a degree of local autonomy as a necessary element of local implementation. And while it does not deny the need for a central role in leadership education, it suggests that this will be much more effective and much more sustainable when it better understands the leader's perception of the challenges they face.

PART TWO

The Meso-Context of Sustainability

CHAPTER SIX

The Singular Contexts of Organizations

Introduction

This book has argued that while the concept of 'leadership' can have a number of different meanings, a fundamental element of the leadership role is the personality of the individual, wrapped up in different experiences, values and ambitions. Individuals can, and do, develop strong leadership abilities with very different approaches. However, any investigation of leadership sustainability cannot rest with an examination of individual approaches, for individuals are not islands of self-sufficiency. Personal sustainability is partly a function of personal individuality, but it is also a function of the contexts that impinge on such individuals. In the next two chapters we therefore look at how the organizational contexts within which people work can affect personal and role leadership sustainability.

In this chapter, on the role that organizations play in sustainability, we begin the process by examining how a number of key elements of organizational functioning which have been identified in organizational literature, impinge on individual sustainability. From this, in the next chapter, we trace these elements through an examination of two real-life organizations, and use this organizational analysis to present an overall picture of how the manipulation of these elements can change the sustainability of organizations themselves. This particular chapter then provides the theory by which organizational impacts on personal sustainability can be traced in the empirically based chapter following. In the final, concluding chapter of the book we align this argument with other contextual factors to present a typology of how such changes can affect the sustainability of different kinds of individuals.

The three organizational elements to be examined

There are many elements of organizational functioning which can contribute to or detract from personal sustainability. The expression of such elements is likely to be unique to an individual organization, just as particular combinations of elements may synergistically produce stronger effects. This chapter examines three particular organizational elements, in order to create a strong analytic focus for exploring the impact of organizations on individuals within them. A first and overarching element is the *form* an organization takes: so when people talk about organizations, what are the most frequently used metaphors or images used? This is important, because the words used suggest the colour, the direction and the hidden curriculum of the organization which all affect how decisions are made, and why the organization is steered in a particular direction. If, for examples, an organization is described in words suggesting it functions like a machine, because it has strongly interlocking parts, which perform in strongly determined and highly predictable ways, what the organization produces is likely to be highly predictable, as are the tasks given to individuals within it. For some people, this may seem a safe, supportive and personally sustainable environment to work within; others may feel that it cramps their creativity and inventiveness. One group may feel sustained, the other may not. But what if the environment changes, so that predictability is no longer a virtue in a competitive world? In the longer term, this type of organization may not be internally or personally sustainable for either. Knowing what metaphors or images are used to describe an organization can then facilitate reflection upon what kinds of individuals are likely to be more or less personally sustained by working within it; and it allows us to better position the organization within its larger cultural and societal context, and to better understand how changes to these will affect its own sustainability.

Related to such metaphors and images is a second element, that of organizational focus. While metaphor and image provide a broad description of organizational direction, organizational focus asks what matters most to those who control and direct the organization. There are a number of foci that could be chosen, for example:

- The control of others in the organization;
- The facilitation of participation in the workforce;
- The promotion of greater creativity and out-of-the-box thinking;
- The predictability of functions and products;
- The achievement of assigned tasks;
- The nurturance of individual physical, mental and spiritual growth.

This chapter examines two of these possible foci by reviewing a long-standing debate in the history of organizational analysis: the primary concern and emphasis in organizations of results, as opposed to a primary focus of achieving better relationships. The analysis will suggest the complexity of debate in this area, and how different organizational and societal contexts can promote greater or less personal sustainability.

The third element examined in the chapter focuses upon the changing nature of organizational discourse. Rather like organizational focus, the dominant discourse of an organization can be one of the principal means by which the messages and values of an organization are communicated. Many times this discourse is unrecognized, or simply seen as 'this is the way we do things round here'. But in an age of major change, involving the alteration of organizational metaphors and focus, discourse can become an essential tool in facilitating such change – and in the opposition to such change. Discourse change, then, may be acceptable to some, and enhance personal and role sustainability, but for others it may be highly problematic and personally very damaging. An examination of organizational discourse change, and of the stages through which it can be developed in the attempt to change the nature and function of the organization makes it a very important area for the discussion of personal sustainability.

This chapter then uses this three-pronged analytic framework to explain how such elements can impact on organizations, and as importantly how they can impact differently on organizations, and then on the people within them, and in so doing facilitates an understanding of the dynamics of organizational sustainability.

A final couple of points need to be made. A first is that this book has so far adopted a positive meaning for personal leadership 'sustainability', by equating it with a numerically satisfactory presence of individuals in the leadership role. A lack of such sustainability has been viewed negatively, suggesting that some combination of physical, emotional and mental pressures has led individual leaders to feel their continued presence in the role is not viable. This understanding of negative sustainability now needs expanding beyond its physical, emotional and mental components, to include ethical consequences. Some of these ethical aspects have been alluded to earlier in discussions on the effects that the creation of guilt and blame cultures can have on individuals. Such effects suggest that diminished sustainability cannot be simply viewed as a practical consequence of the problems posed by threats to leadership sustainability in populating the senior hierarchies of schools. One also needs to be highly cognizant of the damage to the mental, emotional and physical well-being of individuals if an ethic of care is abrogated. As Hodgkinson (1978) noted, organizations, *qua* organizations do not possess consciousness, they do not have values, and they cannot be held morally responsible for actions performed within them. It is those at the apex of organizations, and those who impose rules on organizations from outside, who have the greatest ethical responsibility for the welfare of others. This consideration has led to examinations of 'toxic' leadership (Kellerman, 2004; Lipman-Blumen, 2005), one potential result being acts created by the 'banality of evil' (Arendt, 2006), as individuals adopt what Milgram (1974) termed the 'agentic state', and are tempted to accept their role as mere organizational functionaries, and as such feel absolved of responsibility for acts committed within and through such organizations. Alternatively, of course, organizational functioning can make people feel valued and self-actualized, and can encourage their moral responsibility and future participation in organizational purpose and impact. Organizations then can play their part for both good and bad, in the furtherance of personal sustainability or psychic damage.

Finally, whereas working towards personal sustainability is almost universally seen as an ethical injunction, organizational sustainability is not. As mentioned above, organizations are not conscious, they do not possess values, and cannot feel physical mental or spiritual pain. But they can be used to elevate personal spirits, they can be used to inflict pain, they can be used for unethical purposes. People can be sacrificed for organizational purposes; people can be led into believing that they *should* sacrifice themselves for the sake of the corporate culture; and they can be sacrificed by governments who may require organizations to pursue ethically dubious policy objectives. The desirability of organizational sustainability, then, will depend upon the nature and objectives which that organization promotes, and of how it changes these to accommodate or assimilate external pressures.

Organizational forms and personal sustainability

Individual and corporate acts can have very large effects upon the forms that organizations take, and therefore the messages they send to those within and outside them. One way of approaching the nature of such forms is to examine the metaphors or images used in attempts to encapsulate the wide variety possible. Morgan (1997), for example, suggested that organizations can take at least eight different forms:

- **As Machines:** where an organization is envisioned as composed of interconnected and interlocking parts, and the people within it as cogs in the wheels of this overall machine. When organizations are viewed in this way, dominant terms used to describe the organization include: efficiency, order, standardization, inputs and outputs, control and measurement.

- **As Organisms:** the use of this image suggests that organizations need to be viewed as living beings, which have life cycles, and which can therefore be viewed as evolving, developing and adapting, and which will eventually die. When they are viewed in this way, the dominant terms used in describing them include: environmental conditions, homeostasis, evolution and survival of the fittest.

- **As Brains:** Those organizations visualized as brains are seen as essentially concerned with gathering information, and in the process, they attempt to cognitively adapt to their external environments; key terms then used for this image include learning, knowledge, intelligence, networks and feedback.

- **As Cultures:** Organizations are here seen as characterized by the expression of particular values, norms and rituals; the organization is essentially the enactment of these. Besides using terms like values, norms and rituals, other words commonly associated with this image are: traditions, history, beliefs and shared visions.

- **As Political Systems:** The central idea here is one of organizations as locations of power, and so issues of contestability, personal interest and conflict are seen as predominating. Key terms used with this image then are: power, authority, conflict management, interests, hidden agendas, alliances and gatekeepers.

- **As Psychic Prisons:** Here, organizations are seen as being dominated not by an actual reality, but by the reality that people construct and bring with them, which can take on an existence and power all of its own. The notion of a psychic prison suggests that rational planning as a description of organizational functioning is insufficient, and that unconscious or repressed mental processes need exploring. Terms associated with this image include: ego, coping and defence mechanisms, repression, denial, projection, conscious and unconscious processes.

- **As Flux and Transformation:** Over recent years, many organizations have experienced dramatically changing and complex external landscapes, and have needed to transform themselves in

Table 6.1 Forms of organization and the individuals within

	Damage to government/ educator relationships	Differences in perceptions of purposes	Depth of accountability and surveillance	Increased use of power rather than persuasion	Complexity seen in tasks or problems	Degree of blame and guilt cultures	Excessive workload	Insufficient preparation for the role
Machines: efficiency, order, control standardization, inputs and outputs, measurement	Very Likely	Strong differences	Likely strong use	Heavy use				
Organisms: evolution, environmental conditions, homeostasis, survival of the fittest					Likely emphasis			Likely
Brains: learning, knowledge, intelligence, networks, feedback					Likely emphasis			Likely
Cultures: values, norms and rituals, traditions, history, beliefs, shared visions								

Political systems: authority, conflict management, interests, power, hidden agendas, alliances, gatekeepers.	Very Likely	Likely strong use	Likely heavy use	Likely heavy degree	Likely	
Psychic prisons: ego, coping and defence mechanisms, repression, denial, projection conscious and unconscious processes, regression.	Very Likely		Likely strong emphasis	Likely heavy degree perceived		Likely strong
Flux and transformation: systems, chaos, complexity, wickedity, permanent change, emergent properties, butterfly effect, paradox	Strong		Strong emphasis		Likely strong	Likely strong
Domination: compliance, power, alienation, force, value imposition and corporate interest.	Strong	Very Strong differences	Very Strong use			

order to adapt to new environments. Terms used with this organizational image then include: systems, chaos, complexity, wickedity, permanent change, emergent properties, butterfly effect and paradox.

- **As Instruments of Domination:** Organizations seen in this manner are essentially characterized by issues of power, and particularly by the exploitative mechanisms used to dominate and subdue others; key terms here then tend to be words like compliance, power, alienation, force, value imposition and corporate interest.

As with all such suggestions, these metaphors or images are both permeable and changeable, but they can provide a framework within which the effects of personal sustainability may be examined. Table 6.1 then takes each of these, and examines their impacts on the major threats to sustainability discussed so far.

A number of things become clear through this examination. A first is that the majority of the intersecting squares in the diagram remain blank. This does not mean that a particular organizational form will not accentuate or remedy particular sustainability threats. Rather it means that to understand the degree of threat, the organizational form has to be much more contextualized. For example the reasons that none of the squares for Morgan's cultural form are filled in is because there is nothing implicit in the notion of 'culture' per se, which affects sustainability. Instead, it is the context, nature and practices of particular organizational cultures which affect personal and role sustainability. If, for instance, an organization had a long history of maintaining strong surveillance on the activities of everyone in the organization, this practice *might* become a threat to personal sustainability, particularly if individuals then felt spied upon and untrusted. However, if this practice was maintained in order to support and develop individuals, and was accepted as such, it might accentuate rather than reduce trust, and so might facilitate greater personal sustainability. In other words, one needs to be fully aware of individual contexts – to drill down into particular organizations, and look at the various factors operating upon and within them, and see whether, on balance, these factors combine to threaten or facilitate personal sustainability. Broad conformance to any particular image or metaphor will not provide sufficiently fine-grained information to make judgements on sustainability. A generalized model or image then provides too 'tame' a picture to provide adequate information on the reality of sustainability threats.

Having said this, there are some organizational forms which seem predisposed *by their very nature* to exacerbate threats to personal sustainability. Those characterized by Morgan as machines, psychic prisons or instruments of domination then seem highly likely to threaten sustainability because their basic concerns with power, domination and control are directly oppressive, and therefore very unlikely to support the individual sustainability of many of those within such organizations. However, one still needs to be very careful here, and not make claims based upon personal cultural predispositions. It might seem to many that championing the development of organizations which encourage personal autonomy, organizational participation and personal fulfilment are by their nature highly sustainable. However, those based predominantly upon notions of hierarchy within organizational power structures which clearly differentiate between those at the top and the bottom, would be low on personal sustainability. But this is almost certainly too simplistic: as the following chapter will demonstrate, many Eastern cultures are based upon hierarchically structured relationships, and many individuals within them find such structures entirely conducive to personal sustainability: they know their place within the organization, their role is spelt out, and so is the nature of their interactions with others. Hierarchy in organizations might then only become a threat to personal sustainability *if* those who possess most power abuse it to their own benefit and advantage, and by the degree to which those below them feel intimidated, lack trust or recognition. In extreme cases they may even be led to believe, as Arendt (2006) and Milgram (1974) suggest, that they are absolved of moral responsibility by their position in such a hierarchy. Once again, the effect of an organizational form on personal sustainability can only be finally determined by examining the context of individual organizations. Personal sustainability is a function of the interaction of many contexts, but it is certainly a function of real individuals dealing with real contexts, and while some may find it difficult or impossible to deal with new threats, others may not have this problem.

In sum, organizations can take many forms on a continuum from functional to dysfunctional, from moral to immoral, from apithological to pathological (Varey, 2008), and in the process may have marked effects – both positive and negative – upon the sustainability of those working within them. And while organizational metaphors or images can provide overviews of possible sustainability threats or facilitators, organizational sustainability will not be defined at the level of Morgan's metaphors: it will be defined by the form that an organization actually takes, and this is likely to be much more complex and wicked than can be described by any overarching metaphor.

Organizational focus

Nested within the notion of organizational metaphors and images then is that of organizational focus. This asks specifically: what matters most to those leading an organization? One could ask this question of all the organizational forms just discussed, but with particular reference to personal sustainability, it is worth going back into the history of organizational analysis, and recognizing that many debates have centred around whether organizations are or should be more concerned with achieving results or achieving better relationships. One of the earlier pieces of work here was that by Douglas McGregor (1960) with his description of Theory X and Theory Y-type managers. Theory X-type managers, he suggested, assume that workers really don't want to work, that they aren't interested in organizational purposes, and don't want to take on any major responsibilities within the organization. Because of these assumptions, Theory X managers then go about their role by trying to control and coerce workers into performing acceptably. Conversely, he suggested, Theory Y managers assume that people do want to work, they are interested in organizational purposes, and will gladly accept responsibility if it is offered to them. Such Y managers then provide greater encouragement and autonomy to their workforce to help them develop themselves within their roles. Given such different views of the nature of workforces, it is perhaps unsurprising that Theory X managers are seen as more likely to focus on completion of tasks, and to give less time to the feelings and aspirations of their workforce than Theory Y managers, who are more likely to see the benefit of devoting time and care to their workforce, even if such attention may only be another way of achieving organizational results.

One of the problems with this approach is that it seems very black and white, very either/or: either managers are predisposed to be relationship-oriented, or they are predisposed to be work-oriented, when in actual fact it may be that they adopt highly individual combinations of these two approaches, including the possibility that they may be quite heavily results oriented, but believe they can only achieve this through better relationships, or that they are heavily relationship-oriented, and it is the achievement of these relationships which drive the focus on certain tasks. Relationships and tasks then become means to ends, rather than the two possessing equal status. Furthermore, it may well be that some leaders change the priority of one or the other, depending upon the context they find themselves in.

A much more nuanced approach may then be necessary. A similar, if rather more developed, variant of this kind of paradigm was seen in the managerial grid described by Blake and Mouton (1985) when they suggested that managers will tend to emphasize either results or relationships in the way they work, and depending on the balance between these two factors, a number of different forms of management are likely to emerge, of which Blake and Mouton thought 'Team Management' probably the best, as committed individuals accomplished tasks interdependently through the sharing of a common vision of organizational purpose, leading to relationships of trust and respect. The implications for personal and role sustainability seem fairly clear: if one plots the major threats to personal sustainability mentioned so far (excessive workload, different purposes between management and workers, degrees of accountability, trust and surveillance, depth of wickedity, and degree or blame or guilt in culture) against these two foci, the evidence points towards a focus which doesn't deny the need for task completion, but does this through a strong emphasis on good relationships in the workplace leading to shared goals, as well as both organizational and personal sustainability.

So far, perhaps, so good, but there are still wrinkles to this idea which need ironing out, and once more they suggest that fine-grained levels of context are needed to fully understand if sustainability is to be a problem. Mohamed and Nor (2013), for example, have argued that any consideration of the two axes of results and relationships need also to factor into an employee's 'psychological contract': what Rousseau (1989) termed 'the beliefs which individuals hold regarding the terms and conditions of the exchange agreement between themselves and their organisations'. Mohammed and Nor suggest that the issue of a psychological contracts has become much more prominent since the economic upheavals and downturns of the 1990s, because the large number of mergers, restructuring and downsizing consequent upon them have undoubtedly had damaging effects on the achievement of Team Management, as such changes are highly likely to threaten the degree of trust in organizational relationships. It may well be then that many managers come to hold a Theory X-type view of workers, not because of any assumptions about the laziness or lack of interest on the part of their employees, but because the changing nature of what is demanded of the organization also changes the nature of the relationship between leadership and workforce. Thus, both in business and educational organizations, an increasing challenge for managers and leaders has been that of persuading workforces of the need to change the nature and purpose of their work in the organization when many within the workforce wish to hold onto traditional purposes. Understandably perhaps, tensions between holders of former values, and those of more current ones, may make it nearly impossible to adopt Theory Y approaches, as the sharing of a common vision of organizational purpose becomes highly problematic, and as relationships of trust and respect are going to be difficult to establish and maintain. Instead, and as argued by one of the authors with respect to schooling (Bottery, 2007), the trust embedded in Theory Y relationships is unlikely to be extended to any significant extent, and Theory X ways of managing are therefore more likely to be used – probably through increased surveillance and accountability, and by punitive measures following lack of compliance.

In such societal contexts, organizational focus is likely to be composed more of elements of Theory X, and is therefore likely to be less personally sustaining for those given the task of implementing it, if their natural inclinations are towards the support of previous values and practices. Moving to a more pronounced Theory Y position, or to Blake and Mouton's 'Team Management' position, will then take more than a predominant focus on relationships per se: at the very least it is going to require a genuine and meaningful dialogue where accommodation is reached which gives some measure of satisfaction to both sides. And once again, the nature of such accommodations is likely to be highly context-specific.

The control of organizational discourse

As important as the structures and focus of organizations are in affecting personal sustainability, quite as important are the messages and values that are implicitly or explicitly sent out – how the organizational discourse is handled. Now much of the literature in this area associates organizational discourse with the control of power, and that such power is located with particular individuals or groups. When this occurs it is argued that they will have the greatest control over what is said and what values are adopted. This, of course, doesn't have to be the case – organizations or larger groups can be organized specifically to distribute power in such a way that no one group has ultimate control, and in this situation, the discourse will very likely be underpinned by such power-dispersal assumptions. Ceulemans et al.'s (2017) study of the Flemish implementation of public educational standards describes precisely such an arrangement. Yet in many English-speaking countries, the adoption of business perspectives by the public sector has seen an increasingly centralized and hierarchical location of power, and this has likely had considerable effect upon personal leadership sustainability. To understand better the dynamics of this, it is useful to refer to Lukes' (1974, 2005) argument that in such circumstances, both power and control can be exercised in at least three different ways:

(a)   By directly imposing one's wishes upon others through threats, coercion or bribes; in such situations, people are conscious of what is going on, but can do little about it;

(b)   By excluding other's views and interests from discussion; sometimes these others may be conscious they have been excluded, but sometimes they may not;

(c)   By determining and then controlling the discourse through which issues are debated, such that individuals or groups may never hear alternative points of view, sets of values or arguments. The aim here is to ensure that these others are not conscious of how power and control is being exerted.

In organizations and societies where power is exercised in this concentrated manner, all three kinds of power may be exercised. Yet overt power and control can be very counterproductive, and its very public exercise can produce strong and persistent negative reactions, and therefore the third and final kind is probably the most potent, for if it is unrecognized, it can provide an unchallenged form of the discourse. As Lukes (2005, p. 28) argued, by determining the words, phrases and concepts which define how an issue should be viewed:

> Is it not the supreme and most insidious exercise of power to prevent people ... from having grievances by shaping their perceptions, cognitions and preferences in such a way that they accept their role in the existing order of things, either because they can see or imagine no alternative to it, or because they see it as natural and unchangeable, or because they value it as divinely ordained and beneficial?

This is all very well if discourse can be so completely controlled, but if it is not, if people recognize what is happening, it will likely increase feelings of deception, distrust and suspicion, and in the long term may be more damaging than the two other more overt kinds. In the circumstances, strategies less focused on control and power, and more on persuasion, reward and the creation of more personally fulfilling organizational cultures (Peters and Waterman, 1982) may be used instead.

Furthermore, where an institution is located within a larger corporate organizational structure, those who mostly determine what 'the organisation' says, may be located beyond any particular institution, and the 'leaders' of that institution may not only be asked to comply with this discourse, but promote it as well, with the potential then for developing conflicting feelings of differential purposes, and less personal sustainability. For some public sector educational leaders in English-speaking Western democracies, the attempted control of educational discourse may be extremely challenging if the attempt is made to replace traditional public sector educational values with private sector ones.

Of course, some may see education as essentially a private sector activity or as an individual item of consumption, rather than as a form of public endeavour, and who may believe that business styles of thought and management are the most appropriate or necessary in the present political and economic climate. They may then embrace or accept what they see as the inevitably of such change, and see little problem in it. For them, personal sustainability is likely to be more threatened by the amount of work demanded by 'greedy organisations' in the pursuit of these aims. But for those educators holding different kinds of values and discourse, personal sustainability is more likely to be threatened by the strong differences they feel lie between what they perceive as the purpose of their role and those purposes expressed by government policies. Moreover, if they express such disagreement, and attempt to translate such purposes into practice, they will probably attract greater surveillance, accountability and accompanying workload. And those imposing such greater surveillance and accountability will likely feel that a low-trust regime is inevitable, given that such practitioners do not hold the values which current discourse suggests should underpin the leadership role. As discourse changes, then, so do the values promoted, and when this happens, the sustainability of those who attempt to hold onto a former discourse is likely to be seriously threatened.

Discourse control and the loss of sustainability

The organizational threats to individual sustainability discussed so far may seem wide-ranging in nature, yet in terms of the control of professional work in neoliberal organizational and policy contexts, there seems clear strategic intent, based upon moving such control from being largely external and public in nature, to being internalized and then finally invisible. In this way, not only is discourse controlled, but so, it is intended, are values and the practices as well. In the process, the sustainability of many of those who adhere to different educational purposes is likely to be gradually undermined. This seems likely to be accomplished in three different stages.

Stage 1 occurs when extensive external inspection systems are put in place, and institutional managements then have the responsibility for ensuring that all those to be inspected are informed of and are prepared for the inspection. In the first instances, notice of inspection may be a matter of months, and institutions will probably plan to fill that time space. These first inspections will also normally be perceived by the inspected as being a response to those external to the organization, even if much of the inspection is likely to be concerned with the actual work that the institution does. It is important to note here that this stage of the inspection procedure does not have to comprise an 'us' and 'them' mentality, where the external inspectors are perceived as 'the enemy'. As will be seen in Chapter 9, it is perfectly possible in some cultures for these inspections to be seen as helpful, and conducted by fellow peers who are perceived to be there to help the school, rather than as in some cultures, being seen as highly adversarial and threatening. In both positive and negative cases, however, sustainability may be threatened by the increased workload required, even if it is only in adversarial cases that one is likely to see the sustainability threats of different value purposes imposed through inspection, a perceived lack of trust, and the creation of blame and guilt cultures. In neither case is the degree of wickedity involved in the process likely to be perceived as a threat, as most inspections may demand plenty of preparation, but the tasks involved have tended to be relatively 'tame' – producing documents, talking to inspectors and having lessons observed.

At Stage 2, the length of notice of inspection is curtailed to perhaps only a week or a few days; this is in line with the belief or expectation that after the first couple of inspections, school managements should be very clear on the nature and culture of the inspection process, and therefore should understand much better than formerly what is required for subsequent visits. Indeed, rather than waiting to adjust practice and performance upon the announcement of an incoming inspection, most senior managements will have begun to steer existing school policies to greater conformity with perceived external demands, and will have formulated and developed new policies, practices and strategies which they believe better reflect what future inspection teams want demonstrating. At this second stage, then, the internalization of external inspection requirements has begun, but may still be largely located at senior management level, who now likely feel the need to pressurize those less senior to conform to these new expectations.

The final stage, Stage 3, will occur if all those within the institution come to understand, and then internalize, what is required of them. In effect they will be monitoring themselves and their own practice in order to ensure that they conform to external expectations. In the process, they will be practising surveillance upon themselves, and so will learn to increasingly discontinue those practices which don't conform with external expectations, and will adjust others to be similarly closer. As one English head teacher said of herself and her staff,

> Whatever we're discussing, it always got the Ofsted element there ... 'we can show this to Ofsted' always comes up, no matter what you're doing.'

Indeed, if external authorities believe that this stage is well embedded, and staff can now be expected to replicate required practices as a matter of routine, they may see little or no need for prior notice of inspection, and a phone call the day before may be all that is used. Or the team may turn up with their boxes and briefcases in the school car park on the morning of the first day of inspection.

If all of this happens, three strategies of control and steerage through inspection would be completed. A first would be the Foucauldian rendition of Bentham's 'Panopticon prison' (1979), and the kind of psychic prison that Morgan (1997) described. Practitioners would now know that through a variety of different formats, they are constantly being observed, and their efforts recorded, but do not know exactly when this will occur. So surveillance changes from being a series of actions by external forces, and becomes an internal series of actions practised upon themselves. In so doing, the nature of control changes, because, rather like riding a bicycle, when such self-surveillance is used constantly, it moves from being a conscious if stuttering process of learning, readjustment and adaptation, to being a much more efficient and streamlined, fully learned, unconscious process – unless, of course, parts of what is required are changed, and then those new elements will need to go through much the same stages once more.

In moving through these stages, then, the very language of practice and values would be changed and both might ultimately be accepted, leading to the external control of educational discourse through such unconscious adoption. One would then see the realization of the Aristotelian belief that values do not create practice nearly as efficiently as practices create values. If values and purposes need to be changed, then the best way to achieve this is to simply get people to do the same thing, time and time again. As Fergusson (1994, p. 113) argued some time ago with respect to English schools

> As sceptical teachers ... comply with the National Curriculum programme of study, test their pupils, accept appraisal, as reluctant heads sit on sub-committees of governing bodies to apportion the school's budget ... they come gradually to live and be imbued in the logic of their new roles, new tasks, new functions, and in the end to absorb partial redefinition of their professional selves, first inhabiting them, eventually becoming them.

In the process, it is argued, some threats to personal and role sustainability cease to be important, either because those who continue to resist are identified and are eventually forced out, or they leave of their own volition; or those who originally resisted, through such practice, come to live these different values, and gradually conform or even identify with them, or fail to remember why they seemed so important.

Conclusion

Well perhaps: sometimes this is the way that things work out, but it seems very unlikely that they always work this way. In many societies, such power-oriented control of discourse can be modified or minimized by the way in which organizations are structured to prevent such power centralization. Once again, one needs to be aware that much of the leadership and sustainability literature is embedded within Western cultural norms and practices, and it is important to understand and see the linkages not just between the individual and the organization, but also how organizations are nested within larger cultural values. In the next chapter, then, we shall see how two organizations in two different cultures paint very different pictures. In part this is because when organizational purposes and individual values show a strong match, this use of discourse to exert greater control and power is unnecessary and inappropriate. But it is also in part because of the nature of larger cultural values, and how they can affect organizations. This is the subject of the next chapter.

CHAPTER SEVEN

Locating Personal Sustainability within Two Organizational Contexts

Chapter outline

Introduction

The previous chapter examined the contribution of important organizational elements to both personal and organizational sustainability. The analysis of organizational forms or metaphors demonstrated how some of these forms, through the very essence of their meaning, can contribute to greater or less sustainability. However it was also argued that such typologies are only a first step in understanding the dynamics of real organizations. The consequent analysis of task versus relationships in organizations re-emphasized this: this simple idea needs to become much more nuanced, much more contextualized before its effects on real rather than 'typological' organizations are fully understood. Finally, the examination of organizational discourse suggested that hidden power agendas affecting individual sustainability are always possible, but will very likely vary with the context of the organization, and the nature of the organization itself. Each time then the analysis of different organizational elements is attempted, one will almost certainly need to dig deeper into actual realities, to deeper complexities, to deeper individualities.

This chapter then takes the examination of such individuality deeper by examining the effects of these elements on two real-life organizations. The two organizations selected are not seen as outstanding exemplars of any particular positive or negative characteristics: rather they are organizations whose dynamics were 'discovered' during two particular portrait projects, and which threw important light upon how organizations can support or detract from the sustainability of the individuals within them. The quotations are taken from three different sources: the first are taken from full transcripts before selection for portraits; the second are from actual portraits; and the third are from discussions either singly or in groups following the portraits. All are anonymized.

The organizations

One of these organizations was located in England, the other in Hong Kong. The English organization was a large multi-institutional private organization, one branch of which employed a small team of head teachers, contracted out to a LEA, to deal with particularly difficult schools. The composition of this team was in large part serendipitous. It originated through the appointment of one head teacher, experienced in dealing with difficult situations in schools, who was asked to deal with a particularly challenging school; her success led to the appointment of other practiced head teachers to do much the same thing at other schools in the area. They were what the research team (Mike Bottery, Nigel Wright and John Smith) would come to call 'trouble-shooter head teachers', because these individuals would be 'helicoptered' into a school at a moment's notice, with little or no knowledge of the school, or of its problems, and not knowing how long they would be there for. Indeed, their stay could be a couple of weeks, months, or even in one case, a couple of years. Their job essentially was to restore order in the school and get it back on track. The call for them to go in could be very urgent. As one of the team remarked, when she got to one school:

There were police at the gate escorting staff and pupils on the premises and eight out of the twelve teachers were off sick ... emotions were very raw and staff were fighting with each other, parents were literally fighting, children were literally fighting.

We were invited to work with this 'trouble-shooter' team after one of these head teachers, who previously had two separate portraits of her written, had found the experience rewarding and thought that the portrait exercise would constitute a useful development and reflective exercise for the other members of the group. After discussions were then held on who would actually conduct the interviews and write the portraits, an invitation was extended to the research team. The project ran for 2–3 months: after preliminary discussions, and an introductory session on the portrait approach, six 'trouble-shooter' head teachers were interviewed, their portraits were written, after which a final follow-up interview took place. As will be explained later, it is important to note that there was something of a disjunction between the culture of the private organization and the shared culture of the head teachers. The shared culture of the head teachers – and of its sustainability – will be the major focus in the analysis.

The Hong Kong organization, in contradistinction, was an overarching body overseeing the work of a group of special schools, within which the principals worked. For this particular analysis, we want to make a distinction between the wider organization, and the institutions within it, but focus primarily on the relationship between its principals and the wider organization, as this seemed to us to be the key relationship with respect to the sustainability of individuals, institutions and organization.

This organization oversaw the functioning of schools, which catered for children with mild, moderate and severe learning difficulties. The research team (this time, the authors of this book) were invited in through securing a Hong Kong government grant to help develop the specials schools, and one important part of such development was felt to be that of the school principals, particularly as the organization had at that time seen the departure of a significant number of experienced principals, and the subsequent movement into the role of a number of relatively inexperienced individuals. In this study, all principals were interviewed, portraits were written, and then each principal re-interviewed two to three months later to enquire about their reactions to the portraits. In addition, a further set of interviews was conducted afterwards to study the impact that the interviews and the portraits had had on these principals – a study of portrait impact to be covered in Chapter 11 of this book.

These two sets of portraits then throw important light not only on the personal sustainability of the individuals, but also, and a little surprisingly and serendipitously, on the sustainability of the organizations as well. As elements of organizational functioning are examined which can contribute to or detract from personal sustainability, an analysis of the sustainability of these two organizations will also be developed. The comparative sustainability of the two organizations is shown in Table 7.1 where not only are the forms, focus and discourse of these organizations examined, but so also are the threats, support and improvements which might be made to them, and to the individuals within them.

Table 7.1 Comparing personal and organizational sustainability: Two case studies

	EnglishOrg	HKOrg
Organizational form	Tensions between local organic and standardized machine	Strong continuous culture of child care
Task/person focused	Tensions between relationship and task/results focus	Heavily relationship (child) centred
Discourse use	A tension between person and task/results focus	Child-centred/personal responsibility
Individual types and responses	All relished difficult challenges; all aware of need to 'heal' problems before other concerns addressed	All child-centred and focused; many had to learn to grow beyond classroom-focus into teacher-growth focus
Personal sustainability threatened by	Premature moves from healing the organization to results emphasis	Premature induction into leadership; need for greater adult care discourse
Personal sustainability supported by	Initial autonomy for context-appropriate responses to problems; enjoyment of challenges	Personal embrace of organizational philosophy; autonomy permitted to act contextually
Personal sustainability would be improved by	Greater recognition by external others of need for healing process and contextualizing of judgements	Talent spotted early and mentored; personal horizons stretched; more devolved responsibility granted
Organizational sustainability threatened by	Premature movement by others demanding 'results' rather than 'healing' focus	Premature induction of inexperienced leaders; cultural context undervaluing SEN
Organizational sustainability supported by	Initial emphasis on healing within context-bound timeline	Overarching organizational focus, discourse and philosophy on care
Organizational sustainability improved by	Reducing results focus; permitting greater appreciation of contextual nature of many challenges	Developing organizational as well as institutional support; increaseing scope and quantity of devolved leadership

Organizational forms in the two organizations

The two organizations had some strong similarities, but also some strong differences. The leadership and ethos of the Hong Kong organization was very widely respected by the principals working for it. One principal described it as

> the greatest association working with the mentally handicapped in Hong Kong … . [the organisation] is a good, good boss … they want their schools to improve.

The organization had a very strong and continuous culture of responding to the needs of individual children. All of the principals and all other members of the organization with whom we talked expressed their commitment to this goal with considerable conviction:

> We believe that people with disability still have their potential, or their ability, so we try our best to provide school education or training, and then after that they can live independently, and they can serve our society.
>
> They [the children] really need our love, our companionship with them, our understanding of their challenges, to help them step by step, to be their companions and to move on with them through challenges.

The pursuit of this mission was felt by all the principals interviewed to be immensely rewarding to them and their colleagues: 'If money is your reward, you can get the satisfaction once a month … But if you like the children, you get the satisfaction every day.'

Leaving the classroom to become principal, however, meant for many a step away from such personal fulfilment. One principal recalled the pleasure he gained from his time in the classroom, by simply saying 'I miss it … I miss it.' Another said that being in the classroom was 'the happiest time of my career' but now as a principal, 'You don't have a lot of chances to stand in the classrooms, you know, work with them.'

It was clear then that this was not just an intellectual philosophy; it was a deeply felt emotional commitment to which all principals were strongly wedded. Most of them had their happiest times in these one-to-one relationships with these children, driven by the desire to make a difference to their lives. This meant that there was a strong cultural focus to which all subscribed, and which built a strong culture.

Yet the commitment to the children, and the love of being in the classroom could have its problems. It meant that many didn't look on the principalship as a move upwards, but as a move away from where they really wanted to be. It could also mean that this culture of child-centred care might reduce attention from a focus on teacher development and support for new principals. One said, almost apologetically, '*It's very obvious the children come first here ... all of us know that the vision is children come first.*'

Another felt that some redress in the balance might be necessary as:

'*I think the colleagues are also just like my students before ... I have to take care about my colleagues.*' And just as all the children needed individual educational plans (IEPs), '*so we can have also IEPs for my colleagues, for my teachers, so I can give them personal support*'.

Finally, in a highly competitive culture like Hong Kong, where everyone '*is moving very fast, everybody walks very fast*' a greater focus on changes in that society, and of the need for linkages with other organizations might not only develop personal leadership sustainability, but might help the organization to develop greater awareness of threats to its sustainability coming from beyond its boundaries. This was then a healthy organization, but one which probably needed to be alert to potential external problems.

The English organization was rather different. There seemed little in the way of a corporate educational culture, other than it being a private company contracted to 'deliver' results to a client. However, our interactions with the principals suggested that a culture had gradually been formed by the 'trouble-shooter' head teachers without formal recognition by larger corporate perspectives. It was initially a largely organic and evolving culture, which recognized the need to adjust to the particular circumstances of a school as need arose:

> *You can't have too formed an idea in your head of where you're going because it's very turbulent and things change very quickly.*

The shared culture stemmed, it seemed, largely from two elements. A first element lay in their approaches to the role; while these head teachers were very different in personality, all seemed to demonstrate considerable resilience, all had strong self-belief, and all had a sense of compassion for those in the troubled schools. Perhaps most noticeably, however, all *enjoyed* the challenges presented by such problem schools, which many other head teachers might well have found overwhelming. In a previous interview Mike Bottery had had with the head teacher who suggested this exercise for the group, he had listened to her talking about the enjoyment she felt going into such difficult situations, and had suggested to her that there was an element of the '*adrenaline junkie*' about her. She had simply laughed and agreed, and there was a similar welcoming of extreme challenge from all in the group:

> *I like challenge, I like turbulence.*
>   *I only ever, ever envisage myself being in a school with difficulty ... .*
> *I just really like the challenge, and I really like that buzz when you go in somewhere , and the place feels like it's falling around its ears.*

> *I'm actually driven by wanting to do things, not necessarily better, but wanting to do them in more difficult circumstances ... it's almost like you test yourself and you want to see how far you can push it.*

As another remarked, her mother had always said of her that she '*doesn't like anything unless she has to wear a safety helmet*'.

The second element of this shared culture was their prescription for dealing with the schools: this was not one of strict discipline, or setting targets and working towards them, or focusing on results: it was in fact a strong belief in the need to '*heal the school*' – to allow the anger and pain to be acknowledged, the feelings of helplessness to be recognized and talked about, and then to be dealt with. Too often, they would go into a school and find morale on the floor:

> *This feeling among staff that they've failed and that they are useless ... a feeling of hopelessness ... a big black cloud over the place ... a sort of emotional paralysis.*

This meant that they felt that the role initially had to be '*about mending broken links in relationships within a school in itself and within the wider community*'.

This did not mean that tough decisions did not need to be taken. One head teacher talked of the need to have two teachers leave the school: '*It needed doing ... it was the only way the school could survive*'. Another simply said that both '*compassion and toughness*' were essential hallmarks of doing the job well.

Only in this way, then was it felt that a school would be able to get back on track. This was something of a surprise to the research team: so often the recommendation from governments and media is for charismatic individuals to go into problem organizations and lead them forward by sheer force of personality (a characteristic of leaders seen in many business books where the organization is brought back from the brink). Yet few of the head teachers in the group matched this characterization, and even fewer believed that this was the appropriate way forward:

> *We're not super-heads, we're not super humans ... we struggle as well sometimes.*

And this was an important part of the healing mission because '*the one thing you can't do is allow people to become dependent on you*' and coming into a damaged school with a charismatic super-head status might just lead to this unhelpful and unsustainable development. It was perhaps then unsurprising that one of the head teachers said:

> *It's my bounden duty to show from day one that I've got feet of clay.*

So a different kind of approach was needed:

> *I'm not an imposer really. I'm much more a facilitator in finding the way ... I don't have a tick list ... typically what I do is give time to people to talk to start with. ... You gather information that tells you about other things that you need to do in order to heal those relationships.*

And the end result?

> *You see things flower that you've sown the seeds for ... people do say 'Oh I've done this and it worked really well' and you think that's because I've put everything in place for that to happen ... and it just makes you smile inside.*

Another head teacher said much the same thing:

> *I get a lot of satisfaction from [healing the school] ... it is just fantastic going in there [now], it has this buzz, because we have managed to get the children excited about their learning ... for the staff to be so proud to see what they have achieved.*

The initial culture then was a highly contextualized, listening and healing approach, with, almost by default, a great deal of autonomy devolved to these head teachers. In a highly difficult role, this 'healing' culture seemed to have strong elements of sustainability about it. However, there were indications that external pressures were leading to a change of organizational focus. It is to organizational focus, then, that we now turn.

Sustainability in the two organizations: Forms and focus

The English head teacher group then appeared to be evolving an organic and heavily context-specific response to local organizations, which initially focused on healing the institutions in their care. The English organization, perhaps almost by default, seemed to have aided leadership sustainability through permitting a considerable degree of autonomy to the head teachers, thus allowing them to contextualize problems, and to adopt specific healing approaches to the schools within which they were asked to work. As one said:

> *There's a danger in thinking 'because that worked in that school, and you recognise certain characteristics, then it's going to work the same in this school' ... because it doesn't.*

In these particular contexts, then, a focus on relationships was seen by the head teachers as absolutely paramount, with a results/task orientation needing to be delayed until the schools were judged by them to be ready for a different kind of focus. As one of them remarked, if you don't mend these first,

> You can't hope to make any impact on achievement ... you have to have those things in place first.

However, a tension was noticed throughout the project, as the head teachers spoke of concerns about external pressures on the schools, in particular a greater emphasis on schools to achieve results earlier than they felt appropriate, putting into the question the sustainability of the schools and the viability of their role. As one head teacher said, she wasn't *anti-government* or *anti-accountability*, but she felt that '*I'm being asked to do a job I don't in my heart believe will improve things for children* [even if] *it might improve standards on paper*'.

Her greatest dissatisfaction then was '*the frustration of thinking you know what's to be done, got to be done, but you can't actually do it, either because the staff are not yet able to, or because you're not actually allowed to because of the external accountability*'.

The result was that '*you're put into a school to do a job, but actually sometimes the job that you're asked to do has no integrity*' by which she meant if she was driven by an external imposed agenda which didn't match the needs of the school, for her, then, the danger was that '*it's like pouring things down a bottomless pit because those structures are not there to keep it and underpin it ... . I just know that if they* [the school staff] *are asked to fill another grid to be accountable then you know one or two of them are going to crack*'.

There then seemed to be a real threat not only to the sustainability of the people and the institutions which these head teachers were trying to heal, but very likely to their own personal and role sustainability, stemming largely from pressure from what was viewed as a premature movement of focus from healing relationships to harvesting results.

The Hong Kong organization, on the other hand, seemed at the time of the portrait project to have a strong and continuous culture of child-centred care, even if it was one which might need a greater focus on adult-centred care if the principals' role was to be made more sustainable. It was also located within a wider educational culture, which our research suggests was not as results – and accountability – driven as for instance in England (see Chapter 9 of this book). The Hong Kong societal view very likely helped the sustainability of the organization, as relatively less task-oriented pressure seemed to be exerted on the organization than on its English counterparts. Little challenge then seems to have been made to the organization's heavily person-centred focus by a more results-oriented emphasis. If there were issues of leadership sustainability, they seemed to come from an insufficient organizational focus on the support and development of the school leaders. As one principal said, the organizational culture had to be '*also about caring about teachers, not just caring about students*' and this did not seem reflected in its discourse. It is to this subject that we now turn.

Discourse and sustainability in the two organizations

The type and use of discourse reflected the forms and focus of the group of English trouble-shooter head teachers, and of the HK organizational values, shared by its principals. Neither conformed to the power-based use of discourse, which both Foucault (1979) and Lukes (2005) describe. Instead, in the English organization, the discourse of these head teachers, largely originated and was then owned by them, rather than being imposed on them, and it was a collective discourse of 'healing' the institutions in their care. However, it was apparent that this discourse was challenged by a wider legislative results/ accountability focus, which was seen not only by the demands made by external authorities on the schools they were dealing with, but also in the speed with which they were being asked to move to this larger discourse. Their organic discourse then was being challenged and a real threat lay in its being replaced by a more centralized power-based discourse. In Hong Kong, the organizational discourse as noted, was highly child-centred, and there seems little doubt that such discourse both attracted and selected most of those who worked there. They worked there, then, because they identified with and were so emotionally committed to the discourse that there was no need for the discourse to be determined or imposed upon them by others. In both organizations, then, there existed discourses which seemed to support both personal and organizational sustainability, though the English discourse was challenged by a results-oriented discourse which made the realization of the 'healing' discourse problematic.

It seems clear then that the power-oriented control of discourse described by Lukes and Foucault is not a *necessary* consequence of working in an organization; new discourses can be invented, or existing discourses can be modified or even minimized by the way in which structures are organized to prevent such power centralization. What also seems clear is that while the two organizations addressed very different issues, the organizational purposes and individual values of both showed strong coherence at that time, even if the future of the English headteachers' discourse looked increasingly threatened.

In the HK organization, throughout the length of the study, there was no observable change in the discourse used. One principal, in describing one of his colleagues, simply said that '*he's a very good principal, and very* [name of organisation]'. To be able to use such a phrase makes very clear a belief in a strong and identifiable set of values, and a commonly accepted discourse, which are both assertive of the rights of people with disabilities, and fully committed to the organization to realizing such rights. For the reasons given above, such discourse was part of the emotional framework which all the principals expressed, and which underpinned their sense of achievement. This, then, was no exercise of power by those at the top of a hierarchy on those below: it was a commitment which all shared. As one principal noted, the overarching organization was not top-down, focused upon *'control'* of ideas and people, but instead was *'very supportive and trusting'* of its principals. The discourse then supported both organizational and personal sustainability. If there was a problem, as suggested above, this seemed to lie in the lack of emphasis on the organization's commitment to the personal development and sustainability of its school leaders. It then seems highly unlikely that Luke's three-stage discourse model would develop in this HK organization in the short to medium term.

In the English organization, the tension between the tightly held values and purposes of the head teachers with a larger political educational discourse seemed clear, and likely produced pressures on the purposes of the overarching organization within which the head teachers were situated. This other discourse had for a number of decades in England been one of low trust, high stakes and results accountability. However, in this organization, the innovative project the head teachers were employed to implement had provided a degree of autonomy to these individuals, which as one of them remarked, many new projects do:

> *I've always seen when the government have an idea in the first year or so, you have much greater freedom [before] they actually work out what it's for and setting the regulations.*

The group of head teachers then seemed for a while to have escaped some of the pressures from the larger accountability culture. However it was also clear that the schools to which they were assigned were still subject to these external pressures, largely because of the continued presence of Ofsted. So when these pressures are combined with a settling down of the organizational models, which Weber (1947) pointed out over a century ago, organizations tend to retreat from or discourage large-scale experimentation, and move towards a greater emphasis on the standardization of rules and procedures. In such circumstances, one suspects that the larger political educational culture might reassert itself, and in so doing, move the head teachers away from a focus on healing relationships in these unsustainable schools, towards a greater emphasis on the generation of results.

With such pressures, there must therefore be some concern not only for the sustainability of these schools in difficulties, but also for the sustainability of the 'trouble-shooter' head teachers' role, as envisaged by the group at that time.

Threats, support and improvement to organizational sustainability

The argument has been made throughout the book that personal and role sustainability will ultimately only be fully realized when the individuality of the leadership role is recognized. This requirement largely applies to organizations as well, with the recognition that organizational differences also require nuanced responses as well. Organizational sustainability, then, is likely to be better improved by measures suited specifically to the nature and context of a particular organization.

Now if the threats to organizational sustainability are examined in the Hong Kong organization, the induction of relatively inexperienced individuals into the principal's role seemed the most pressing issue at the time of the research, and in large part appeared to stem from the teachers' greater fulfilment in the classroom. As one new principal remarked:

> *I prefer to be a teacher ... I enjoy teaching really ...* [the principals job] *is not an easy job to do.*

Another was quite blunt about the reluctance felt at taking on the role:

> *I think I'm a teacher only ... . I like to be number two always, not number one ... . No planning at all* [for the role of principal] *... . I don't think about this ... . I rejected and refused to try at first ... a lot of pressure ... suddenly I become a principal.*

A similar response came from another principal, but this time with explanation of why the post was reluctantly accepted: '*I had never even thought about it* [becoming a principal] *because I think I am not ready.*' However, '[the organisation's] *schools really needed a principal, and I know it is very difficult to find one*' and he was '*really committed*' to the organization. Another principal said that the role of principal was '*a challenge that I don't want ... [but] I have to face it*'. Out of a sense of duty and responsibility to the organization, then, the role was rather reluctantly taken up.

Other threats to the organization's sustainability seemed to come from beyond its boundaries. Three of them are mentioned here. A first was the gradual contraction of the special needs area: '*The inclusive education is the main change in education theory after 1997*', and the consequent '*immigration [from special schools] into the mainstream schools*'. This may have been exacerbated in the past by feelings of inferior status for SEN schools, and one principal thought that '*maybe they were like this ten years ago*' but '*nowadays they don't*'.

Another external threat was the undervalued nature of SEN activity. In part this was because of the competitive nature of Hong Kong society; in part because of a cultural embarrassment of children with such needs. One principal talked of how one mother had told him that *'whenever they* [she and her children] *went inside the lift* [of her housing block] *people who were inside would get out and say' 'don't infect us, please don't come in'*. And when there were family gatherings the response to the presence of disabled children was direct and unpleasant: *'Please don't come again.'*

Another principal, however, took a longer historical view and suggested that things had changed in the 1990s, and the parents then *'fought for their rights, and they would voice out what they needed'*, but after the handover in 1997, *'the trend changed again because most parents come from mainland China ... they are afraid to let others know they have special children'*. However, he suggested that even this was now changing as they had quickly adopted the political habits of Hong Kong: *'They know more about the rights and fight for their rights more.'* The organization then had to handle two almost contradictory attitudes; one was the embarrassment felt by some about SEN children, the other was the rights-demanding parental voice.

A final external threat, and a surprising one given how strongly many interviewees felt, was the message of child care transmitted by the organization, stemmed from the pace of change in Hong Kong. One principal said that *'the society has changed, the environment has changed, the atmosphere of society has changed'*, and a consequence of all this change was that people were now much busier than previously, with demands not only from work but social life as well. He suggested that this meant that the management board of the organization couldn't spend as much time with the organization as they might have done previously. He also felt that this problem was compounded for the organization by the fact that the board had very few educators: *'Only one lady comes from the education field.'* This meant, he thought, that despite the fact that he *'didn't doubt the devotion of the management of* [the organisation] *... most of them have less time to contribute ... they are too busy'*.

These changes, these challenges, this busyness, he thought, contributed to a surprising but major problem for the organization in that he thought *'it shares less vision or mission than the one I entered twenty five or thirty years ago'* and the result was that *'... I think most of us are puzzled where we need to go or the direction ... 30 years ago, we had a clear direction and mission to do the job. Only one aim and one direction'*, strongly suggesting that in a faster-changing, higher demanding, more immediately communicating world, the complexity and speed of demands had increased dramatically, such that it was now no longer possible to focus on just one area of concern. This then was a problem not just for the organization, but for society as a whole, and once more points to the need to place not only individuals but organizations in their full cultural, political and time contexts, if one is to completely appreciate the full range of threats to organizational sustainability.

As in Hong Kong, external pressures were also coming to bear on the English organization. External political pressures in England have, for nearly three decades, been committed to raising educational standards through external imposition, backed up by regular and punitive inspection regimes. So the schools with which the English head teachers were dealing not only had various pressures from within, but continuous pressure from without. In such a societal context, the major threat to the success of the 'trouble-shooting' activities of this group of head teachers seemed to be potentially premature movements by the larger organization, prompted by government pressures, to increase emphases on improving school results. This, we have seen, was leading to an incommensurability of values and visions between these head teachers, and the larger organizational demands which mirrored governmental requirements. Thus, there was an interesting similarity between the Hong Kong and English organizations: despite very different emphases and foci, both organizations, and those working within them, were facing conflicting visions of educational purposes, which were unlikely to help the long-term sustainability of either.

The support and improvement of the sustainability of both organizations then follows from what has been written above. In the English organization, sustainability of the head teacher group would seem better supported and improved by the continuation of a healing rather than a results emphasis within these damaged schools, and by the greater appreciation of the contextual nature of many challenges, as well as by the need for a continued degree of autonomy to experienced educational leaders in their remediation of the problems in individual schools.

In the Hong Kong organization, there seemed little doubt that the sustainability of the overarching organization was supported by its philosophy, and by its focus and discourse on the care for its charges. It was also clear that when support was provided to these principals, it was very much appreciated:

> *When I first pick up the principalship, I have intensive meetings with the [organisation's] administrative group almost every two weeks.*
> *When I need to make some important decisions I can cooperate with some principals for advice.*

Moreover, principal autonomy was also felt to be very supportive. One principal had developed his own strategy for dealing with the parents of SEN children, by allowing them '*to enter the classroom*' and help there. This, he felt, had really helped relations, and then '*you find that you're helping not only the students but the whole family ... and that's a very meaningful job*'. Yet such autonomy could result in variation in both strategy and level of support, which might then be more effective and more sustainable through greater attention to the developmental state of each principal. By focusing support on the various stages of development of the principals, organizational sustainability would also be strengthened.

Individual sustainability: Threats, support and improvement

Considerations of sustainability should then not remain at the organizational/institutional level. Retaining the organizational values, strategies and practices which promote sustainability, while altering or eliminating those which decrease it, and introducing other sustainable measures, not only increase overall organizational sustainability, but can increase individual sustainability as well, and the interaction between these levels of sustainability is therefore critical to understanding individual sustainability.

Threats to personal sustainability, as we have seen, to some extent stemmed, a little paradoxically, from what were perceived by many as strengths of the organization or group. The strong child-centred organizational metaphor in the Hong Kong organizations, and the strong team ethos in the English organization, underpinned by strong, shared collective discourses, made it very likely that this marriage of collective and individual purposes aided personal sustainability in the role. Indeed, despite the concerns of one HK principal about the diminution of organizational vision, most others thought that the philosophy and values remained strong and clear. The threat to personal sustainability seemed to stem for many from never having wanted to leave the classroom and take on the leadership role. As one principal noted, reflecting on his own career:

> 'It's very happy when you're in the classroom. I feel very happy.' It was not then surprising that he went on to say that 'the teachers like the teaching, so they foresee the principal's job is not an easy job ... so they prefer to stay in the classroom.'

Another principal also remarked on how she loved her time in the classroom, not only because 'I can have contact with all my students ... but because [the organisation] gives us that flexibility ... we can have our professional judgement'. The problem, as the previous principal had noted was that 'if we feel comfortable, then maybe we don't want to get the promotion'.

For many, then, fulfilment was still seen as coming from interactions with the children; institutional leadership was much more of a duty, fulfilled out of loyalty to the organization, but not sought after or welcomed:

> It's my responsibility to take up the school for the school improvement.

Feelings of responsibility didn't then always translate into sustained feelings of satisfaction in the role. The challenge for the organization seemed to be to help develop all principals to a level where they felt fulfilment from leading. One principal exemplified this when he said, '*I like working with people ... . I can give some advice and suggestions for the teacher*' after which '*the teacher will impact on the students ... that's not an impact just on the classroom ... . I can impact on the whole school.*'

A similarly strong set of shared values and purposes pervaded the English headteacher group, who, as we have seen, relished the challenge of what many others would regard as a highly stressful role, who were resilient, and believed in the need to heal schools before addressing other concerns. So, the main threat to personal sustainability here seemed to come, not from overwork, or the stress of dealing with such schools, but from what was perceived as mounting pressure on them to move from healing institutions to generating better examination results before the schools and their inhabitants were ready.

In sum, then, in both organizations, a prematurity of organizational movement seemed to be the main threat to personal sustainability. In Hong Kong, threats to personal sustainability seemed to come from the need to promote individuals to the position of principal before they were ready, either because their hearts and heads were still in the classroom, or they did not feel they had sufficient experience or training to meet the role. In England, the prematurity took a different form: a pressure on them to focus more on delivering externally verifiable results, rather than getting the relationships in the schools right. In the light of these analyses, approaches to support and develop personal sustainability would likely to be more effective if the measures adopted were designed to suit the needs of particular individuals and the contexts they found themselves in, rather than ones designed for more generalized application.

Levels of individual support, it seemed clear, differed between the two organizations. The strong similarity between the philosophy and purposes of the Hong Kong organization and individual philosophies and purposes meant that personal sustainability was strongly supported. It also permitted a considerable degree of personal autonomy to school principals. For some this was highly welcomed, though for less experienced principals, more support and direction would probably have been more appropriate. In England, as the individuals interviewed were experienced head teachers, the autonomy provided to them to devise context-specific remedies was seen by these individuals as very helpful, though it was unclear whether the larger organization understood or appreciated the need for these head teachers to focus in the first instance on 'healing' institutions, rather than engaging in some charismatic leadership exercise of leading all to attaining better grades.

How might personal sustainability then be improved? Improvement was likely to come in Hong Kong through a stronger organizational policy of spotting talent early, and of such talented individuals being mentored through a formal organizational mentoring policy rather than through principals spotting talented staff and doing this individually. The comments by one principal, that '*we don't have good policies to cultivate or train the staff to be a principal*' suggested a useful area for improvement.

There was probably also need for staff personal horizons to be stretched beyond a focus on the child, the classroom and the individual school, and for the development of a greater awareness and involvement in organizational level problems and beyond. This might be facilitated by what one principal called an '*exchange programme*', where more teachers (and principals) saw and compared the practices of other schools, both within and beyond the organization, with the result being '*If a principal gets experience from different schools ... I think it's better because he can get more experience to share with different people*'.

Greater sustainability might also be developed through a greater devolved responsibility in some areas – such as in welcoming the input of principals on selection panels for the appointment of new principals. In the English organization, personal sustainability would probably have been improved if principals' autonomy and the need for contextualized judgements was consciously recognized by the larger organization, rather than apparently default-based, and of the need to heal organizations and the relationships within them.

Conclusion: Locating the micro- and meso- within macro-contexts

In these last two chapters, the effects that organizations can have on the personal and role sustainability of educational leaders have been examined. Through scrutinizing different organizational forms, their major purposes and the discourses used within them, we have seen how two particular organizations could be very distinctive yet could share some strong similarities. While they had very different goals, they were both sustained by the shared commitment their members had to these goals. Moreover, organizational and personal sustainability in both seemed affected by different kinds of premature action. In England, this seemed to be a premature movement from a healing to a results focus. It is a prematurity which cannot be understood without an appreciation of the high-stakes/low-trust political and legislative context within which the organization existed, and which ran against many of the policies and perceptions of those trying to 'heal' the schools in their charge. In the HK organization, both personal and organizational sustainability was weakened by the appointment of principals before some of them were ready or willing to take on the role.

However, even here, where the main presenting problem seemed to be internal to the organization, many of the other suggested threats to their sustainability stemmed from larger contextual factors. It is to the influences of cultural factors on personal and role sustainability that we now turn. While there has been some research on such effects, it is a relatively neglected area, and the majority of educational leadership writing, and particularly its sustainability, has failed to engage with these influences. As with the organizational focus, this examination of cultural effects on sustainability is divided into two chapters. The next chapter then contrasts the underpinning values and practices of two sets of broad cultural norms in Western and Asian countries, the examination of which provides the means to focus better on personal sustainability, and these are then used in the following chapter to contrast the views of English head teachers and Hong Kong principals on the challenges they face. The results suggest that there are both major differences and some surprising commonalities between the two cultural groups. It is then to an examination of the effects of this macro-context on personal and role sustainability that we now turn.

PART THREE

Macro-Contexts of Sustainability

CHAPTER EIGHT

Cultural Influences On Leadership Sustainability

Chapter outline

Introduction

It was suggested at the beginning of the book that there exist a number of different threats to the personal and role sustainability of educational leaders:

- The increased damage to government/educator relationships, and particularly the loss of trust between them, over the last few decades;

- Differences in governmental and professional perceptions of the purposes of the leadership role;

- Increased accountability and surveillance of the leadership role;

- The greater use of power rather than persuasion by governments to effect changes;

- A failure to recognize the increased complexity of the role, in particular the increased influence of more and larger contexts;

- The growth of guilt and blame cultures;

- The development of excessive leadership workloads;

- Insufficient preparation for the leadership role.

It was also pointed out that the strength and combination of these causes may well vary from culture to culture, particularly if some elements within a culture exacerbate particular threats, while others ameliorate them. It would then be dangerous to assume that the threats to leadership sustainability in one culture are the same as those in another, just as it would be inadvisable to uncritically adopt remedies used elsewhere. This chapter then begins by first discussing the meaning of the term 'culture', before contrasting the underpinning values and practices of two sets of very broad cultural norms with respect to issues of educational leadership. One set, seen in most 'western' countries, is also that which is most represented in the educational leadership literature. The other, rather less well covered, is that sometimes claimed as being exhibited in many 'Asian' countries. The chapter will suggest that many of the sustainability threats reported in this leadership literature are exacerbated by current ideological and legislative trends within this 'western' culture, and particularly within an Anglo-American subculture, and that these threats have the potential to be exported elsewhere. On the positive side, it will also be argued that a degree of nuanced cultural borrowing might help to remedy such sustainability problems.

Defining 'culture'

'Culture' is one of those words, the meaning of which many people think they understand, but usually find it hard to pin down. This is not surprising; the map is always more simple than the territory it describes, and 'culture' has many meanings, many approaches and many values underpinning descriptions of its use. It is also a word which historically, has gained considerable negative connotations, and has been used to discriminate against minorities within a country, to promote conservative functionalist views of society as opposed to more conflict-based ones, as well as being used as an ideological tool in the imposition of colonial and neocolonial rule on others. It is not then without its problems, but its mis-use should not prevent investigation of its more constructive qualities, and it continues to be of considerable interest in a large number of academic disciplines: anthropology, archaeology, sociology, social and cognitive psychology, linguistics, business studies, comparative education, educational leadership – all of which will likely come to its study with different framings of problems and questions, underpinned by different interests and values. Thus when Kluckholm and Kroeber in 1952 reviewed existing definitions in the anthropological literature, they counted 162. And in Keasing's (1974) magisterial review of agreement on the meaning of the term, he suggested (pp. 81–2) that one needs to begin 'with no expectation that an eclectic composite can be reached with which they [different anthropologists] would agree'.

Finally, anyone browsing current introductions to an anthropological study of culture (e. g. Hendry, 2016; Eriksen, 2017) will find descriptions of a complex historical development of such study with all the differing arguments, perspectives and values normally found in any academic discipline.

However, this is not meant as a counsel of despair, but as a warning of its wickedity – that if we try to 'tame' the concept, we end up with something insufficiently rich and nuanced to reflect its complexity, and which therefore lacks any real practical value. And there does seem good reason to believe that it has value in helping to explain how individuals come to behave in certain ways, and to hold particular values and beliefs. If there is difficulty in pinning down its central meaning(s), there still remain helpful ways of approaching this issue, and the one used here is to ask the following set of questions:

- What do cultures consist of?
- What are the dimensions of culture?
- What are the functions of cultures?
- How big are cultures?
- What do researchers regard as the most significant aspects of 'culture'?

Each will be dealt with in turn.

1 So, what do cultures consist of?

Because here there are so many things that could be written down, there is a real danger of simply supplying lists of actions or practices performed, or of values held deeply by different groups of people. Fox (2014, p. 18), for example, quotes a list of seventy-three cultural universals by Murdock (1945), but which provides little help in getting to grips with connecting concepts. Fox's (2014, p. 16) own more focused suggestion is that culture consists of 'the sum of a society's or social group's patterns of behaviour, customs, way of life, beliefs and values'. Dimmock and Walker (2005, p. 13), two educational leadership writers, suggest that societal culture consists of 'those enduring sets of values, beliefs and practices that distinguish one group from another ... which include' 'how they dress, what and how they eat, marriage, customs and family life, their patterns of work, religious ceremonies, leisure pursuits and works of art'

It might well be argued that *all* lists may amount to little more than stipulative definitions, but it is worth noting here that both of these definitions suggest that cultures consists of both surface behaviours and practices, and deeper issues of cognition and values, and perhaps of an interaction between surface and deeper manifestations. While both elements seem essential to any comprehensive definition, rather than trying to enumerate them all, perhaps a more useful exercise than working from any particular list would be one of being aware of a range of possible elements, and using these to iteratively interrogate social practices.

Nevertheless, this joint focus on the behavioural and the cognitive, the practice and the value suggests a way of understanding cultural dynamics. For example, Nisbett (2003, p. xx), a cultural psychologist, has suggested that different cultural groups not only have enduring observable behaviours and practices, and world views, but that they think differently, and therefore act differently. Cultures for him, then, are essentially self-reinforcing homeostatic systems where 'the social practices promote the worldviews; the worldviews dictate the appropriate thought processes; and the thought processes both justify the worldviews and support the social practices'.

Yet one needs to be careful here; what he says may be interpreted as 'fixing' individuals and groups into particular thought patterns and behaviours, which can lead down the mis-used roads of stereotyping and standardization. A better way, it seems to us, would be to regard cultures as group orientations to certain values, ways of thinking and behaving. On such an account, the degree to which an individual or group conforms to such an orientation, or adopted elements of other orientations, would depend on other factors, such as individual personality traits, the strength of this cultural influence, and the level of exposure to other dissonant orientations. So, while most individuals in a group would likely embrace this orientation, at no time would it be expected that any one individual or group would conform completely to such an orientation, and at no time would they be completely determined by it.

2 What are the dimensions of culture?

Hofstede is famous in the business community and beyond for suggesting five basic dimensions to a societal level of culture, which he described as:

- Social inequality, including the relationship with authority;
- The relationship between the individual and the group;
- Concepts of masculinity and femininity;

- Ways of dealing with uncertainty, relating to the control of aggression and the expression of emotions;

- A long-term orientation in life to a short-term orientation. (2003, pp. 13–14)

Since publication, his claims have received some fairly withering reviews about his sampling, methodology and analysis (see, for example, McSweeney, 2002). But others (e.g. Trompenaar and Hampden-Turner, 2004) have produced not-too dissimilar lists, while Dimmock and Walker (2005, pp. 29–31) from an educational leadership perspective, suggest six dimensions of their own:

- Power-distributed/power concentrated;

- Group oriented/self-oriented;

- Consideration/aggression;

- Proactivism/fatalism;

- Generative/replicative;

- Limited relationships/holistic relationships.

As with cultural content, arguments can be made for a combination of many different dimensions. For instance, such lists might also include *change versus stability, tameness versus wickedity*, and *inward-looking versus outward looking*, and the reader will probably be able to supply a few more. A deeper concern lies in the point made by Eriksen (2017, p. 33) that these dimensions are abstract concepts, used primarily by American and European researchers to select and organize data, but where 'corresponding concepts do not always exist in the life-world of the informants'. A possible danger here then is the real if unconscious imposition of neocolonial mental structures on the thinking of others in different cultures.

Perhaps the best approach, rather than attempting to come up with any definitive list of dimensions, would be to keep these suggested dimensions in mind, but also look at the work, concerns and concepts of the particular group with which one is working and studying, and then to create a formative list, which can be interrogated by further research, and amended accordingly.

3   What are the functions of cultures?

For functionalists, the definition of culture lies in how it helps groups to adapt to their environments. For example, Binford (1968, p. 323), an American archaeologist, suggested that 'culture is all those means whose forms are not under direct genetic control ... which serve to adjust individuals and groups within their ecological communities'. The business writers Trompenaars and

Hampden-Turner (1997, p. 6) similarly suggest that culture 'is the way in which a group of people solves problems and reconciles dilemmas'. And from an educational leadership perspective, Heck (2002, p. 88) conceptualizes culture as a system through which 'groups adapt to the challenges of their particular environment'.

Adaptation is undoubtedly a useful function, but it may be unnecessarily limiting. For a start, it takes a functionalist perspective, and assumes that societies have cohesive and homogeneous cultures, which may then fail to address any conflict inherent within that culture (see the introduction by Karabel and Halsey (1979) (eds) for an excellent introduction on this). Moreover, cultures do a great deal more than help groups to adapt to their environments or solve problems – they may facilitate the development of world views, may promote the creation of works of art, or help develop perspectives on what constitutes the 'good' human being. All of these may be applied to challenges and problems, but may be used in other ways as well. We may be dragged into lists, once again, this time of perceived cultural functions, and it seems that the same caveats as mentioned for content and dimensions need to apply here as well.

4 How big are they?

A little reflection on what is meant by the term 'cultures' suggests that all 'cultures' are not necessarily the same size. If 'culture' is normally seen as a national- or societal-level phenomenon, it can be seen in other ways as well. Many individuals may belong be **subcultural groups** whose orientation 'nests' them within a larger cultural group. Such subcultural behaviours and beliefs may then only be shared – to a greater or lesser extent – by a small group of people (a football team or book club), by an organization (a school or a university), or by those in a local area, even while all continue to see themselves as part of a larger culture.

Even societal-level expressions of cultures in places like England and Hong Kong may not be the highest level use of the term; most people talk about (and we shall shortly discuss) notions of larger 'western and 'Asian' cultures. Even here problems are encountered: such cultures may not be situated within any particular society or nation state, and may be seen as shared attributes by particular groups of nations, even as some nations seem better described by some of the shared attributes than do others. 'Western culture' for instance seems as a term to include not only nation states but also groups of nation state variants like Northern European, Anglo-American and Southern European. 'Asian' as a cultural term is also generally recognized, but Chinese, Japanese and Indian may all be seen as subcontinental variants of this larger conception, and they may also be broken down into further smaller enclaves.

Another potential level is a potentially **pan-cultural** level. In the following chapter, after we have reviewed the findings of the two sets of educational leaders in England and Hong Kong, we introduce a table (Table 9.1) concerning the implicit values that these two groups seem to hold. The really interesting thing here is the considerable agreement between these two groups, as if the professional values they jointly hold transcend any national or broader set of cultural values. This suggestion requires a great deal more research to see if it holds up at a wider level, but it nevertheless suggests an extra 'wicked' component to any notion of the levels of culture.

Finally, it would also seem inadvisable to ignore descriptions of an increasingly influential **global** culture. As will be discussed in Chapter 10, the technological, economic, political and social aspects of globalization may move individuals and groups towards other value, thought and behavioural orientations, and thus condition and even reduce the influence of other levels on a leader's work and role (see Bottery, 2004). Moreover, the more levels of culture and subculture there are, the more complex and wicked the lenses are through which we need to understand the world, and therefore the challenges that educational leaders face. 'Culture' as a term may then need to be viewed not unlike the way in which Heater (2004) sees the term 'citizenship': as a term denoting loyalty of an individual to a larger group, but needing to be seen, not as definitive at any particular level, but as consisting of different levels 'nesting' within larger conceptions of the term. This suggests that both 'culture' and 'citizenship' are not fixed terms, but orientations, in dynamic relationship with other levels.

5   What have researchers regarded as the most significant aspects of 'culture'?

To some, it may seem slightly odd to place significance on the beliefs of a particular sub cultural (or pan-cultural?) group. Yet the opinions of this group are important, because it is the group which has most studied – and defined – this phenomenon. In so doing, they have not only been highly influential in defining what is generally understood by the term; but the considerable variety of opinions produced provide a means for reflecting upon what may be its most significant elements.

This is not the place for a history of academic disciplines concerned with the notion of culture, but it does seem possible to pick out aspects that key thinkers have focused upon. It might be then, that you resonate with the views of someone like Levi-Strauss (1966), who argued that a comparative exploration of the nature of thought processes in order to explore the degree of their universality is the really critical issue in exploring cultures. You may however feel more inclined to the views of Radcliffe-Brown (1957) whose pivotal concern was in understanding how cultures and societies are integrated, where different institutions fit together almost like pieces of a jigsaw, but where the function of individuals is little more than being bodies occupying different status positions. You may be unhappy with such a view of the individual's role, and like Barth (1966), think that societal and cultural phenomena are best explained by examining the aggregated effects of repeated transactions by individuals within particular groups. The view of this book, it will be clear, takes a mid-way position between these views, and somewhat like Homans (1967) or Giddens (1984), argues that the essential dynamic of culture and society is that of the interrelationships between actors and structures, in which individuals can and do make their own decisions, while also being constrained and limited by the structures around them.

'Culture', then, needs to be recognized as a complex and changeable term, where the kind of 'definition dementia' Shallcross and Robinson (2007, p. 138) talk of is avoided. While it may not be possible to arrive at a definition generating full consensus, we shall use as a working definition of 'culture' the following:

> *Culture is the study of the orientation of particular groups' thoughts, values and behaviours, and of the interrelationships of the individual members of these groups with wider social practices and structures.*

This definition fits well with the argument of this book: the portraits used in it provide descriptions of the practice, values and thought processes of educational leaders, while also examining how these individuals are affected and constrained by the social structures, norms and legislative architecture within which they function.

So, with this definition in mind, we move to a consideration and comparison of 'Western' and 'Asian' cultures, before focusing upon two particular subcultures within these. We will examine the interrelationships between the behaviours, practices and values of educational leaders and the social frameworks within which they function, to finally arrive at a better understanding of how these may affect leaders' sustainability.

Western and Asian philosophical inheritances and cultural differences

A number of writers (e.g. Nisbett, 2003, 2010; Wei-Ming, 2000; Dimmock and Walker, 2005) argue that to understand the largely unrecognized and unspoken differences between Western and Asian cultures, one has to go back to the major thinkers of the Greek and Chinese societies of 2,500 years ago, and examine the influence of Aristotle and Confucius. They suggest that it was the kind of thinking of which these two individuals were the most prominent and influential proponents, which ultimately led to very different orientations in looking at the world through Western and Asian cultural perspectives. It is then argued that Aristotle and the large majority of ancient Greek philosophers were particularly interested in using observation and logic to understand the nature of individualized 'things', and also how these 'things' worked, while Confucius and other ancient Chinese philosophers were much more concerned with pragmatic issues of cultural and family cohesion. So, the argument goes, a tradition has evolved in the West of a perceptual focus upon individual and discrete objects, where stasis rather than change is seen as the norm, which is then translated into the moral and political idea of human beings as individuals, possessing freedom from communal constraints and thus separable from their social and cultural groups, who then embraced the virtues of independence and individual liberty. One cannot of course adopt a purely Aristotelian focus in explaining this Western emphasis on individual freedom and responsibility: one also needs to work into this argument the influence of the Renaissance, the Enlightenment, the growth of capitalism, and of the personal moral responsibility engendered by Protestantism (Weber, 1947), all of which have built upon the Aristotelian ideological substructure.

A very different 'Asian' tradition, it is argued, has evolved from a focus on, and valuing of group cohesion, where it is felt that change is ever-present, and where the role of the individual is understood and located through its function and relationship with the larger group, and with the context within which it is positioned. Nisbett (2003, p. 50) suggests that on such a viewpoint the conception of what a person *is*, is then summarized very differently in the two cultures. From a Western viewpoint, the person is 'bounded, impermeable ... free', while from an Asian viewpoint, the person is 'connected, fluid, and conditional' (ibid.). In the same way, in contrast to the Western emphasis on a person being an autonomous individual, Marriott (1976), writing about Indian social relations, describes persons as 'dividuals', because their personhood is created through their relationships with others.

Now, clearly, such orientations will likely be expressed differently in different individuals; yet if such tendencies do exist at a shared level, then they may well, over many generations, lead to very different political and moral foci and values. An 'Asian' focus on community may then have led to a valuing of *interdependence* and shared responsibility, a 'western' focus on the individual, to the valuing of *independence* and personal responsibility. An 'Asian' focus would also see the needs of the group normally taking priority over those of the individual, whereas the reverse would generally be true in a 'western' one. Interpersonal harmony would also likely be a dominant concern in Asia, while individual liberty would be predominant in the West. Studies of the views of managers in selected businesses have tended to support this notion of Asian/Western differences (e.g. Trompenaars and Hampden-Turner, 1997). Interestingly, and supporting the notion of subcultural groups, Trompenaars and Hampden-Turner also found that the cultures of business and management practices seemed located along a spectrum, with the majority of individuals from the United States oriented to 'Anglo-American' individualist self-achievement, with individuals from a continental European subgroup espousing both individual and communal values, while 'East Asian' individuals (predominantly Chinese) were more normally oriented to the end of the spectrum where the success of the group was given priority over any individual achievement. This suggested location of subgroups along a cultural spectrum has also been supported by the work of Meyer (2015) with business groups on how the meaning of the same English words can be perceived differently.

However, while we seem to be dealing with two different orientations to the nature of ontology, epistemology and social behaviour, there also seems to be a broad spread of opinion within such sets, with some 'western' individuals expressing opinions much nearer to those of someone with an 'Asian' orientation, and for 'Asian' thinkers to sound very 'western'. This is not very surprising – not only are cultures permeable to other influences, but historically, one also finds that an ancient Greek philosopher like Heraclitus had a very 'Asian' concern about the nature of change, which contrasts strongly with a more traditional 'western' belief in stasis, just as one finds the ancient Chinese philosopher Mo-Tzu concerned with many of the issues focused upon by 'western' philosophers. This conflation of views along this spectrum is probably even more pronounced today, with the global spread of different cultural views, particularly through hyper-connected means. One then finds some 'western' individuals wedded to notions of hierarchy, and some 'Asian' individuals fixated on goals of personal achievement and success.

However, one other qualification needs making, and that is that both 'Western' and 'Asian' tendencies can be seen in the same individual depending on the conditions under which they are working and thinking. As Morris and Peng (1994) have shown, individuals from Hong Kong can be encouraged to think and resolve issues using either Asian or Western perspectives when they are presented with images suggesting one culture or another. This is a particularly important point, given the amount of cultural borrowing of Western, mainly Anglo-American, influences that have been seen over the last few decades, as it implies that cultures are not only permeable and changeable at a societal level, but that such influences can produce cultural change within individuals – which can be reversed given the right circumstances.

Nevertheless, the evidence still seems strong that real cultural differences do exist. As Fox (2014, p. 15) argued when talking of the use of implicit rules by English people:

We do not mean ... that all English people always or invariably exhibit the characteristic in question, only that it is a quality or behavioural pattern that is common enough or marked enough to be noticeable and significant.

The same argument applies to notions of culture: even if individual variations within a cultural group do occur, this does not invalidate the idea of larger cultural influences and orientations.

With such caveats in mind, a number of tentative cultural generalizations will now be examined, in order to 'examined' used four words earlier; use 'assess' here instead how they might impact on leadership sustainability.

Issues of cognition

Nisbett (2003) has examined the cultural and subcultural expressions of a number of cognition issues in Asia (particularly East Asian views) and the West (particularly Anglo-American views). From his analysis, he suggests that people from 'East Asian' cultures may better detect connections and relationships between people and objects than their Anglo-American counterparts, because they are inclined to attend much more to the context within which events occur. In addition, he proposes that 'Anglo-Americans' tend to believe that it is possible to have a greater degree of control over their environment than those from an East Asian culture normally would. Anglo-Americans, he argues, also tend to have a less complex view of causality than do East Asians, believing that to resolve issues, general rules of logic can (and indeed should) be applied to virtually all situations in order to resolve difficulties, while their East Asian counterparts may have a more complex view of causality, which involves recognizing more connections and relationships within a situation, driven by a desire to achieve a harmonious end result, rather than being 'right' in some strict logical sense.

Now while the formal rules of logic seem fundamental to much Anglo-American thought, East Asian thinking, he suggests, is less likely to separate the truth of a proposition from its moral effects, as it tends to be believed that if the logic of an argument leads to immoral ends, the stricter form of logic needs rejecting, not the morality. Nisbett (2003, pp. 26–7) therefore suggests that East Asian cultures tend to view reasonableness as more important than reason, rationality or logic per se, as any application of abstract rules which fails to take into account an issue's contextual circumstances is likely to lead to grave mistakes.

These issues and their potential implications for leadership sustainability are summarized in Table 8.1, where the final column suggests a number of possible differences between populations of educational leaders in East Asia and Anglo-American cultures, differences which may in part derive from different ontological, epistemological and perceptual cultural orientations. Indeed, while allowing for individual variation, East Asian leaders may be more likely to see their role as dealing more with complex problems and resolutions than their Anglo-American counterparts, in part because of a tendency to more strongly consider the influence of surrounding contexts

Table 8.1 How different cultural patterns of cognition affect perceptions of leadership role and challenges (after Nisbett 2003)

Cognitive aspect	Asian	Western	General Implications	Asian Leadership (AL) v. Western Leadership (WL) Approaches
Patterns of attention and perception	Attending more to environments	Attending more to objects	Asians more likely to detect relationships among events than Westerners	AL likely to see more complex problems and explanations than WL
Basic assumptions about the composition of the world	Seeing substances	Seeing objects	Asians see connections; Westerners see discrete objects	AL likely to see wider pictures to problems and responses than WL
Beliefs about the controllability of the environment	Less control	More control	Westerners believing in controllability more than Asian	AL likely accept reality of less control in problem situations than WL
Tacit assumptions about stability versus change	Tact assumption of environmental change	Tacit assumption of environmental stability	Westerners seeing stability where Asians see change	AL accept more easily reality of change and lack of control than WL
Preferred patterns of explanations for events	Events happening in a complex and systemic environment	Focusing on discrete objects and simple linear causality	Asians see a more complex, less controllable world	AL likely to see more complex problems and explanations than WL

Habits of organizing the world	More likely to focus on relationships between things	Preferring abstract categories	Westerners see a world of simpler explanations than do Asian	AL likely to see more complex problems and explanations than WL
Extent of the use of formal logical rules	Stronger use of harmonious responses than logical response to resolve problems	Westerners' strong use of logical rules to resolve problems	Westerners more inclined to use logical rules to understand events and resolve issues	AL focused more on relationships, WL on results

on a presenting problem. They may therefore be more likely to accept that reality is less controllable than many Anglo-American leaders might believe.

However, given the argument of previous chapters, perhaps the most interesting implication is how East Asian leaders may be more likely to adopt a 'wicked' view of reality, and of the nature of problems faced. Their governments may also be less likely than their Anglo-American equivalents to adopt policies based upon 'tame' assumptions of reality, though it seems highly likely that other issues – like those of power and control – will reduce this effect. If this line of reasoning is correct (and this would require research so far not undertaken) then East Asian educational leaders may be faced by fewer of the sustainability challenges of a tame and wicked kind than many Anglo-American leaders currently seem to (though as we shall see, they may have other, different challenges to confront).

The final aspect noted in Table 8.1 – the extent to which formal logical rules may be used – suggests the possibility of a greater preference by Anglo-Americans for universalizable logical rules to resolve problems, compared with East Asian cultural preference for working towards more harmonious relationships in resolving problems. This might also lead to a greater leadership focus on developing good relationships in a team, compared with a greater focus on the achievement of results by Anglo-American leaders – and their governments. Once again, though, the situation is highly complex: debate over leadership focus on relationships versus results is also to be seen *within* a business literature focused upon an Anglo-American perspective – as we saw in Chapter 6 with Blake and Mouton (1985).

Independence and interdependence

This kind of cross-cultural analysis can be taken further by looking at how the concepts of independence and interdependence could affect cultural orientations to the leadership role. Table 8.2 suggest the possibility of different implications for East Asian and Anglo-American leadership practice, with Anglo-American notions of independence seemingly associated more with preferences for the freedom of individual action, the self as a free agent, the valuation of personal distinctiveness, success as a measure of individual merit, and debate and disagreement as the best ways at arriving at some 'truth'. By contrast, East Asian notions of *inter*dependence seem more closely associated with a preference for collective action; for seeing the self as a contributory part to the success of the whole group; where group hierarchy is accepted as the norm, and where people adopt behaviours appropriate to their place in this hierarchy; and where 'excessive' debate and disagreement may be seen as a threat to group harmony and hierarchy.

Table 8.2 How the concepts of independence and interdependence affect leadership perceptions in Western and Eastern cultures

Aspects	Western Independence	Asian Interdependence	Implications for Leadership
Preferred form of action	Insistence on freedom of individual action	A preference for collective action	Personal forms of individual leadership action favoured in West: more subsumed collective forms in Asia?
Nature of personhood	The self is a unitary free agent, and individual distinctiveness is desired and valued	The self is part of a larger whole; individuals are viewed as contributing to harmonious group blending	Distinctive individual leadership forms preferred in West; Asia prefers leadership forms channelled more into group cohesion
Role in group	A preference for egalitarianism in group membership	Greater acceptance of group hierarchy	Group composed essentially of equals in West; group composed more by hierarchy in Asia?
Reason for success	Success valued as an indicator of individual merit, achieved through competition and ability	Success valued as reflecting well on the group individuals belong to	Leadership success achieved more by talent in West; achieved more by designation in Asia
Nature of behaviour and decision-making	Strong belief that the rules govern-ing proper behav-iour should be applied universally	Preference for approaches that take account of the context and the nature of the relationships involved	Tamer application of rules in West: more wicked application through consideration of context in Asia?
Value of debate	Debate and controversy seen as best way of arriving at 'truth'	Debate and controversy seen as disruptive to group harmony	Different emphases on usefulness of disagreement and debate
Empathy for others	Westerners are concerned with knowing themselves and will sacrifice harmony to 'fairness'	Highly attuned to fostering group dynamics and will avoid actions or attitudes which prevent this	Different degree of emphasis on empathy because of different focus on self or group

Implications for educational leadership

If such differences do tend to work in the ways suggested, the implications for educational leadership may be both interesting and important. Group preference rather than individualism, hierarchy rather than equality, role assignation rather than role achievement by talent, may be more pronounced in East Asian leadership settings and role expectations than in Anglo-American contexts. A number of pieces of research support this. Morris and Lo (2000) for instance found that the implementation of Anglo-American-style reforms in Hong Kong was blunted by the hierarchical, non-consultative style of the principal in whose schools the reforms were taking place. Yet, in contrast, Hallinger and Kantamara (2000) found that implementation of reforms was successful in three Thai schools because of the use of a hierarchical style of leadership, and other more traditional practices, to rather paradoxically implement a more participatory style of teacher engagement.

Finally, and utilizing the concept of wickedity once more, Anglo-American leaders may then show a greater preference for the application of universal rules, and thus may be more inclined to lean towards 'tamer' applications of such rules, if they downgrade the importance of a problem's context, and adopt an either/or type of rationality. East Asian leaders on the other hand, may better appreciate that situations need greater account taken of such contexts, and of the nature of the relationships involved. They therefore may well be more likely to include in their approach to leadership a greater appreciation of the possibility that both sides can be 'right' in a discussion. With such an approach, it seems likely that they may better appreciate the 'wicked' nature of many challenges than their Anglo-American counterparts. As Aquila (1983, p. 182) said of Japanese managers, they are more likely to accept that '*human interaction and behavior are so complicated that it is impossible to formulate specific rules for all occasions*' (italics in original).

Yet once again, we need to be careful, and avoid any suggestion of cultural exclusivity. Much present Anglo-American economic thinking, for instance, is based on market principles, taken supposedly from the thought of Adam Smith, who famously wrote (1976, pp. 26–7) that

> it is not that he cares for you, the customer, that the brewer, the baker or the butcher provides for your dinner, but because he cares for himself.

Now it may be pointed out that an either/or logic is unnecessary here, for those selling their services or products may want to profit from such ventures, but also will feel more fulfilled if they help their customers to benefit. Adam Smith himself recognized this danger, even if the weakness of either/or logic has been ignored by many of his (mostly Western) advocates. With any discussion of cultural effects, then, we need to be conscious of the differing voices within the same culture, just as we need to accept that such cultural trends can have widespread effects.

Cultural differences and leadership sustainability

So how likely is leadership sustainability to be affected by cultural differences? It was suggested that there are at least eight different causes for greater personal and role unsustainability:

i **Excessive increases in the workload of educational leaders;**

ii Increased differences between the purposes attributed to education systems by governments, and the purposes held by some professionals in those systems;

iii Accusations by governments of a lack of professional competence and trustworthiness in implementing agendas;

iv An increased degree of accountability and surveillance of professional work;

v The increased use of hierarchical power to enforce change;

vi The increased 'wickedity' of many of the problems faced;

vii An increase in the growth of 'guilt' and 'blame' cultures;

viii **Insufficient preparation for the role**

This section now discusses the extent to which each of these causes is likely to be exacerbated, ameliorated, or only slightly influenced by factors in East Asian and Anglo-American cultures. Now, the highly qualified nature of any discussion on the meaning and impact of culture, and of the large effects of other factors discussed in this book, necessarily limit the claims that can be made. Nevertheless, what follows at least raises the question of whether the nature of cultural orientations could potentially have important influences on leadership sustainability, and what kind of further research would be needed to further develop such understandings.

i *Excessive Increases in the Workload of Educational Leaders.*

As we have seen, there is good empirical evidence that over the past few decades a substantial increase in the workload of educational leaders across both cultures has occurred. Not only have governments acknowledged this phenomenon, but so has much research, including our own. The causes of this increase seem to have stemmed largely from the national level, in the form of government legislation, but there is good reason to suggest that national increases at least in part originated from demands at higher levels – such as within trading groups like NAFTA or the EU, or from the competitive demands produced by free trade agreements. Until there is research on educational leadership comparing the perceived pressures on such Anglo-American and East Asian leaders, or of the degree to which such pressures are caused primarily by cultural or other issues, it remains difficult to say whether there are similar levels of pressure on leadership sustainability in both. It is clearly an area ripe for future research. Our feeling currently, however, is that it is possible that some aspects of East Asian cultures could have greater ameliorative effects than are present in Anglo-American cultures, but considerable caution needs to be exercised in generalizing here.

Threats to leadership sustainability from excessive workload
                                                    Anglo-American?
Less Threat———More Threat
                                       East Asian?
There is evidence of both cohorts reporting strong pressures from increased workloads, though evidence is lacking on comparative evidence on where such pressures emanate.

   ii *Increased Differences between the purposes attributed to education systems by governments, and the purposes held by professionals in those systems.*

East Asian tendencies to embrace the cultural importance of harmonious relationships, and for more concerted attempts to work towards harmonious solutions, suggest less divisiveness of purpose than Anglo-American governments and their educators. This would also suggest that the kind of neoliberal market imperatives which have formed the basis for much globalized economic policy over the last few decades would be better mediated by such governments, and by implementers themselves, than their Anglo-American counterparts, as the kind of individualist, self-serving imperatives behind much market thinking seems less pronounced in East Asian than in Anglo-American cultures, with different kinds of economic approaches used. However, it would be foolish to totally discount the effects of global economic tendencies, and so while pressures on East Asian educational leaders might be less than their Anglo-American counterparts, they are still likely to have an effect.

Threats to leadership sustainability from differing purposes between government and professionals
                                              Anglo-American
Less threat———More threat
                                       East Asian
There seems a greater separation of purposes between parties in the Anglo-American context than in the more communal East Asian, but

Anglo-American market influences still occur globally. More research is required here.

iii *Accusations by Governments of a Lack of Professional Competence and Trustworthiness in Implementing Agendas.*

Issues of lack of competence and trustworthiness seem to stem in part from the different purposes ascribed to education by governments in contrast to the beliefs of at least some of their educational leaders, and governmental accusations of incompetence and untrustworthiness may stem from educators not engaging fully with governmental agendas. As already noted, these seem less pronounced in East Asian educational systems than in Anglo-American ones, and this may be in part because of a greater East Asian cultural stress on community and harmonious relations, and in part because of a cultural dislike for the kind of disagreement, argumentation and debate which characterizes much Anglo-American discussion. There are however, exceptions to this rule, and this may well come down to national or even regional differences. Walker et al. (2011) suggest that in China blame has also been inappropriately attached to educational leaders for failure in implementation, when in fact the problems seemed to lie more in deep-seated cultural values. Nevertheless, at the same time, global free-market policies may strengthen the influence of Anglo-American cultural norms, which may 'leak' into other educational systems.

Threats to leadership sustainability from accusations of incompetence and untrustworthiness

Anglo-American

Less Threat—————————————————————————————————More Threat

East Asian

Accusations tend to stem from professionals not engaging with government agendas, rather than incompetence or lack of trust per se; these seem more marked in Anglo-American than in East Asian systems. More research is required here.

iv *An Increased Degree of Accountability And Surveillance of Professional Work.*

Unsurprisingly, given all of the above, it might also be the case that less threat to leadership sustainability came from an increase in accountability and surveillance measures in East Asian educational systems than in Anglo-American systems. Threats to leadership sustainability stem in part not only from the higher workload associated with increased accountability measures, but also from the stress and loss of trust caused by public judgements of capability. The drive in Anglo-American cultures towards the greater accountability of its educators has led not only to more frequent acts of surveillance, but also to deeper forms. So while workload, lack of trust, and greater accountability may all be functions of extended governmental intervention, the more frequent and deeper surveillance demanded by government of professional work can add to personal leadership pressures, because they tend to lessen the personal space which the Anglo-American culture values highly. Many educational leaders in East Asian cultures, working with a more communal and collectivist sets of values, may then feel less pressured by such governmental interest.

Threats to leadership sustainability from greater accountability and surveillance

Anglo-American

Less Threat————————————————————————————————*More Threat*

East Asian

These pressures stem in part from higher workloads associated with higher accountability, and from stress caused by lack of trust. Anglo-American systems suffer from both of these; East Asian systems probably suffer less, though globalization exports some of these pressures.

　　v　*The Increased Use of Hierarchical Power to Enforce Change.*

While it may well be the case that neoliberal Anglo-American governments have used the power of the state to enforce much market-based legislation, and in many cases have done so with a marked decline in the consultation with those affected, this is not the only form of government likely to impose such strategies. Indeed, any greater cultural utilization of hierarchical relationships, and the existence of one-party governments, may well produce similar results. This is another area requiring much more research

Threats to leadership sustainability from the increased use of hierarchical power to enforce change

Anglo-American?

Less Threat————————————————————————————————*More Threat*

East Asian?

Anglo-American governments adopting neoliberal approaches have tended to use state power to enforce markets reforms; a greater utilization of hierarchical relationships may produce a similar threat to leadership sustainability. More research is required here.

　　vi　*The Increased 'Wickedity' of many of the problems faced.*

The discussion earlier in the chapter suggested that much Anglo-American thought has tended since ancient Greek times to focus on the linear, the singular, and perhaps the tame, with a logic which dislikes paradox, the possibility that two ostensibly different positions may both be right, and which tends to pay only limited attention to the context within which actions and problems occur. East Asian thought, on the other hand, it was suggested, may be more aware of, and work within a holistic, complex and contextualized understanding, and therefore may live more comfortably with paradox and the possibility that two ostensibly different positions can both be valid. In such circumstances, it may be that East Asian governmental policies if influenced by such cultural values (and this is a large 'if'), would be less likely to view problems as tame, and their educational leaders therefore less likely to feel guilty. In such circumstances, then, many Anglo-American educational leaders may feel more personally and role-threatened by 'tame' policies than their East Asian counterparts, and so may be likely to feel less sustainable. Again, comparative research is essential here.

Threats to leadership sustainability from increased wickedity
Anglo-American
Less Pressure————————————————————————————*More Pressure*
East Asian
If Anglo-American thought tends to focus more on the linear, the singular, and the tame, and East Asian more on the holistic and the complex, then increased wickedity may be coped with better in East Asian than Anglo-American contexts. More research is needed here.

vii   *The Increase in the Growth of 'Guilt' and 'Blame' cultures in Education.*

This book has argued that both 'Guilt' and 'Blame' cultures appear to be grounded in 'tame' thinking: in believing that most problems are relatively simple and can be resolved by relatively simple measures. 'Blame cultures' then develop when governments believe – and communicate this belief to educators – that individuals can and therefore should manage and control more of the targets, challenges and problems that they are set. 'Guilt' cultures would then arise if professionals also adopted tame beliefs about reality. If they then accept that such blame is legitimate, and internalize such blame to the degree that when they fail, they feel that they are to blame, then they are likely to feel guilty. On this basis, blame and guilt cultures seem less likely to be pronounced in East Asian than in Anglo-American educational systems, because of the belief that individual actions cannot be understood without a deep knowledge of the contextual grounding and of the influence of external factors on such actions. One final point is needed here. As noted earlier, Walker et al. (2011) suggest that Eastern governments can be as guilty of tame policies as their Western counterparts, though the causes of these may not stem from the wicked problems seen in Anglo-American cultures, and the means of redressing them may also be dissimilar.

Threats to leadership sustainability from the growth of 'guilt' and 'blame' cultures
Anglo-American
Less Threat————————————————————————————*More Threat*
East Asian
Blame cultures can arise when governments believe that individuals should better control role responsibilities; 'guilt' cultures develop when professionals accept such blame and internalize it. These seem less

pronounced in East Asian than in the Anglo-American contexts, because of East Asian beliefs in less possible individual control. However, governments in both contexts can create tame policies which lead to professional blame.

viii   *Insufficient preparation for the leadership role.*

The UK government was the first to establish a national leadership college in response to what was seen as insufficient preparation for the role, and a number of other countries have since followed suit. Now it might be assumed that simply having such a preparation programme is better than not having one. Yet this has to be doubted, and for two reasons. A first is the argument made throughout this book about the necessarily 'wicked' nature of much leadership work; for if existing programmes cater to 'tame' perceptions of the nature of leadership problems, and then provide only 'tame' prescriptions for them, the cure may be worse than the disease. A second is the preponderant influence of Western academic literature on the nature of the role, and on the threats to its sustainability; because there is little by way of alternative views, such partiality is likely to have an effect on leadership programmes both in terms of the selection of threats and how to deal with them. Yet, if the analysis of this chapter is correct, threats to leadership sustainability in other cultural contexts may be very different, and if programmes were then created which were inappropriate to cultural needs, they would likely be more damaging than remedial. More research also seems required here.

Anglo-American?
Less Threat—————————————————————————————More Threat
East Asian?

Threats through insufficient preparation do not stem just from (a) a lack of courses and programmes; they could also stem from (b) reliance on tame perspectives and insufficient wicked materials, and (c) addressing threats seen more in other cultural contexts than their own, and not addressing their own cultural specific threats. Particularly, given the preponderance of Western literature on this issue, how much do other systems adopt Western perspectives on such threats?

Possible remedies

The varied and in some cases fairly intractable problems of lowered personal leadership and role sustainability are more wicked than tame, strongly suggesting that in many cases more wicked than tame responses will be needed as remedies. As argued elsewhere (Bottery, 2016) however, wicked responses, no matter how much care is taken, do not guarantee successful solutions, as they consist of at best a collection of 'messy' efforts at resolution, and therefore more like silver buckshot than silver bullets. As Table 8.3 suggests, the eight causes of sustainability pressures have varied effects on personal and role sustainability, and effective remedies will likely be responses which appreciate better the nature of wickedity; which improve communications and shared purposes between governments and professionals; and which re-appraise current modes of accountability. Interestingly, and somewhat wickedly, this analysis also suggests that social democratic rather than neoliberal policy approaches may be better for sustainability.

East Asian cultural threats to leadership sustainability?

The analysis of this chapter so far has led to the conclusion that some aspects of different cultural tendencies can contribute to greater or lesser educational leadership sustainability. Yet because such cultural influences may be increased or decreased by other personal, local and global influences, it is highly unlikely that a simple, predictable or controllable prescription will emerge as any final best balance of forces to foster greater personal and role sustainability. This is likely to be highly contextualized, highly personal and highly changeable. Once again we are dealing with a wicked rather than a tame problem. Yet it would be a policy of despair to think that nothing could be done to remedy sustainability problems, particularly if there is evidence that some factors can inhibit the development of sustainability threats more than others.

It also seems to be the case, judging from the foregoing analysis, that a number of Anglo-American values and practices have created major threats to leadership sustainability, and more so within Anglo-American cultural contexts than in East Asian ones. It would however be easy, very tame and probably very wrong to suggest that such Anglo-American values are the only potentially cultural threats to leadership sustainability. East Asian governments, like Anglo-American ones, also seem capable of producing tame policies. And it also seems equally plausible that some East Asian values, if similarly over-stressed, could be the cause of some forms of leadership sustainability not seen in the Anglo-American context. If one returns to Tables 8.1 and 8.2, and looks at some of the values suggested as being favoured in East Asian cultures, it seems possible that the following could in some contexts constitute real threats to educational leadership sustainability:

a   An over-stress on the belief in limited individual control could lead to this becoming a self-fulfilling prophecy, where educational leaders then adopted fatalist perspectives to many problems, and instead of trying to resolve these, allowed them to get worse;

Table 8.3 Threats to personal and role sustainability, and possible remedies

Threats to sustainability	How personal sustainability is affected	How role sustainability is affected	Possible Responses
1. Damage to government/educator relationships	Negatively affects self-concept through loss of trust, lowered self-esteem and enhanced self-blame	Poor personal sustainability inevitably leads to lowered role sustainability	Better communication and appreciation of difference in governmental and professional approaches
2. Differing purposes for leadership role from governments	Negatively affects self-concept through personal purposes not valued, and enhances self-blame	Poor personal sustainability inevitably lowers role sustainability	Better communication and appreciation of difference in governmental and professional approaches
3. Increased accountability and surveillance	Increases workload and conformity, lowers trust relationship and morale	Pressures towards role conformity	Better communication and appreciation of difference in governmental and professional approaches
4. Increased use of power rather than persuasion to effect changes	Takes away personal visions and autonomy in decision-making	Reduces personal commitment, increases conformity	Better communication and appreciation of difference in governmental, stakeholder and professional approaches
5. Increasing complexity of the role	Wickedity of role not fully appreciated	Wickedity of role not fully appreciated	Rethinking of ontology and epistemology; greater appreciation of wicked nature of much of the role

6. Growth of blame and guilt cultures	Lowers self-concept, enhances self-blame	Increases tame nature of the role	Better appreciation of wicked nature of much leadership work by all parties
7. Excessive workload	Individuals feel over-stretched, over-stressed and over-tired	Inability of individuals to cover full range of role responsibilities	Better communication and appreciation of different approaches and causes of overwork
8. Insufficient preparation for the role	Increases workload and stress	Increases workload and stress	Recognition by all parties of the kinds of preparation required for leadership in a 'wicked' world

b An over-stress on the belief in the ever-changeable nature of the world could lead to the same kind of self-fulfilling fatalistic perspectives which suggest that whatever one does, things will change, and likely are beyond one's control;

c An over-stress on a preference for the maintenance of harmonious relations rather than the resolution of problems could lead to problems being ignored, leading to much larger problems later on;

d An over-stress on the preference for conformity, hierarchy and appointment by patronage could lead to the appointment of inappropriate individuals for a post, reducing the ability to resolve problems;

e An over-stress on the preference for group determination, rather than the value of individual solutions could lead to the suppression of minority creative ideas, which again would likely reduce problem-solving abilities.

The point here then is not to criticize any particular set of cultural value orientations, but rather to suggest that orientations in any culture, if taken to extremes, could produce the kind of sustainability threats which have been seen in the Anglo-American context. It also suggests that the literature on leadership sustainability would benefit by recognizing that much of it is largely Anglo-American value-based, even if not always acknowledged as such, and therefore of the need to examine how the more careful examination of other cultural values and practices might help in viewing threats to sustainability from other perspectives. In so doing, it may well be that, with an appropriate degree of caution, some degree of cultural borrowing might improve a situation. This book has already advocated an ethic of humility as crucial to educational leadership; an ethic of cultural humility also seems highly appropriate.

Conclusion

We hope it is very clear that this chapter has not suggested that one 'set' of cultural values is superior to another, nor that 'culture' should be viewed as a monolithic and deterministic concept. Rather the chapter has proposed that an in-depth examination of different cultural orientations might lead to an enrichment and greater sustainability of one's own cultural approach to the leadership role. But most of the current literature on educational leadership sustainability is heavily Anglo-American oriented and culturally derived, and much more comparative research is needed. Cross-cultural research on threats to leadership sustainability has only just begun to scratch the surface.

Nevertheless, this chapter has suggested that because different cultures have different orientations, and tend to place different emphases, and different importance, on some important issues of ontology and epistemology, and on social, political and ethical values and behaviour, it seems likely that threats to, and support for leadership sustainability, may differ from culture to culture, and may also depend upon the extent to which personal and role leadership flow with, or flow against, these cultural emphases, particularly as expressed through educational policies.

Finally, we have been at pains to point out how permeable, how contextualized, how individual the causes of lowered leadership sustainability may be; they may then not only differ from culture to culture, but also from person to person, and it is hugely important not to impose personally held cultural assumptions about threats to leadership sustainability upon the policies and practices of others. They may not have the same threats to their sustainability, and they may not require the same remedies. It is then to a comparison of how individual leaders function, and how they do so in two different cultures, that we now turn.

CHAPTER NINE

Patterns of Individual Responses to Challenges Across Two Cultures

Introduction

Educational leaders exercise their role not only within local and organizational contexts, but in national, cultural and global contexts as well. They then are the recipients of a large amount of policy borrowing, as governments attempt to transplant what they regard as 'best practice' into their own systems. So what have been the attitudes of educational leaders to these changes, and has their personal sustainability in the role been affected?

Have they, for instance, mediated these changes in different ways, depending upon the cultural/legislative context within which they work? The research in this chapter reviews the portraits of two cohorts of leaders in England and Hong Kong, and asks what they tell us about the effects of these changes on individuals and their sustainability in the role, with a focus upon:

- Legislative changes;
- Inspection procedures; and
- Marketization, parental choice and school competition.

All individuals quoted are anonymized.

The extent to which these changes have had effects upon individuals' time and energy will be examined, as well as their ability to act on personal priorities. We begin then by comparing the effects of legislation on these two cohorts.

Educational leaders' attitudes and responses to legislation

Despite the desire by some individuals to challenge aspects of the legislative architecture within which they worked, all those interviewed accepted their national legislative context as general frameworks in England and Hong Kong within which they positioned themselves, their practice and their school. There were however different perceptions of these two architectures, particularly with respect to legislation and inspection. Perhaps the most prominent difference was the more critical and embattled approach by English head teachers, and the low-trust relationship they felt they had as a profession with their government. The most public example of this was probably Michael K., an English head teacher who some years prior to the interview had suspended the National Curriculum at his school. Michael said, '*I refuse just because somebody says that this is the latest idea ... to be moved on that. If somebody can do it better, they can come in and show me how they can do it better ... but I am not going to implement it [simply] because somebody says this is the latest thing.*'

Michael was not alone in this view. Joanne F. had similarly challenged legislation by taking a third of her year 6 students out of National Curriculum provision because '*they just could not access the curriculum*'. She, like Michael, was aware, however, that such school initiatives needed to be backed by evidence: '*If you can prove that what you're doing is going to make [the results] better, that's fine. So we monitored it carefully and the maths ages of all those children went up significantly by the end of the year.*'

Roz. L. was similarly resolute: '*I would not be defeated by someone who told me I could not do something ... . It would make me more determined* to *actually do it.*' She was also very concerned at '*how desperately boring [the curriculum] had become for children*'. However, she believed that any alterations at the school needed backing up by '*all kinds of systems and procedures that make sure it works, and lots of record keeping systems, because ... that will be my evidence to Ofsted*'.

Such embattlement was displayed by many English head teachers, and was probably felt most by those with least experience in the role. We have already seen the intense pressure on Harry C.: with only one year's experience as a head teacher, in a school with very low socio-economic status and poor exam results, his LEA had been heavily criticized for its own performance, and Harry was being pressurized by it to raise his standards, partly in order to raise their own.

Similar pressures were felt by James R., another newly appointed head teacher to a school with a declining population. He felt that despite suggestions of local financial autonomy, this was mostly an illusion; his budget was so tight that there was little room for movement. He felt that '*either they want locally managed schools, or they don't, and at the moment, they want locally managed schools, managed in their [the government's] way*'. He expressed similar feelings of powerlessness to much current legislation: '*to be honest you just nod and say "well we're going to have to make the best of it"*'.

The attitude of Hong Kong principals was rather different. Most were favourably disposed to the direction of educational reforms, despite the fact that there existed a critical academic literature about educational policy changes in Hong Kong (e.g. Choi, 2005) which suggested that the kind of legislative mechanisms so criticized in England – privatization, managerialism, competition, standardization and surveillance – were also being used in Hong Kong. Such criticisms, however, were seldom expressed by the principals, part of the reason for this seeming to lie in the attitude that their government took towards them. Susan H. said that she *could not think of any examples* where she had been in conflict with the legislation. '*It is very difficult for me to find ... . I agree with the guidelines and also the ordinances ... .* This was largely because *usually I agree with the rationale behind the policies.*' In like manner, Peter L. said that '*the requirements and guidelines* of the territory's Education Bureau (the EDB) ... [were] not too many, and they were also rather *reasonable ones, and therefore I seldom have problems in this respect*'. Moreover, he felt that even if '*your satisfaction differs for each guideline*', these were not cast too rigidly, for '*actually you can still have some flexibility in implementing these guidelines*'.

This flexibility was also mentioned by Emily W., who said that '*you don't need to listen to all of the things they say: you need to distinguish what is right and which is wrong ... . No matter what they want you to do, you still can find some ways to deal with them, right?*' Finally, Sandra W. was very clear that '*I do not think that so far I have come across an instance where*

I have had to make a decision which is conflicting with the educational ordinances.'

These principals, then, felt in tune with the direction of educational reforms, and seemed to feel trusted by their government. The English head teachers, by contrast, generally felt more distrusted, and that much legislation expressed that distrust. Such critical perceptions of governmental attitudes towards them also affected the way they viewed evidence of good practice in their schools. While English head teachers tended to describe 'evidence' as a form of *defence*, the Hong Kong principals tended to see it as *confirmation* of the success or failure of an approach, which was then shared with interested outsiders. There were, then, distinct differences between the two cohorts with respect to the legislative contexts within which they worked.

Educational leaders' attitudes and responses to inspection procedures used by their governments

Unsurprisingly, the embattled attitude of English head teachers to legislation was reflected in their feelings to inspection, and particularly towards Ofsted, the Office for Standards in Education, created in 1992 to inspect schools. While its processes and priorities have changed over the years, there remains a general feeling of concern, and in some cases of fear, of Ofsted, especially as at the time of writing (2016–7), when the format allows no time for preparation for a visit. These head teachers however did agree with the need for an inspectoral body. David G., for instance, believed that this was needed in order to achieve '*a sort of quality assurance right across the nation ... as well as seeing what works well in school ... of being able to disseminate good practice*'. Yet he felt that Ofsted had adopted the wrong approach from the start: '*It became a threat when it didn't have to be a threat.*' As we have seen, Harry C. also agreed: '*People feel that careers are made or broken on the strength of a group of people for a few days in your school looking round.*'

Despite the perception of Ofsted as a threat, some interviewees still felt in control of the situation. Michael K., for instance, said that '*when you've been through it once or twice, it certainly takes away that sense of fear and suspense*'. But his strategy went further, such that he had been '*an Ofsted inspector for about eight years*' – and that, '*when it came to an Ofsted inspection*', letting them know that *he* knew what they were about warned them against taking any liberties with the process.

Nevertheless, Michael seemed an outlier: many of the English head teachers interviewed felt that Ofsted was a genuine threat because of its punitive nature, and it was therefore seldom far from their thoughts. Penny R., for instance, said that '*whatever we are discussing, it's always got the*

Ofsted element, it's always there ... "we can show this to Ofsted" always comes up, no matter what you're doing'. Once again, evidence which supported practice was largely seen as being used for defence rather than for developmental discussions.

The danger of such a defensive attitude is, as Lauder et al. (1998) have argued, that people become so used to control and direction that a 'trained incapacity to think openly and critically' (p. 51) is created. There was research evidence to support this view. Penny R., then, was concerned that her (younger) teachers were reluctant to adopt more creative approaches to teaching, for while she said she *'would not be intimidated by [Ofsted]'*, she thought that *'it is very scary stuff for my young staff'*. Building a more creative school might be essential for good learning, yet she also believed that it meant keeping one wary eye on Ofsted, and the other eye on a staff who *'don't want their subject to be the one that goes down'*.

This kind of concern was developed by Alison L., who argued that there was a real temptation *'to stick to the tried and tested'* which was particularly true *'in year 6'* (where published testing occurred), and so there was *'a big reluctance to alter anything at the top [of the school], unless it is dramatically poor'*. The temptation was then to *'use other children who are not going to be publicly acclaimed just yet, as guinea pigs'*. The overall result then seemed to be that such a climate limited both creativity and experimentation at both high attaining and struggling schools. As Alison said: *'I think a high attaining school would have felt that [an innovation] was a risk because they had something to lose ... if your standards are pretty good ... then you are reluctant to really try something else in case they do fail.'* In a struggling school, the situation was likely to be even worse. As we saw in Harry C.'s school, for instance, while he felt the critical question for his school was *'what is it that would bring parents into school?'* the reality of Ofsted *'drives me more than the needs of the community'*.

Such comments suggest that while some English head teachers overtly championed new approaches, others were aware of the dangers of doing so, and not all felt such embrace a wise move. Even when they did, they all knew that any experimentation needed to be backed by evidence and support. Nevertheless, strong planning ability doesn't completely explain why some did and some didn't explore more creative roads: it seemed also a matter of personality and courage. Some, of course, might call it foolhardiness: Jill S. said that any innovation *'might take two or three years to see the benefit of doing something differently'*, and results might even dip. Yet she also felt that as a professional with a commitment to her students, *'you've got to be brave'*. The dilemma was clear.

This ability to do something different then seemed driven by a number of factors. One was in believing strongly in the role of the creative arts in the curriculum; a second was in being sufficiently experienced to have amassed enough evidence to defend the practice. A final factor seemed to be having the personal courage to dare such things. The likelihood of individual opposition, mediation or experimentation were then not easily predictable, for the factors generating such actions were complex, and seemed a fusion at any moment in time of complex personality and contextual elements.

Attitudes to inspection in Hong Kong generally paralleled the principals' approach to legislation, though there was variation in their views. Eva L. felt there were two reasons why inspection procedures were manageable. One was that they were not too frequent: 'The EDB (Educational Bureau) seldom inspects schools'; the other reason she gave was that 'they usually come to school because our schools are doing some good practices, not the bad ones ... . they have good intentions, not pick your faults'. Like Eva, Susan H. said that 'I know the ESR [external school review] is a friend to me'. She saw external inspection as a way of helping self-examination, for it 'is good to let us know what we are going to do'. She also felt that it was 'a good means for the school to do something after [listening to] their expertise and ideas'.

Other principals were generally positive, though with notes of caution. Phillip H. said that 'I don't fear the ESR because I don't think they are our enemies'. He thought that 'if inspectors were to come like a friend, and had the background of a very experienced teacher or educator ... the general picture is OK'. However, he also believed that if a school was struggling, 'then I don't think they would be our friends: they would be just like auditors'. John L. expressed a similar caution, but for market-oriented reasons. While saying that 'I am not worried about external inspection because I can justify what we did' he felt that keeping a school open in an area of declining population required a good reputation, and 'if your school does not have a good report from the EDB, that may mean that parents do not like your school'.

Finally, Mary N. was relaxed about the activities of the EDB, including inspection, but felt that inspections added pressure to what she regarded was an already over-burdened school. So while with respect to the government reforms, she felt that all things are good, she also felt that 'all the things put together are not good'. Sandra W. developed this point when she said that an external inspection 'does put a kind of pressure on the school' and as she talked, concerns voiced in England were mentioned:

- The paperwork: 'There are lots of paperwork that the school will need to prepare';

- The uncertainty attached to the process 'because they are not telling you how much you need to prepare, so actually you are using a lot of resources doing that';

- Complaints from teachers that this was taking them away from their 'real' job: 'a lot of teachers I think they wanted to just do the operational work';

- And finally, the need to provide proof for what they were doing 'they have to keep a record, because this is evidence'.

There was then a reasonably clear divide between English head teachers and Hong Kong principals in their views of inspectoral bodies: in Hong Kong, they were generally regarded at best as friends, at worst as neutral observers; in England, they were at best an ever-present threat, at worst the enemy. There were, however, similarities, the strongest being the perception of an excessive investment of time and energy needed to meet such demands. This question of time and energy will be returned to later as it has a wider, and more critical, impact upon individual sustainability in the role.

Educational leaders' attitudes and responses to school numbers, parental choice and competition

Both sets of interviewees showed a keen awareness of these issues, but varied considerably in the importance they attached to them. Mary and John L. in Hong Kong, and James R. and Jill S. in England, all took these very seriously because of declining numbers in their schools. For Mary, such diminishing numbers meant that 'parents will compare this school, this school, and this school' and would ask 'why do my daughter and my son study in your school, why can't I find this (in your school) but I can find it in that school?' This led, she felt, to a need to 'sell' the school and publicize its achievements, and Mary thought that these were things a school should not be involved with, but were now things '*I simply have [to do]*'. John L., in Hong Kong, while also principal of a school facing closure due to declining numbers, didn't appear to be as conflicted in having to address such issues. He simply said that '*I do my best to keep my school open, and I will try anything to do that, provided it is in the interest of the students*'. but all designed to bring the school to prospective parents' attention. This involved, he told us, working extraordinary hours at his school; yet he was so motivated, he seldom felt a sense of exhaustion. In England, James R.'s school was also losing students, largely, he believed, because '*houses no longer belong to first-time buyers and owner occupiers ... there's a much bigger turnover of people, and many of them don't have children, so there are only single people left*'. This led to expressions of exasperation: '*It's not that we have done anything in particular that has upset people ... it's just that the area is drifting away.*' In this situation, he felt himself being pressured into starting initiatives like '*breakfast clubs*' with which he was not in total agreement, but which he knew other schools in his area were adopting, and thus was torn between wanting '*to run your school in the right way ... and yet on the other hand, you've got to try and sustain your numbers*'. Finally, Jill, being head teacher of an English denominational school, did not have the benefit of a catchment area – that geographically bounded area within which children were expected to go to a designated school. The result was that *when anybody rings up the LEA, and says, "can you tell me a catchment school", we're never mentioned*. Because of this, *marketing for us is big* and Jill had sent out leaflets to households in the local area, *but I got told off for that by the other Heads because they said it's our catchment, and they see us as poaching ... it's just that if we didn't get them from somebody's catchment, we wouldn't have any children at all*.

Others were aware of the danger of declining numbers, but for different reasons. Penny R., in England, felt that her problem was not declining numbers, but *a lack of confidence in our feeder secondary school ... . So I lose children from the top of year 2, and then into key stage 2*. The critical issue then was that *they are looking at the secondary school, not the practice of the primary*. She was also a little conflicted because she had lost some parents due to her firm approach to pupil behaviour, but generally the parents *love our calm beautiful school, and I have to say to them: you can't have the one without the other*. Finally, Clio C., principal of a private school in Hong Kong, was seeing her numbers constrict, in part because of declining numbers across the city, in part because of parents finding it difficult to afford private school fees, and in part because of the perceived attractiveness of the new part-government-funded schools. This squeeze on numbers led to a greater need to accept students on the basis of ability to pay, rather than on aptitude, *Now we do not have such luxury to choose.* Furthermore, while she felt that the best form of advertising for the school was word-of-mouth personal recommendation, she felt the need to develop more commercial ways of attracting students – even though she thought, *education is not something that you packaged*.

There were also a couple of individuals who had market concerns, but who were steered by more potent forces. As already seen, Harry C. received intense pressure from his LEA to raise published results, rather than the more critical issue, as he saw it, of developing relationships between home and school, and in the process preventing a decline in numbers. In somewhat similar vein, Emily W.'s 'PM' Hong Kong school suffered from declining numbers, yet most of her attention was focused on the stranglehold that the 'AM' principal, the 'senior partner' in this arrangement, exerted over both schools, which prevented Emily from developing innovations which might have helped to halt this decline in numbers. For both, market issues were over-ridden by more pressing concerns.

Rather differently, Susan H., a Hong Kong principal, did not regard market issues as a major consideration at the time of interview, even though she was in an area of declining student population. However, fortuitously for her school, *six* others schools in the area were in the process of closing, and while she felt this was *very cruel* for the staff and the students at these institutions, it meant that her school would be a major beneficiary from the redistributed numbers.

So there is plenty of evidence to suggest that market issues were critical concerns for some in both cultures, if for others they were not, the dominant reason being that the schools had stable or increasing populations. Thus, in Hong Kong, Sandra W., Julia B., Phillip H. and Eva L. were principals of schools in precisely this situation. Sandra, for instance, recognized that *'the market consequences now have become a lot of the drive of most schools in Hong Kong,* and this was largely *because they have to survive'*. However because of a variety of factors – the larger number of applicants than places available at her school, the school's high reputation and strong academic results – she did not see this as a problem. Phillip, similarly had high application rates for places, good academic results and *'many newspapers, radio and media ... always report our school'*. Moreover, while he did believe in publicity, *'The most important thing is that when you work, you must do very well, and then everyone knows your school is a good school ... it's the results more than anything else'*.

On the English side, Michael K. also didn't see market issues as a problem. This was firstly because of a partnership he had engineered with other local schools: *'We have tried very hard not to play at pulling the children from each other's schools.'* The other reason was simply because *'we have had increasing roles continually ... and while we remain buoyant with numbers'*, market issues would not be a cause of concern. Julian B. was in a similar position: his school had 570 students when he arrived, and now there were nearly 700. Steady or rising numbers also insulated other head teachers like Frances G. and Tim L., who had relatively stable school populations, and so 'market' issues tended to take a backseat. Frances nevertheless recognized that *'we have to be realistic and maintain our numbers, purely for the fact that children have a price tag on them'*. Both of them thought there were educational reasons for discounting the importance of the market. Frances said that *'I don't believe it is a major part of my thinking because I am driven by the quality of education that I provide'*. Tim was equally clear: *'I've never thought it [the school] being part of a marketplace ... . I feel that I need to remain aware of what the community is about and that's the part that drives me.'* It would be interesting to see whether such views would change if numbers took a dip.

Results from this examination of pressures from legislation, inspection and markets suggest different trends and considerable variability. First, despite the global/international nature of much of these changes, there were marked cultural differences in leadership perceptions of legislation and inspection, with English leaders expressing a more embattled view than their Hong Kong counterparts. Governmental/cultural mediations of such pressures can then have marked effects upon the perceptions of individuals having to deal with them. Yet, second, and in contrast, market pressures produced similar results in both cultures: where schools were undersubscribed, there was considerable pressure to raise student numbers to avoid losing teachers or to avoid school closure; and where schools were comfortable or oversubscribed, markets were not viewed as a problem.

But a further question is then raised: do these changes have effects on an individual's time and energy, and on their ability to act on what they perceive as role priorities? We turn to these questions now.

Effects on Time and Energy

One might assume that more workload simply means more pressure, which then means reduced sustainability in the role. However, one of the key themes coming from these interviews has been the degree to which personality and context make strong generalization difficult, and this is particularly so for issues of time and energy. For example, Phillip H. was a very experienced Hong Kong principal in his mid-fifties, who described a very demanding job, and who said he only got five hours sleep a night, yet found this quite sufficient. He also told us how he had recently trained for and run in a marathon, in part as a mental discipline to ensure that when he set himself a task, he made sure he completed it. Tim L. on the other hand, was an English head teacher nearing the end of his career, who was feeling growing pressure from his role; increasingly he noted that he lacked the energy to do jobs to the degree which had once been possible. He said that he felt that '*I've got much less energy now, physically, I have less energy in terms of being able to coordinate mind and body,* and admitted that *I need somebody who could actually be my legs*'. Pat L., the head of a small school, smiled and said that '*we haven't even got time to think about the fact that we haven't got time*'. Yet, being so involved could have an upside as well. Michael K. said that '*I really feel that trying to do all those jobs ... . I've probably got a finger on the pulse with things*'. The head of a large school, Michael was grateful he was no longer head of a small institution, as '*I do not know how I would cope as head of that school now*'. Nevertheless, this did not mean he was not busy – '*I think that any head that says that they have time on their hands is lying: we are all under immense pressure.*' However, he did seem to be a good time manager, and he had '*learnt slowly over time to delegate*'. Others seemed to have similar demands, and also seemed to be coping pretty well: David G. said that '*there are huge demands made upon schools nowadays,* and that you *have to use your judgment in picking out what you're to go with*'. So while he believed that he was '*pressured for time*' he felt that he was '*not stressed by it*'. In similar vein, Joanne F. said that she was '*not the kind of person to do things half-heartedly*', and this meant that she needed to adopt the strategy of finding the time to deal with the issue there and then, or that you needed to '*postpone it until you do it properly*'.

Comments by some other English head teachers were more concerning. Angela M. felt that her problems arose less from the legislation itself, than from the fact that there was *a surfeit* of it. '*Everything comes in great big piles. I take home boxes of the stuff.*' The result was that it produced '*huge amounts of reading matter*', which in turn '*necessitates huge amounts of time to assimilate and transform it into action*'. Penny R. also talked of '*countless, countless, countless initiatives ... and sometimes you come in and the desk is a heap, and I'm desperately toiling away and getting tired*'. And while Jill felt that she still managed to get her priorities right, nevertheless '*there are so many other things that come into school ... then it takes longer to implement things that are really important*'.

There seemed little doubt then that lack of time and energy were perceived as serious issues by virtually all the English head teachers, though some found them more problematic than others. When we look at the Hong Kong situation, it is noteworthy that while most Hong Kong principals were generally happy with the direction of legislative reforms, there was also some worrying replies, based around the accumulated pressures the reforms generated. Susan H., for instance, thought that the reforms were generally progressive, but thought there were simply too many of them: '*It is too many things, and also a lot of changes, something done in this way, tomorrow another thing comes out ... . I can do things very quick, very fast, but you see coming a lot of papers, circulars.*' Another concern was that while she personally had developed coping strategies for these pressures, she was concerned that '*not many deputy heads want to be principals nowadays ... it's too hard for them*'. Peter L. also felt that '*it's a tough job (to be the principal), so no one wants to take up this position*'. He also said that '*mainly because of my health, I can no longer endure the workload in the school*', and so had decided that '*I am going to retire soon*'. Peter was not far away from formal retirement, but Eva L. was only just into her first headship, and apparently doing a good job, yet she said she was greatly dissatisfied by her inability to '*reduce the workload of teachers*', and when asked about her own situation, her reply was simply that '*actually we are on the same boat*'. And at the end of the interview, and much to our surprise, she told us that '*I have just quit my job*', the reason being largely that '*for the principal, everything you have to handle, complaints from parents, other things*'. This picture of overwork was added to by Gloria L., who felt that being principal of a DSS school gave her the creativity she wanted, yet she was resigning from the post: '*Time and effort are the main issues that I am concerned with ... even when I'm not working, you have to think all of the time.*'

A picture is then beginning to emerge of a variety of mediations of higher level pressures, and it is important to ask to what extent these individuals felt their mediations were successful. An initial area to explore then is to see what priorities they personally held, and how far they felt they managed to translate these into practice.

What were individual priorities when it came to their leadership?

A major finding of this research was that one area of practice and value was prioritized across both cultures: all were agreed on **the priority of the local.** David G., an English head teacher, said that his first priority was *'what is important in this school'*; this came before *'what is important to the LEA'*, before, last on the list, *'what is important nationally'*. This concentration on the needs of the local is perhaps unsurprising, given that school leaders generally work long hours on issues at this level. However, this prioritization of the local seemed also to be held because they believed that as leaders in their schools, they were in a better position than most to understand the school, its locality and its problems. This was behind the comment Harry C. made with respect to Ofsted inspections when he said that *'their view is too wide. They are looking at too big a picture;* while his job was concerned with *these pupils in this school.'* This being the case, *'I can narrow it down a lot more than they can.'*

This mediation of central directives and legislation by an understanding of the local was seen in many responses. Eva L. described her school's problems primarily in terms of its location and its pupil intake: the students came from a housing estate in a fairly run-down part of Hong Kong, and because *'most of the residents living here mainly come from mainland China ... the students do not have a high aspiration for the future ... the motivation to learn is not so high'*. So Eva was aware of wider contextual challenges, but her greatest satisfaction, she said, came from achieving a better future for this group of students.

David G. also placed his concerns within a wider context by remarking that *there are huge demands made upon schools nowadays,* and he felt that *you can't respond to every one of them*. In such circumstances, you *'have to use your judgment in picking out what you're going to go with'*. David then felt that he needed to be very clear about his values in order to perform such mediation: *'If you don't have a vision of every child coming through the school, succeeding to the best of their ability, and putting into place the best that you can, then I don't think you should be a head teacher.'* This kind of philosophy was also expressed by Julian B., another English head teacher, who said that whenever he was asked to consider an issue, or to adopt a new initiative, he would measure the importance of such things by asking himself over and over again: *'What relevance has this got for the children at this school in terms of raising their attainment and achievement?'* Crucially, if it didn't have immediate or obvious impact, then it was *'really back-burner stuff'*.

This prioritization of the local in most cases came down to **the prioritization of the students,** a view fairly frequently and perhaps unsurprisingly expressed through an educational philosophy underpinned by moral or religious values. Mary N., a Hong Kong principal argued that while academic performance was hugely important, more important was the '*nourishment of the moral development*'. Jill S. said that she became the head teacher of her English primary school because for her the role was about, '*is this going to make a child who comes into this school feel valued and important … do children leave this place feeling confident in their own ability, and feeling that they can go and achieve?*' '*If they don't, we're getting it wrong*'.

This very moral notion of making a difference to the lives of the students in their care came across strongly in most interviews. However, it is important to note that their concern did not just focus on the students. As noted in the chapter on organizational sustainability, being a good principal meant changing focus – the welfare of students then increasingly came from caring for and developing the teachers in their schools. Thus, Julia H., a Hong Kong principal, believed that while her greatest satisfaction came from '*the students' performance*', she felt this was only possible through developing the right *school culture,* and here, her '*main concern*' was '*the teachers' development, because teachers are the ones who face the students, they are the front line … . If you want good students, you need a team of good teachers*'.

Two comments need to be made here. A first is that attaining the head teacher or principal role did not seem to have diminished their commitment to making a difference to pupils' lives, even if now it might need to be achieved through others. There seemed little cultural difference in this. However, a second observation raises a more worrying question. Given this understandable focus on the personal and the local, did they have sufficient understanding of the forces that were acting upon such personal priorities? If these pressures ultimately derived from global forces, did they have a sufficient grasp of these to be able to embrace, mediate or counter these, as appropriate? Did they, in other words, feel that they could exercise such personal priorities in the role?

Managing personal priorities in the leadership role

Across both cultures, there was a wide spread of opinion on this issue. For example, some head teachers expressed great confidence in their ability to steer their schools. We have seen how Michael K., an experienced English head teacher, felt it necessary to suspend the National Curriculum –*We saw from the start that there was not joined up thinking between the different groups that had put together the documentation.*' There were similarities here between him and Philip H., the Hong Kong principal with long experience in the job, who displayed the same kind of strategic view. Being chairman of an influential educational association was a job he said which provided him with '*many chances, many opportunities*' to gain a wider picture: '*If I have a good plan, and I have the practice, I can make it.*' Michael and Phillip both seemed ahead of the game, and intended keeping it like that.

However, it didn't seem necessary to be the principal of a well-appointed school to believe that one could have strong influence on a school's direction. Joanne F., in England, and John L. in Hong Kong, both worked in challenging schools, and yet both claimed strong steers on their school's direction. Joanne said that inspection teams '*on the whole are fine ... what they want you to do really is to make things better for the children. So if you can prove what you're doing is going to make them better, that's fine*'. Like Michael K., some time previous to the interview, she had suspended a number of National Curriculum activities, knowing that Ofsted would quickly be down to see why she had done so – and like him, had survived the encounter.

A different kind of confidence was shown by John L., the principal mentioned earlier whose school, like many others in Hong Kong, had faced closure due to declining pupil numbers. '*In Hong Kong ten years ago, the birth rate is 2.2 per family; now it is 0.9.*' John could not prevent closure if numbers dropped below the minimum legislated level ("*a school must enrol at least twenty-three pupils in order to survive*"), but there was a lot he believed he could do to attract the extra numbers needed. Once again, part of this seemed to be down to experience – he had been a schoolteacher, college lecturer and school inspector, before becoming a school principal, so '*I think that has given me great advantages*'. Yet, like the other three, there was the strong feeling that his energetic, never-say-die personality had a great deal to do with his success in keeping the school afloat.

Yet while there were individuals with such confidence, there were also some who at the time of interview had felt under much greater pressure. As already seen, Harry C., the English head teacher of only one year's experience, felt that his role at times was being reduced to '*raising standards by paperwork*', rather than the critical one of developing better relationship between home and school. A similar feeling of relative powerlessness was also echoed by Emily W., as the well-established AM principal prevented her from developing innovations, and undermined her with her own staff.

If the AM/PM school arrangement was a culturally specific context, another strong contextual factor in Hong Kong was the effect of diminishing school populations, and therefore of increased market pressures on many schools. Yet such pressure did not necessarily produce standardized responses. With John L., this produced a spirited response. With Mary N., however, the reaction was rather different, and seemed part of a gradual accumulation of pressures, which her eighteen years of experience in the role did not seem to help – '*too many things to handle at the same time*'.

A similar level of frustration was expressed by James R., the English head teacher whose school had a declining student population, and which largely explained the school's poor financial situation ... . His feelings of powerlessness extended to a great deal of legislation as well. As noted earlier, he simply said: *to be honest you just nod and say, 'Well we're going to have to make the best of it.'* Like Harry C., he thought he had the local knowledge to address the school's real problems, but felt prevented from exercising that knowledge.

There seem then some strong similarities across the two populations with respect to their ability to achieve personal educational priorities; some felt they were doing this strongly, some felt very constrained and a fair number occupied a middle ground. However, a couple of things need noting. One is that experience can be an important factor in how principals/head teachers cope with the situations they find themselves in, for it can provide ways of dealing with issues to which the less experienced simply do not have access. This, of course, is not always true: the case of Mary N., for instance, suggests that when new contexts clash with long-held values and visions, not all are able or willing to adapt. A second factor is that the local context in which a principal or head teacher finds themself can have very uplifting or very depressing effects on their morale. Yet contexts do not need to be decisive: similar contexts can generate very different reactions, due to different personalities. There is then no simple explanation for individual perceptions and behaviours: one has to know both the person and the context to understand why they feel the way they do about their ability to influence the school's goals.

Conclusion: What do these patterns of response say about role sustainability?

The results so far suggest strong concerns were felt by members of both groups about a decline in school numbers, and for many, these issues caused real stress and were a contributory threat to their sustainability in the role. Clearly, however, where numbers were more buoyant – again a phenomenon seen across both cultures – personal sustainability was not threatened from this direction, though all were aware that market issues might become a problem in the future. The threats to personal leadership sustainability from the rise of competitive school systems and declining school numbers were then real ones across both cultures, but differentially affected leadership according to the local context.

In terms of the pressure generated by new and increased amounts of legislation, and the demands that came from it, this resulted for many in greater demands on time and energy, and was again seen across both cultures. However, such demands did not fall on one or two unlucky head teachers or principals who happened to inhabit unlucky contexts: pressures of time and energy were recognized and felt almost universally, even if some seemed better able to cope than others. The issue of individual difference will be discussed shortly, but the unanimity of opinion and concern across both cultures was both striking and worrying. While some governments have responded to this concern, for instance through espousing models of distributed leadership and hence distributed responsibility, it appears to continue as a major threat to leadership sustainability, in part because both delegation and redistribution of work entail other problems of time and energy, including the checking that both are properly implemented.

Looking now at pressures in the two cultures, there seemed very different perceptions and responses to the intentions of legislation and inspection. The data suggest that English head teachers experienced a more threatening regime of legislation and inspection than did their counterparts in Hong Kong. Indeed, the English legislation and inspection seemed to be framed and implemented in a manner which sent messages to educational professionals that they were not particularly valued or trusted, and this left many English interviewees feeling angry and insulted. Issues of lowered trust and morale were then more frequent with English head teachers than with Hong Kong principals, leading to the view that personal leadership sustainability in the English context was more problematic than it was in Hong Kong.

Yet the data also clearly illustrate two other issues concerning leadership sustainability. One, already mentioned, is the effect of the local context. This is clearly implicated in the workings of the market, and in the implementation of legislation, and suggests that those working in local contexts with stable or declining populations normally have very different foci. Similarly, English head teachers inheriting schools with strong or poor Ofsted records almost certainly also prioritize different issues. Finally, Hong Kong teachers who ascended to the principalship of either 'AM' or 'PM' schools were also very likely to have different issues to deal with. There are of course a host of other locally specific issues that could arise in a school and which are not replicated elsewhere: disputes between teachers, parental neglect of children or problems with neighbouring schools can all produce unique pressures. Understanding the challenges of the local context therefore seems vital both to individual sustainability, and to the sustainability of the quality of the role.

One other issue concerning leadership sustainability returns the discussion to the contribution of personality. Both cultural groups were composed of a spectrum of different individuals: some were happy to stand up to and publicly oppose policies; others felt that while some pressures were unacceptable, the best strategy normally was to keep one's head down and adopt a 'safety first' position; and there were those in both cultures who struggled in the role, and felt that the combination of pressures faced was taking them to breaking point. The data then suggest that irrespective of cultural differences in response to pressures, there will always be a difference in individual responses *within* cultures to these pressures. The different kinds of responses seem a function of the complex of factors that make up an individual and the contexts they inhabit.

Table 9.1 Nine implicit leadership rules potentially impacting on individuals' sustainability in England and Hong Kong

Implicit rule	Rule origins	Seen in England or Hong Kong	Effects on leadership sustainability
1. Having a personal philosophy of education is an essential compass in conducting the leadership role	Personal values and professional socialization	Seen in both cultures	If central directives prevent the operation of such a personal compass, personal sustainability may well be threatened
2. The priority is to make a difference to students' lives	Personal values and professional socialization	Seen in both cultures	If insufficient time is spent on this priority, this may lead to less sustainability
3. Personal and local concerns are the major foci of attention	Personal values and presenting issues	Seen in both cultures	These take large amounts of time and energy; if leaders cannot spend enough time on these foci, they may feel less sustainable
4. Central directives should be mediated by leaders' understanding of personal and local issues	Personal values and professional socialization	Seen in both cultures	If central directives prevent such mediation, personal sustainability may be threatened
5. The national legislative architecture is accepted, even parts which are disagreed with personally	Personal values and socialization	Seen in both cultures	The more individuals disagree with such architecture, the more likely they are to feel less sustainable
6. School practices and results are viewed as defence against external inspection	Professional experience	Seen mostly in England, much less so in Hong Kong	When viewed in this manner, this is likely to increase personal pressure and reduced sustainability

7. School practices and results are viewed as discussion points with external authorities	Professional experience	Seen mostly in Hong Kong, less so in England	When viewed in this manner, this is likely to reduce individual pressure and increase sustainability
8. When school numbers are threatened by market forces, these should be taken seriously	Professional experience	Seen in both England and Hong Kong	In many cases, market forces may lead to more pressures and less personal sustainability
9. When school numbers are not threatened, market forces need not be a major focus of interest	Professional experience	Seen in both England and Hong Kong	Absence of market pressures does not add to leadership pressures

A major conclusion from this chapter however must also be how much more these two groups of leaders had in common than in how they differed. As Table 9.1 demonstrates, of nine implicit rules of leadership derived from the data reviewed, only two – how school practices and results were viewed – were different between English head teachers and Hong Kong principals, and these differences seemed to arise from different contextual experiences impacting on their values and practice. Of the other seven, five (having a personal philosophy of education, making a difference to students' lives, the personal and local being the major foci of attention, central directives being mediated by such local understanding, and the acceptance of a national legislative architecture) all seemed to stem primarily from personal values and professional socialization. The final two (both concerned with school numbers and market forces) seem to be essentially pragmatic rules: that if there is a market problem, it should be taken seriously, but where it isn't a problem, then one should get on with the rest of the job.

It is also worth noting that these implicit rules seem to be shared more closely by English head teachers and Hong Kong principals than earlier comparisons of Anglo-American and East Asian cultures suggest. This may be due to Hong Kong having been strongly influenced by its history with England over the last 150 years; but it seems at least plausible that sets of deeply held professional values may tie groups together across larger cultural contexts more than might be anticipated. It also cannot be assumed that just because a level of culture (the East Asian) has more adherents, and is more widespread geographically than another level (for example, that of East Asian head teachers' professional values), that the larger/wider cultural level will necessarily have the most influence upon an individual's behaviour and thought. This may instead depend upon the particular context and situation within which an individual makes choices or judgements. The impact of different levels or kinds of culture then generates important questions and areas ripe for further research.

Yet, finally, despite the evidence from these last two chapters that cultural issues might have profound effects upon leadership sustainability, it is clear that impacts upon individual sustainability are not just cultural in nature. The influences and impact of other levels of context can leak into and change cultural values and practices. Thus, the personal, organizational, local and national contexts so far described are all likely to permeate the cultural, and change its nature and impact. Yet at this moment in time, it could be argued that some of the forces having the most profound effects on cultures, and on political systems, are found at the global level, in part because of the manner in which they impact on contexts below them, and also in part because of the extra complexity and wickedity which such global forces can add to the demands of the leadership role. It is to this area's impact that the next chapter turns.

CHAPTER TEN

Global Influences On Leadership Sustainability

Introduction

The previous chapter dwelt principally on the potential cultural effects on the sustainability of the leadership role. It was situated within a wider picture of the growth of national educational systems, and of the need to recognize the 'wicked' nature of many leadership problems, in order to give some understanding of the complexity of the forces that impact on educational leaders' work. While a leaders' attention may be focused primarily on the personal, institutional and local, many forces which steer and constrict (and on occasions, liberate) their work occur at higher levels of context. The complexity and wickedity of their challenges, have, if anything, increased over the last few decades, because of an increase in global influences on educational leadership. It would therefore be under-describing the challenges that educational leaders face if these influences were not examined. This chapter then will scrutinize a number of these, to examine whether there are any underlying similarities between them, and to see what impacts they might be having on leadership sustainability.

However, one needs to be cautious of lists: their contents can seem to be separate and separable, permanent and impermeable. Yet the forces discussed in this chapter seem highly permeable, and to have strong influences on one another. It can therefore be very difficult knowing where one force begins and another ends, and this makes the job of understanding their boundaries, and of dealing with them, all the more complex. Is global warming, for example, an example of environmental change, or better categorized as a consequence of human use of fossil fuels in the pursuit of global economic growth? Are the greater steering and control of professional work by centralized online monitoring and the global dissemination of comparative national curricula achievements better characterized as examples of technological globalization or as one aspect of political globalization – the greater monitoring and steerage of electorates? The answer is likely to be more Asian than Western in character: each is likely to be a fusion of more than one or two forces, and as they combine, they increase the interconnectedness and wickedity of the forces acting upon nations, institutions and individuals, their sustainability, and upon the leadership role itself.

From the national to the global

As noted earlier, the historic role of most public education systems over the last two to three hundred years has been to inculcate the notion of citizenship loyalty, and to identify such citizenship with the nation state. However, there has been an increasing awareness of a number of global forces which appear to be undermining the hegemony that nation states have tried to achieve. Ohmae (1995), for instance, entitled one of his books 'The End of the Nation State'; and Fukuyama (1991), in triumphal hubris after the fall of the Berlin Wall, assumed a convergence of social and political systems to more closely match that of the United States. This is a view developed further by Bobbit (2002, p. 211), who argued that all nation states were transforming into 'market states':

> Whereas the nation-state, with its mass free public education, universal franchise, and social security policies, promised to guarantee the welfare of the nation, the market-state promises instead to maximise the opportunity of the people and thus tends to privatize many state activities and to make voting and representative government less influential and more responsive to the market.

But such apparent inevitabilities have been hotly contested. Huntingdon (1988), for instance, has argued that cultural values are so ingrained that he sees a continued clash between civilizations as almost inevitable – though why this has to lead to conflict and confrontation and not greater understanding and reconciliation is never quite spelt out. There has also been a greater recognition of the abilities of some nation states, through their considerable economic, political and military power, to mediate such global trends (Palan, 2002). And lately, there has been an increasing anti-globalist feeling by elements of electorates in economically developed countries, who have felt economically disenfranchised after losing their jobs to cheaper labour in less developed parts of the globe – the election of Donald Trump to the US presidency seemingly being the most significant recent reaction.

Globalization has certainly influenced educational reforms, but in different ways. Astiz et al. (2002) have shown how globalization pressures have led to very different degrees of centralization and decentralization in education systems, as these countries have mediated the pressures to their own cultural imperatives, rather as Hallinger and Kantamara (2000, p. 202) have suggested that leadership needs to be very subtle in its understanding of situations 'where the underlying assumptions are foreign to prevailing norms of the local culture'. Ribbins and Zhang (2006), Preus (2007) and Law (2012) have all demonstrated how the various components of Chinese culture ensure that educational leadership looks very different from its UK and/or US counterparts. So this is not a simple picture of global domination or universal national defence. As Zhong (2006) and Yin et al. (2014, p. 307) argue, while many 'global' ideas may be largely Western in origin, 'the reform process is by no means a simple cut and paste exercise, but a subtle fusion and modification according to the local cultural context...'

Yet there seems little doubt that the influences caused by global policy borrowing, and by global movements, have had, and are continuing to have effects on national cultures, on public educational systems, on their institutions and on the individuals within them. Even then, there are probably many individuals, including educational leaders, who do not recognize the extent of these influences upon their values and practices. There is then real need to understand this level of context much better.

Now it is important to recognize that 'globalisation' can have a number of different meanings. It can simply refer to the perception of the earth as a physical whole, a planetary object whirling through space, both greater and different from the sum of any number of politically invented entities upon its surface. It is a geological, geographical and ecological body, the fragility of which humanity is only just coming to realize. 'Globalisation' then can be a perspective of the whole being greater than the sum of the parts. However, the term is more usually used to suggest two other things. A first is in terms of the effects that human functioning has had on planet Earth, such as in the way and degree to which human beings have used fossil fuels, in the process significantly contributing to the rate of global warming. 'Globalisation' can also be used to describe the way in which global changes (whether natural or man-made) alter the way in which humans view themselves, their potentialities and their future actions. Waters (1996, p. 3) was one of the first then to suggest that globalization is 'a social process in which the constraints of geography on social and cultural arrangements recede *and in which people become increasingly aware that they are receding'*. (our italics) This second meaning then suggests that while global changes alter human lives, part of the change comes from human awareness of such change, which then leads to further change because individuals now plan their lives differently. A simple example would be the use of an internet communication medium like Skype: its invention has meant that human beings can communicate in ways not possible before, and who now plan their lives in ways very different from how they have done in the past. Ritzer's (2004, p. 160) definition of globalization captures many of these nuances, when he suggests that the term now involves

> The world-wide diffusion of practices, expansion of relations across continents, organisation of social life on a global scale, and the growth of a shared global consciousness.

Such 'shared global consciousness' might well be another way of talking of a 'global culture'. However, one needs to be careful here, because, as noted above, a backlash can occur because the new opportunities for some created by global movements can be seen as threats by others. Huntingdon (2004), for example, has written of his concern that the culture of the United States is fragmenting, and he explains this in part through the way many US immigrants no longer need to become or adopt American values or an American identity. Instead, because of the strong ties to people 'back home' which can now be maintained through these new communication media, they can remain loyal to their birth nation, sustained by such technologies in their communication with their family and friends. 'Globalisation' here then includes both the globalization of technology, and the paradoxical retrenchment and sustenance of nation state identities.

Moreover, as the Huntingdon example shows, definitions may simply fail to capture the richness and complexity of interactions that occur in such global changes; one needs to look in detail at the specific global forces which lead to changes at national levels, and in educational systems, in order to examine their effects on leadership sustainability. This chapter will then explore the links between four forms of globalization which are having immediate and observable effects on the sustainability of individual educational leaders, and on the roles they attempt to negotiate The four forms of globalizations are:

1 Economic globalization
2 Political globalization
3 Cultural globalization
4 Technological globalization

Economic globalization

Economic globalization is probably the most recognized form of globalization; indeed, it is sometimes seen as the central range of ideas and motivational form underpinning the term 'globalisation'. While such a narrow interpretation is not favoured here, it remains a very powerful force, impacting on and changing all the other forms. It consists of at least four different elements.

A first element has been the widespread adoption of free-market approaches to economic activity, seen by advocates as the best means of generating national and individual wealth. This belief has migrated from a business environment into the public sectors of many nation states, and particularly into public education systems, and has led to policies of greater competition between institutions within the sector, and the much greater use of economic terms to define and then redefine the nature of educational work, with talk of customers, producers, consumers and the creation of internal markets. Over the last forty to fifty years, the force of neoliberal arguments have been accepted by some unlikely politicians: from a previous 'socialist' Prime Minister in the UK, Tony Blair, who talked of the choice between private and public provision of a service as being essentially no more than 'what matters is what works' (quoted in Ainley, 2004, p. 507); to the former Communist Chinese Premier, Deng Xiaoping, who famously stated that in choosing between communist and free-market economics to develop China's economic base, it didn't matter if the cat was black or white, as long as it caught the mice. Market approaches then have been a heavily adopted global economic strategy for a number of decades.

Of course, it remains to be seen whether such influence will continue at present levels, given the political and economic backlash currently being experienced in countries, where the movement of jobs to countries with cheaper labour costs has led, not only to 'rust-belt' phenomena in previously wealthy industrial communities, but also to the leakage of IT skills away from the same Western nations. Yet if such a backlash was to have long-term effect, it would have to affect a second element of economic globalization, the work of highly influential global economic organizations like the World Trade Organisation, the International Monetary Fund and the World Bank. Over the last few decades, such organizations have brokered agreements with nation states, which have steadily prevented many from 'firewalling' their economies against global financial movements. Nation states have then become open to and increasingly vulnerable to global financial market trends, intensified by the global speed of financial transactions.

The power of nation states has also been weakened by a third force – an increasing dependency upon the investments of multinational corporations, who have been able to search out the 'best' national sites for their operations, and have also been able to move these elsewhere when particular national sites have become less profitable (see Korten, 1996). As noted above, Bobbitt (2003) has claimed that such movement is transforming nation states into 'market states', as nation states are increasingly unable to provide the degree of protection and welfare to their citizens that they have historically performed over the last one hundred and fifty years. In the process, such nation states may be increasingly limited to providing opportunities for citizens to generate individual wealth, in part through the provision of an increasingly privatized range of different educational mechanisms. If this happens, the nation state will lose its protective function for citizens, and instead as the ETUI (quoted in Ainley, 2004, p. 501) suggests, it will become little more than:

> the body for monitoring and controlling 'good behaviour' on the part of its citizens. Its role is to distribute not wealth so much as opportunities; it becomes the 'enabling' or 'empowering' state which rewards the most dynamic.

This helps one to understand why many public sector workers, including educators, would speak as much of state control over their functioning as in their enforced engagement with competitive internal markets. However, probably a more subtle and complex explanation comes from the experience of Singapore, Japan, and other 'Asian Tigers' in the second half of the last century (Ashton and Sung, 1997), who have worked from the belief that if some sense of national identity and power is to be retained, strong government intervention at the national level is needed in order to mediate such external global forces. Palan et al. (2002) described a variety of strategies which nation states were using to negotiate global forces, of which the Asian Tiger/Singaporean approach was but one. Other strategies included the deliberate grouping of nation states into larger trading blocks (such as the EU and NAFTA); the political domination of such blocks by the most powerful of these states (Germany and the US); and the deliberate shielding of some valued social structures and values from globalizing forces (as with Sweden and Norway); it should be noted however that some countries, such as many sub-Saharan states, have never been financially robust enough to engage in this game.

Such strategic mediation, as well as the observation by Stiglitz (2002) that global economic history over the last century has been one where developed countries have deliberately skewed markets to favour themselves, suggests two things. One is that the nation state as an entity is far from dead, though some are in a better state of health than others. The other is that nevertheless, nation states have had to adapt to these global forces, and a standard way of doing so has been, almost paradoxically, to combine approaches which facilitate competitive advantage in global markets with national policies which also increasingly steer and direct the people and institutions within their borders. From an individual professional's point of view, the adoption of market concepts best explains the dual effects of the greater marketization and the greater control of their work, the former being seen as a means of increasing the work and quality of the 'products' being created for a global marketplace, while the development of greater central control ensures that 'producers' conform with what their governments see as the essential skills and values needed for a globally competitive environment.

As suggested in earlier chapters, such forces may threaten personal sustainability and the quality of the leadership role in a number of ways. First, as governments sponsor the entry of economic and business terms and values into educational discourse, such as the replacement of public good values with private interest ones, such terms and values increasingly challenge personal leadership values. For some, this may change their view of what constitutes 'quality' performance in the role, they alter behaviours and practices accordingly, and sustainability is maintained; for others such change may be seen as one for the worse, role fulfilment is reduced, and sustainability decreased.

Second, and as noted previously, the replacement of previously held values and practices has been largely achieved in Western countries through increased accountability measures, which have affected role sustainability through increases in workload, by threats to morale, by greater personal surveillance and by measures of performativity, which run counter to many principals' visions of the purpose and practice of the role (see Ball, 2007). Some of these leaders may then find themselves having to adopt competitive and market-based mentalities, while being steered into actions and functions at odds with deeply held educational values, and they may come to the conclusion that this is no longer the kind of role they want to maintain. Current economic globalization forces then reach down a long way to affect the lives and values of many individuals.

Political globalization

Political and economic globalization forces are closely linked in a number of ways, having similar effects upon the allegiance of individuals to nation states, and upon the sustainability of nation state actors and institutions. Now, both the economic *and* the political power of nation states have been seriously challenged over the last few decades, because nation state power (and therefore its perceived legitimacy by its citizens) has leaked away from it. This leakage has occurred in three different directions.

First, nation state power has leaked *upwards* to larger international bodies. These bodies may be primarily economic in nature, through the actions of bodies like the International Monetary Fund, the World Trade Organisation and the World Bank; or they may be mixtures of the economic and political, through bodies like the European Community. Nevertheless, the effect on many nation states has been for them to cede both economic and political power, in pursuit of opportunities afforded by being a player in a large internal market, and also by the economic and political protections provided by being a member. Indeed, as this is being written, the UK is negotiating its withdrawal from the European Community, one of these economic and political clubs, and a major concern by those UK citizens who wish to remain within it, is precisely the lack of political clout they fear may occasion if the UK no longer has access to political and economic high tables.

Second, however, power can also, a little paradoxically leak *downwards* to local communities, if individuals feel distanced by such large bodies, and may instead come to prioritize the local and personal. This is in part one of the reasons for populist political movement at the present time, as individuals feel that politicians at the political centre do not understand or are not interested in their concerns. Moreover, and as Naisbett and Aburdene (1988) remarked some time ago, when such distancing occurs, individuals may 'increasingly treasure the traditions that spring from within'. This has resulted in calls for greater devolution, and in greater autonomy to regions, and even to the separation of cultural or linguistic groups into new smaller nation states, such as Czechoslovakia into the Czech Republic and Slovakia and perhaps to the breakup of the United Kingdom. In the process, nation states may be threatened by the perceived 'nesting' of citizen loyalties at different levels of political activity (Heater, 2004). Scottish Nationalists, for instance, argue that Scotland (and perhaps the European Union) has the levels of primary citizenship allegiance, rather than the UK.

Finally, as multinational companies influence the economic strategies of nation states, and as these companies can play off one country against another, so power can leak *sideways* to them as well. Indeed, the financial power of larger multinationals dwarfs that of medium-sized nation states. Moreover, because such companies are also able to move assets around the globe in a manner impossible to a geographically bound nation state, they can be more adaptable to changing circumstances, as well as being less accountable.

Many nation states then face the threat of a decline in their power from a number of directions. No longer does Marshall's (1950) argument hold that nation-state citizenship is an evolutionary process which can be traced historically from *civic* citizenship (where only legal protections were granted to citizens); to *political* citizenship (where citizens had the right to participate in political decisions); to that of *social* citizenship (where the state grants supports and protections to citizens). Instead, the history of citizenship may seem better described by Bobbit's (2002) 'market state'. As Davidson and Rees-Mogg (1999) have argued, nation state citizenship may now be little more than another form of market purchase, where nation states increasingly reduce or alter the range of citizenship 'deals' they offer individuals.

Yet once again, it should be noted that nation state governments have not simply rolled over and submitted to such pressures. Many, in mediation of such pressures, have attempted to exert increasing control over internal policies, and particularly over the work of those in their public services. Part of such attempts, as also noted, has come from the perceived need to create and steer economic policies and strategies which can mediate global pressures. But a requisite degree of loyalty and citizenship to the nation state is unlikely to be created solely through the creation of particular economic strategies. It is more likely to come from creating a stronger sense of personal and political identity with the nation state. In the process, the project of citizenship education can then take a number of forms. It can amount to forms of indoctrination, with the non-critical inculcation of nation-state loyalty, and of the responsibilities of individuals to their local communities and to the nation state itself. It can also amount to an education into citizenship as an understanding of the kind of nested citizenship relationship now experienced by many. Finally, and in line with market trends, citizenship education can become little more than a form of consumerism, in which individuals are shown how to 'shop around' for the best citizenship offers. Educational leaders would be wise to recognize such choices, and consider the extent to which their personal values cohere with the models most favoured by their government. These may match the values they want to see underpinning an educational leadership role, but they may well conflict, and such conflict will likely affect personal and role sustainability.

The effects of political globalization on individual professionals may then be closely aligned with those of economic globalization, leading to similar threats to individual and role sustainability. The paradoxical combination of global market values and nation-state internal policy control may not only conflict with personal held values, but may lead to diminishing the quality of the role. Moreover, negotiating a role which has to respond to a political world in which loyalty is nested at different levels may be problematic for many if they are simultaneously required to implement nation-centric political values.

Cultural globalization

Economic and political globalizations are also entwined with **cultural globalization.** This form of globalization also fits well into a world characterized by wickedity and paradox, as it has at least two contradictory forms. On the one hand, cultural globalization can offer a variety of experiences available worldwide, propelled by an economic mechanism designed to facilitate and increase individual consumption of aspects of different cultures. However, while such diversity may be seen by many as a welcome life-changing opportunity, for others it may be seen as an attack on the integrity of deeply held beliefs and truths which need maintaining, and which may also be linked to anti-Western and anti-American feeling. In similar vein, and particularly in Western cultures, such variety may also be seen as damaging and ultimately corrosive to personal values, if it is seen as leading to a relativity of values, creating what Rorty (1989, pp. 73–4) described as ironic individuals, who are 'never quite able to take themselves seriously because [they are] always aware that the terms in which they describe themselves are subject to change'.

Yet this globalization of variety has an oppositional form, a globalization of standardization, which can be seen in Ritzer's (1993) description of McDonaldization. Borrowing from Weber and other nineteenth-century thinkers, this idea is underpinned by the four classic bureaucratic forces of control, predictability, efficiency and calculability. Paradoxically, its current forms are also driven by economic mechanisms designed to facilitate and increase consumption of the experience. Moreover, just as cultural flexibility has its personal and cultural downsides, so does cultural standardization. Thus Ritzer (2004) describes a potential consequence of cultural standardization as resulting in the globalization of 'nothing' – where 'nothing' is a value-less end product, and which needs to be seen as the reduction of culture to its commodification, in order to facilitate its consumption and to enhance profits. Rikfin (2000, p. 247) has also warned that when the commercial tries to reduce the cultural to consumable bits and pieces, 'it risks poisoning the well from which we draw important values and feelings'.

Both forms of cultural globalization can also threaten the status of the nation state. The globalization of cultural variety has the potential to offer rich, invigorating and refreshing insights into long-standing national problems through new ideas and new perceptions. Yet such variety can also lead to forms of fragmentation, as having too much choice can feel overwhelming to many, who then may feel incapable of prioritizing what is most important. Indeed, Ritzer (1993, p. 1) noted that many people 'prefer a world that is not cluttered by choices and options' because 'they like the fact that many aspects of their lives are highly predictable'. This is reminiscent of Fromm's (1942) cautions, when he suggested that individuals may surrender their political freedoms to powerful others when decision-making becomes too difficult. Down the road of fragmentation, then, may lie political forms of society where democratic values are undermined, and instead the views of the demagogue, the authoritarian and the xenophobe are embraced, because they provide simpler answers. When this happens, fragmentation may facilitate a violent swing over to cultural and political standardizations, as the simple, the tame, and the black and white, are vocalized and supported, and the kinds of political and cultural creativity needed to deal with wicked challenges are throttled in their development.

Such challenges are not currently heavily written into the role of the educational leader, but their sustainability is affected by their need in the role to reconcile a number of cultural tensions. First, they need to reconcile the virtues of experiencing a diversity of views and experiences with the potential reduction in the possibility of prioritizing particular values. Second, in a democratic society, their role should require them to articulate a coherent set of liberal and tolerant national and personal values and arguments, in order to challenge the potential proliferation of narrow, exclusionary xenophobic and fundamentalist views within their society. Third they need to understand that despite many current political views, economic values need to be seen as necessarily subservient to social values, and of these in their turn being subservient to environmental ones (see Bottery, 2016, on this). Fourth, they need to articulate the virtues of a coherent national view while recognizing that many in society believe that multiple truths still need asserting. Finally, they need to be able to articulate a coherent view of the world, which can counter an increasing belief in the lack of ultimate truth in any. The educational leader needs to be able to negotiate their way through such conflicts in order to establish a personally coherent position which can be articulated in their leadership role. This has not been something much expected of educational leaders in their role previously; today, it is becoming an imperative.

Technological globalization

Technological globalization tends to be seen by many as a positive good, whose expansion can only help create a better world. Yet if there are increased, confusing and paradoxically 'wicked' connections between economic, political and cultural forms of globalization, technological globalization plays a key role in furthering these connections. It does this in three important ways, and in so doing makes these connections, if anything, less understandable and less controllable. Its ultimate effects on leadership sustainability are then highly important and also highly unclear.

A first way it enhances global connectivity is through the massive increase in the **ability** with which people around the world can now communicate and access information globally. This increase in ability is manifested through the availability of information, through the convenience of that availability, and through the democratization of that ability. Thus, in terms of availability, individuals have access not only to what is immediately present to them, but also to a vast amount that they didn't have before, and probably wouldn't have even thought of trying to access. This **availability** then changes the way in which people think and plan, for with such availability, they can vastly increase their aspirations with respect to what they can affect and achieve. Closely related to such availability is the **convenience** afforded by technology to access such information. This means that they can deal with more knowledge and data through not having to spend vast amounts of time trying to access these. And because technology enhances the ability of many more people to access information than through other forms of communication, the only real hindrances are likely to be literacy, cost and training in using a computer. While all three remain a genuine issue in some parts of the world, access is now much higher globally than previously, and consequently there has been an explosion in the democratization of knowledge that formerly would have been accessed by only the privileged few. Simply put, Chinese and Indian IT experts now no longer need to go to Silicon Valley to be at the forefront of IT developments; comparable centres for development exist in Dalian and Calcutta.

Moreover, while many more individuals now have such increased access, the amazing **speed** at which information can be retrieved means that individuals can make decisions and take action quicker than ever before, and this has undoubtedly changed the way lives are lived, and the way individuals plan for the future. Harvey as long ago as 1987 provided a useful conceptualization of how technological globalization has 'shrunk' the world when he produced different pictures of the globe at various times in history. The picture size – and hence the time taken to communicate to another – depends on the major form of transport used at that moment in time. The message is very clear: the faster we can communicate, the smaller the globe becomes. He stopped his pictures in 1960, the suggestion being that with the almost instantaneous communication now possible worldwide, the world's size is no longer much of an impediment to global communication.

Technological globalization then also **democratizes** access to information to an extent never previously seen. It thus has huge effects on people's understanding of the world, and on their belief in what they can achieve. Professional educators are not the only ones, then, who have recognized and utilized the immense educative, learning and communicative potential from such globalization. For many it may seem an unmitigated good, but there are mixed blessings here. Democratizing access to information can also mean that information may be misunderstood, may be misused and may be accessed by people who are not sufficiently critical of its claimed veracity (and hence the global debate currently about 'fake news'). Moreover, not everything that can be placed in the public domain should be put there. Educators may then be particularly taxed in deciding what students should access and how it should be critiqued, to an extent previous generations did not have to consider. In addition, the democratization of access poses the question of whether the role of the educator needs re-framing: Are they transmitters of information, facilitators of access, or critical guides in the assessment of external information, or a mixture of all three? These are urgent issues for educators to consider, to choose and to justify.

In a similar way, increasing the speed of communication may also pose problems because it normally increases the rate of change. When formerly communication was by foot or by post, a delay, sometimes considerable, would be normal and expected, and would condition the rate at which change could be achieved. When however emails, Facebook or Twitter become standard elements of communication and work for many, and it is realized they can be delivered (and responded to) in seconds, many may also feel that time for reflection is much more constrained, leading to poorer response quality. A key concern for educational leaders, as we have seen, then lies in the sheer quantity of materials and demands they now receive, and the time-limited nature of their expected replies. In the process, many individuals may feel that both personal sustainability and the quality of the role are being threatened.

Finally, when there is much wider access to information, it may democratize in some cases, but it can also reduce proper appreciation of more local information, and add to the problems of accountability. Thus if accountability comparisons are local, comparison of schools can be relatively fine-grained, as local contexts are seen as highly relevant to an appreciation of performance. When that comparison is raised to a national level, the contextualization is likely to be less fine-grained, less appreciative of local concerns. And when the comparative context grows beyond the national to the international, schools begin to be compared with others in widely differing cultures, with very different values and expectations. The pronouncements by the OECD, the comparison of performance by PISA, can be taken as examples of a 'smoothing' out of contextualized information, curricula, values and student performance, and for that matter, individual and contextualized leadership qualities.

Burdens of accountability can also be increased through the greater ease of surveillance. One of the outstanding characteristics of many societies in the last few decades has been the elimination of middle tiers of management, as public and private organizations have moved from Fordist to post-Fordist forms of organization (Amin, 1994). Where once an organization had many levels, in which higher levels maintained surveillance of lower levels through physical presence, now enhanced technological capacity to collect and use information to judge quality of work is speedy, far more efficient, and for those being observed, much more intrusive. It is also more effective, because it tends to result in those being watched moving from merely responding to external demands to increasingly internalizing such demands, as they realize that technology allows for their constant surveillance – the essence as we have seen of both Bentham's and then Foucault's notion of the Panopticon (1979). This may increase the effectiveness of accountability, but it is debatable whether it improves an individual's sustainability in the role, or in the prosecution of the role itself. Being constantly watched oftentimes is highly stressful, and can demonstrate low trust towards workers, which once again can impact negatively on personal morale and role sustainability.

In sum, then, because of its profound impact on both work and thinking, technological globalization has great potential for better and worse personal and role sustainability. Its ability-enhancing nature, its speed and its democratizing tendencies can all help to change the work and role of the educational leader towards the more sustainable, as it can be a huge asset in developing the potentials of students and educators. However, it can also produce more negative outcomes, as it can increase the rate of change to unmanageable levels, add to unsupportable levels of accountability, and promote forms of comparative performance which wash out essential elements of local context.

Finally, through its availability and its speed, it increases the connections between itself and other forms of globalization, and in so doing almost certainly increases the wickedity of the problems society and educators currently face, and its use is then highly likely to generate new forms of challenges not seen previously. These will invigorate some individuals as they re-frame their roles to meet these challenges, but it will likely affect other individuals' morale as they find it hard to accommodate to the new frames needed to deal with such challenges.

Three slow-burning globalizations

The case has then been made in this chapter for a number of forms of globalization having considerable and – to many – noticeable effects on the sustainability of individual leaders, and on the sustainability of the role they occupy. Yet there are other forms of globalization whose effects on individual leadership and the leadership role may not currently be that apparent, but which require consideration because in the long term they are likely to be highly influential, as well as being wicked in effect and response.

The first of these is the globalization of **energy security**. Much of the history of the last couple of centuries could be rewritten as the hunt for the energy to fuel nation state economic growth and consumption (see Klare 2004, 2008, 2012). The political confrontations and environmental threats stemming from this search will likely pose even greater problems in the future. One obvious effect is the increased cost of forms of energy, which is likely to contribute to demands for reduced and more closely monitored public funding, the greater use of privatization to reduce the need for public funding, and an increased pressure on the natural environment as governments are tempted to encourage energy companies to exploit new sources through controversial technologies like fracking. Educational leaders will not be able to exclude themselves from such debate, because these pressures not only affect the financial situation of their own institution, but because the search for energy security raises major debates about nation state security and societal values, and also by the environmental concerns also raised by such searches.

A second slow-burning globalization is that of **global warming**. This is now agreed by most parties to be a direct consequence of the prolonged human use of fossil fuels, and it is now having effects on species diversity, human health problems, sea levels, agricultural productivity and weather patterns – and probably a host of other issues not identified so far. These consequences will very likely make it one of the truly 'wicked' issues confronting societies in the future. There are still some who deny either that global warming is happening, or that, even if it is happening, that it is caused by human beings (Washington and Cook, 2011), and one of the challenges for educational leaders will be in developing a role which help staff and students to critically examine the validity of claims and arguments in such difficult territory.

Finally, **demographic globalization** isn't just about how many developed societies now face the problem of increasingly ageing populations: many are also seeing a reduction in their fertility rates (Munz and Reiterer, 2009). In countries that encounter this situation, more people will need support if they live into old age, and in some countries this will likely be with less people coming into the workforce. Strategies suggested have included: the attempt to generate such provision from a higher tax base; a greater emphasis on people saving more and working longer; and the encouragement of immigration of young skilled individuals to fill this gap (see Leeson, 2009). There will be considerable debate in most societies on these issues, though different countries and cultures will have different views on these problems. Poorer countries, for instance, are only gradually moving to this scenario, and it will likely be a couple of generations before they face declining populations with insufficient birth rates. In the meantime they face the opposite challenge of expanding populations, but without the financial resources to support the requisite education and social care. As about one-third of the world's population fits the first scenario, but two-thirds fit the second, there is likely to be an increase in tensions between such countries, with increased attempts at migration, both legal and illegal, from poor to rich countries, and the high possibility that more developed countries will attempt to put up walls, both physical and metaphorical, against such migration. Public education sectors will probably experience this scenario directly through more ethnically diverse classrooms, which may be seen as opportunities for greater intercultural learning, a challenge to existing practice, or a threat to traditional values, or a combination of all three. It may also be better realized that educational systems could utilize the opportunities presented by ageing populations looking for meaning, and wanting to avoid the loneliness that retirement can bring, through expanded forms of intergenerational learning (Studia Pedagogica, 2016). It is also very possible that educators will find the policies of some nation state governments highly challenging, as the possibility of greater immigration controls, enforced deportations, and increased concerns over terrorist attacks, may lead to opportunist radical politicians exploiting such uncertainties for their own authoritarian and xenophobic ends. Yet again, another highly wicked issue is likely to tax the energy of educational leaders and pose new challenges for those in the role.

Conclusion

This chapter began with discussions on different forms of globalization, and suggestions that the work of educational leaders has increased in terms of sheer volume, but also in terms of its complexity, and in particular in the degree of wickedity its problems pose. It has been suggested that unlike in previous eras, when the pressures on leadership came principally from institutional and local levels, the major pressures now seem to come increasingly from levels above these, and one level – the globalized form – has taken new shapes and produced pressures not met before. While government responses to issues concerning educational leadership sustainability have largely focused on the increased volume in demand on the role (much of which actually comes from the increase in *their* demands), and on a lack of preparedness for the role, such preparedness needs to be not so much a tame as a wicked response. Such preparedness needs to come in the form of a recognition of all eight of the threats listed above, and in particular how different global demands add extra levels of complexity and wickedity to the leadership role, and in the process, more pressures of personal and role sustainability.

Having now looked at threats to personal and role sustainability effects at micro-, meso- , and macro-levels, it is time to return to the individual leader, and examine ways of sustaining individuals in such pressured times. One of the more surprising aspects of this research has been the way in which we have realized that portrait methodology is not only an instrument for better understanding how individuals react to these challenges; it seems also to have the potential to be a major aid to sustainability in its own right, through the way that it focuses on personal issues in guaranteed private settings. It is to its ameliorative aspects that this book now turns.

PART FOUR

Responses and Conclusions

CHAPTER ELEVEN

The Impact of the Research:

Tales of the Unexpected

Introduction

Earlier chapters of this book have examined the sustainability of school leadership across and beyond two particular cultures. The general picture has been one where, at national, local and organizational levels, an increased need for enhancing the sustainability of many individual leaders is suggested, as there are a number of threats to it, particularly those generated at global and national levels. Two factors in Western countries in particular seem to weaken sustainability; a first is the view of individuals as little more than 'human resources', to be used primarily to improve competitiveness on the global stage; the second is the pressure from legislation and inspectoral regimes to improve competitive test scores. In the process, there is a strong tendency to classify learners, teachers and leaders as 'units', and so to divest them of their individuality. Yet the results of previous chapters suggest that a greater recognition of such individuality in the education process – whether learner or leader – is a necessary precursor to the creation of greater sustainability.

Now it is important to remind oneself of the methodology used by the authors: we asked questions in a standard semi-structured interview format, recorded the replies and then attempted to reflect back to the interviewee, through a written portrait, what had been interpreted from such responses. The research was focused upon gaining an intimate understanding of what interviewees felt and thought about their situations at a particular moment in time, and sometimes over a longer period when, on a number of occasions, the process was repeated. This process was seen as significant evidence for understanding the challenges to leadership sustainability, for what a person *believes* to be the case can be every bit as damaging or sustaining to them, their colleagues and their organizations, as what may actually be the case in some 'objective' reality.

To gain such information is never easy, for one is asking for a considerable degree of personal reflection and disclosure, and this is unlikely to happen unless a strong degree of trust is achieved between those involved in the process. As one interviewee remarked, '*The critical thing is the relationship, and whether I trust them* [the interviewers].' And indeed, trust seemed to be gained: many interviewees remarked on how well it described them, and this was unlikely to be the case if they had not been forthcoming to the interviewer. Look, for example, at comments made by Hong Kong principals at a seminar discussion of the effects of the exercise:

'*I was comfortable that I could see myself in it. Quite surprised that you'd actually managed to tease that out.*'

(Mark K., Hong Kong principal)

'*In many ways the portrait came back as a confirmation of what I was and what I always have been.*'

(Priscilla L.)

'*I re-read [the interview] yesterday, and I still feel the intensive emotions at that time.*'

(George R.)

As the reader will see in this chapter, similar kinds of comments were frequently repeated, and this chapter will argue that the evidence suggests that the **effects** of this process on those for whom portraits were written were at least as important as the actual research results. This, we believe, is because the interviews, the portraits and subsequent discussions on the portraits, all seem to have acted as strong personal support for these leaders, and could then play a significant part in the future development of a leader's sustainability. Portrait methodology may then be an important form of personal professional development, as it has the potential to not only enhance a deeper understanding of the perceptions of educational leaders, but may also provide strong personal support through such articulation. Moreover, and significantly for an era in which the concept of 'impact' is gaining increased attention, the analysis of the impact of this research suggests that there were a number of ways in which such impact occurred, which can be extremely helpful in understanding the variety of meanings which may be hidden in current uses of the term.

The impact of the research

So while this research has produced valuable findings at personal, organizational and cultural levels, there is one further set of findings, which was not expected, and certainly not planned for. Almost from the very beginnings of this research, we noted how many of the interviewees who took part in the research expressed positive feelings about the process itself. When this first happened, it was initially noted as interesting if a little unexpected, and a little gratifying, because it probably meant that the interviewees were enjoying the process (a good thing in itself). It also probably meant that the interviewees were more relaxed and trusting in our company, and we therefore could have greater confidence about the trustworthiness of what they were saying. But initially this was about as far as our thoughts went.

However, it gradually became apparent that something rather more significant was happening, because in a number of cases it transpired after the interviews and portraits that some head teachers and principals were making personal and/or career decisions after they had gone through the portrait process, and it seemed as if the process itself was causing such actions. Let us look at two examples, one of a Hong Kong principal, Alan C., the other of an English head teacher, Andrew M., who were both interviewed for portraits. Alan C. was nearing retirement, and reflected during the interview upon the fact that he had started a doctorate with a British university, but circumstances had prevented him from finishing it. He mentioned this a number of times, and this was picked up and there had been a wider discussion about this during the interview. In the discussion subsequent to his reading the portrait, and because of the interview and the portrait, he came to realize that this was something that he really wanted to do, and he therefore had got in touch with his former supervisor at this English University, and had picked up the study once more. The portrait process then seemed to be central to him taking a series of actions that very well might not have occurred otherwise.

The other example is rather different. It is of an English head teacher, Andrew M., who, early in his leadership career, was having difficulty meeting the standards he felt Ofsted would want to see at the next inspection. The interview was clearly an emotionally searching one for him, and there were times during it when he was having to be honest with himself as well as with the interviewer. As he said in the debriefing session subsequent to his having read the portrait,

The portrait is so well thought out and deep-reaching, ...

He then went on to suggest that while Ofsted might not agree with the emphases he placed upon the leadership role, nevertheless the portrait procedure had led him to believe that *'it's something I can hold onto, and can say "hey, that's the best I can do", and if that doesn't fit with the requirements of* [their] *agenda, then so be it'*.

In both cases then the effects of the interview and portrait on the interviewee seemed quite as important as the results of the interview did to the interviewer.

It was reflection on and discussion of such examples that led the research team to decide to embrace this as part of its overall research objective, and to therefore extend its scope. Consequently, the team conducted a first series of interviews in both England and Hong Kong to ask previous interviewees about the experience and impact that the process had had upon them. These interviews confirmed the impressions that the portrait process had been a significant source of support to many of these head teachers and principals, and some of their responses are included in this chapter.

Unsurprisingly then, when the team was invited to develop a research project aiding the reflection of school principals in Hong Kong, the portrait approach was again adopted, but a further element was added. Follow-up interviews 3–6 months after the initial interview and portrait writing were then conducted with the principals, and these were specifically concerned with the impact on these principals of being interviewed, of reading the transcriptions, and finally of reading and reflecting upon the portraits provided to them.

The results from these 'impact' interviews, as we shall see, seem highly significant as for many the process had beneficial and supportive effects. They also re-emphasized the fact that people are differently impacted by research procedures, and interviewers need to be aware of the individual nature of this. But they also threw important light on an increasing demand by governments for university researchers to demonstrate the impact of their research beyond an academic environment (See Stern, 2006). The UK government was the first to require evidence of this kind in its review of Universities' research activities (REF, 2014), and examination of scoring from REF 2014 suggests that the impacts rated most highly could be classed as 'counterfactual': in other words, which could demonstrate that an impact would not have happened without that research taking place.

Now the investigation of impact through the use of portrait methodology suggests that besides the kind of counterfactual impact suggested above, there are other distinct forms of impact, which all seem significant to the well-being of educational leaders – and by extension to any other group which uses similar forms of methodology as a means of professional development. The following six forms for impact from portrait methodology then were exhibited:

(1) *Emotional Impact*: An initial impact was seen in the way many interviewees expressed a simple enjoyment at being interviewed, and of reading their portraits. Jack K., a UK head teacher on the edge of retirement, felt that the interview *'was a conversation asking me to think about who "I" was; it was quite cathartic ... thinking about my time of life, my situation ... . I felt slightly uplifted in that I had the opportunity to talk about how I felt.'* Andrew M., the UK head teacher mentioned above, similarly got a great deal out of reading the portrait, and afterwards wrote, *'I was not sure what to expect but this is far more soul searching and involved than I believed it could have been.'* Others used the occasion to reflect upon their problems and to 'get things off their chest'. Emily W., the Hong Kong principal of Chapter 5, faced with a very difficult school situation, where every plan for improvement seemed to be blocked, commented that: *'I just wanted to have some outburst of my frustrations.'*

Such 'emotional' impacts on the interviewee – feelings that came from being able to talk about themselves, their values and current challenges – were almost always very positive. But this was only the most immediate form of impact: other comments after the portrait process made it clear that other forms of impact had occurred.

(2) Thus, another form was *Reflective Impact*. Like the first 'emotional' form, this impact was almost universal, as the process provoked virtually all individuals into reflecting upon their current values and practices. This is hardly surprising: the questions were designed precisely to probe individuals' feelings about themselves and their job, and while the original intention was for the researchers to gain knowledge of the interviewees, there were plenty of occasions when the interviewees gained new insights into themselves. Some individuals simply said things like *'It gives you time to stand back and think.'* (Jim P, UK), or *'You are stimulating my thinking and give me some thoughts.'* (Karen J. HK). Others, however, were more specific in their feedback, and such reflective impact can then be

divided into at least three smaller categories. A first subcategory is that of *Affirmative Impact,* where interviewees believed that the process supported the values they currently held and the practices they were currently using successfully. David D. (UK), talking about his commitment to sustainable education, said that the portrait approach had '*legitimized in my mind the importance of this area of study*'. Andrew M. (UK), talking about how his values fitted the school he worked in, said that the portrait approach '*reaffirms who you are and what you are*'. Again, for Alan C. (HK) '*it is something concerned with strengthening or reaffirmation*'.

However, Affirmative Impact was sometimes mixed with a second subcategory – a more *Defensively Affirmative Impact.* This occurred when the process was seen as supporting personal values and beliefs when working in negative or challenging environments. Andrew M. (UK), for example, while wanting to assert his conviction in his own values, did so in a situation where his objectives for the school didn't necessarily fit with Ofsted criteria or local authority emphases. His view was then that '*if your values don't fit with a certain organization, it's not necessarily you that's at fault ... [I'm] working in a profession under attack on so many fronts*'.

However, while most reflections were generally positive, some were not, containing elements of a third category which might be described as *Unsatisfactorily Resolved Impact* – where reflection on the process reminded individuals of problems they had encountered, and had not fully resolved. Emily W. (HK), who earlier had talked of needing some '*outburst of my frustrations*' at the situation she found herself in, had gained some cathartic release through the interview and portrait, but during a further interview a couple of years later, couldn't bring herself to see the experience as a very positive one. She then talked of having '*locked [this period of time] up, in a box or something like that. I don't want to recall it, because to me it's quite an unpleasant and maybe unsuccessful experience of my career, so I tend not to recall it ... . When I re-read it, I feel a bit sad about the "me'" at the time, because I recall some of those negative emotions*'. Similarly, Julian B. (UK), while also finding elements of the methodology '*cathartic*', nevertheless was led to recall elements which were less pleasant: '*Opening up this again, maybe I should have handled these [problems] differently ... . I should have done more, I should have done more ... but on the whole I tried my hardest to do the best I could.*' Reflection then doesn't always lead to closure.

(3)   *Third Person Impact*: Such reactions were, however, limited in number, and there was a much wider enjoyment of the process, a stimulus to what many interviewees regarded as useful reflection.

One of the reasons for the dominance of more positive responses comes in a third category of impact, which might be called *Third Person Impact*. This seems to derive in large part from the manner in which the research group wrote the portraits. One of the research group likes to describe the portraits as 'mirror portraits', because for him they hold up to an individual a reflection of how others see them, and a reading of their portrait implicitly invites them to view themselves as others might see them – something which can be a valuable experience for a public figure. Many interviewees recognized this picture in the mirror: Susan R. (UK) thought that *'it was written in such a way that it was almost in the third person, but I recognised the third person'*. Sandra W. (HK) thought that it *'enables me to look at myself as a third party. Therefore I can get to know my own strengths, weaknesses, and working style better'*. However, on a very few occasions, interviewees didn't recognize themselves in the portrait at first, but were surprised – and then tended to reflect on the fact – that when they showed it to others, these others did recognize them in the portrait. Brian L. (UK), for instance, commented on how *'I gave the portrait to my admin officer and she said "yes, that's absolutely you"'*. Third-person impact then seems to provide individuals with the opportunity to see themselves from others' perspectives. Angela M. (UK) felt that this was important because, largely through pressure of time, *'You don't get the opportunity to stand on the sidelines and watch the game'*.

(4) *Developmental Impact*:   Many of these impact interviews then suggest that a number of reflections and feelings are raised at the same time during the portrait process, in part because of the third-party nature of the feedback. Yet any impact seldom stayed there: it normally led to some kind of development in feeling or thinking. Emily W. (HK), for instance, even in the final interview where strong negative emotions were expressed, and who was explicit in saying *'I don't want to recall it that much.'* was nevertheless able to say *'but it doesn't mean that I can't learn something from that ... if you're just being angry, it is not enough'*. The impact here then seems to be caused by a process which not only reaffirms, but also helps an individual to reflect upon and reassess values and practice. David D. (UK), for instance, interviewed over his championing of sustainable education, wrote that *'it made me reflect even more deeply about how my own persona influenced my leadership role and how I perceived it'*. Alan C. (HK) viewed the methodology – both interview and portrait – as a developmental exercise for himself, and he said that this was the reason he had agreed to take part on two previous occasions, and then had agreed to a further reflective interview because *'I have to upgrade myself, or update myself ... so that I can*

be a learned person before my teaching fellows and also my students ... if they know that their principal is still a learning one, a life-long learner, they can also be learners as well'.

(5) *Discovered Impact*: Experiential, reflective, third-party and developmental impact then all seem to be different kinds of impacts, even if they may occur simultaneously, or may be close together chronologically, and one may facilitate the emergence of another. A fifth distinctive form of impact is 'discovered impact' – where the process brings to light thought and action which might not have been realized until much later. Susan R. (UK) was very clear that prior to the process *'I was aware of [my emphasis on a values driven approach] but only in the background, and not to the extent to which it drives my leadership'*. For her, *'the process of reflection emphasized the importance of this, and I became more overt in my articulation of values in leading'*. John L. (HK) described across two sets of interviews and portraits how he had experienced a fairly turbulent career that far, and when interviewed a third time, described why he found the second interview and portrait so useful: *'At that critical moment, I needed to think of new strategies to cope with the situation.'* The effect seemed to be 'discovered' impact: *'When I read the portraits again, I think my past experience could be usefully employed to help teachers succeed, ... so I decided to stay in the education career.'* Finally, for Julian B., the portrait experience had brought to the surface issues of advancing age that had not previously been properly considered, but which now, he thought, required intense reflection. Shortly after, he decided to retire, and in interview after this retirement, described the portrait process as a critical driver in his decision: *'Before the portrait process it might have been a throw-away comment, but now it was something I needed to think about.'*

(6) *Counterfactual Impact*: This final form of impact is distinguished from the previous form because the examples of 'discovered impact' seem to be ones which the process brought to consciousness, but which might have been realized later. This final form is probably the strongest form, and the one most related to the UK 2014 REF conception of impact, because there is very good evidence that action taken by individual leaders would not have occurred *without the portrait process having taken place*. To be a member of this class of impact, there then has to be certainty that any change can *only* be ascribed to the portrait process. Could the case of Julian B. above, recognizing issues of retirement for the first time, qualify? Probably not, because Julian would have retired at some stage in the following few years: the portrait process hastened his reflection on the process by 'discovering' the issue for him, but it did not produce the retirement decision; he would have faced this issue at some stage anyway.

More impressive as an example of counterfactual impact, however, is SR, who described herself as '*a perfectionist*', always driving herself to do her best. In interview some years after the initial interview and process, she described how it had made her realize that the changes that the school now needed were things she no longer had the drive to undertake, and that reading the portrait made her realize that it was time to change her job – which she subsequently did. As she wrote, '*the portrait process had a direct and long lasting effect on my leadership role and I am grateful for its contribution to changing my life*'.

Another strong counterfactual example would be John L. (HK) who, while experiencing 'discovered impact', also seems a little later to have experienced counterfactual impact from the portrait methodology, as the process had highlighted for him the things that he most valued, and that '*mentioning creativity impacted on me a lot...and therefore afterwards I spent quite a lot of time on how to promote creativity in our school*'. Moreover, upon leaving this role, he began working with a theatre group '*to produce new musicals for all students in Hong Kong*' and he was very clear that '*this would not have happened without the portrait*'.

Why did the process have such positive effects?

There seems little doubt, then, that many of the individuals for whom the portraits were written derived a great deal from the process. The impacts were numerous and varied, but the majority of these impacts were very positive in their effects. A critical question then now occurs; why did the process have such positive effects? If this can be worked out, one would be in a much better position to replicate such effects on a deliberate and pro-active basis, and through this, to develop a potent form of professional development to help enhance leadership sustainability.

There seem to be three principal reasons for such positive effects. A first reason for such positivity lies in the research focus; the second reason lies in the manner in which the research was conducted; and a third reason lies in the synergy created by combining both together. These reasons need exploring further.

Now it has already been explained how the nature of the research – gaining private information from individuals in order to write a personal portrait of them – was only going to be possible if the researchers made the interviewees entirely comfortable with the process, and trusted the interviewers in being completely ethical in how they managed this. The steps taken to ensure such comfort and such trust in our actions have been described earlier in the book, though we do feel it was really *very* important to repeat assurances, and provide evidence of our behaviours and actions as we went along.

But perhaps even more important than the strict adherence to the highest standards involved in such qualitative research, was the actual focus of the research. Again, as noted above, these came to be known as the 3 'Ps', and rather more about them needs to be explained here, and importantly, how synergy between them was produced.

The first P: The person

The first P, then, was that both the interview and the portrait were focused upon understanding the Person, rather than assessing them. In other words, the research was predicated upon the idea of finding out how different individuals cope with the leadership role they are performing, but not doing so in order to achieve some form of comparative assessment of their coping abilities. Rather, these interviews and portraits were recognized and designed from the outset as being focused on how particular individuals coped with the challenges of their leadership position. Such portraits depended at least in part on the issues that gave the individuals the most concern, and these did not have to be what some would regard as predictable issues (for example, for English head teachers, Ofsted inspections). This being the case, it was made very clear that the interview would be concerned with what the interviewee wanted to talk about, rather than with focusing upon an interviewer-specified agenda, and such assurance was given not only when first contact was made, and when the interview questions were sent out, but also at the beginning of each interview.

Certainly, there were areas of discussion of which an interviewer would expect such leaders to be aware, and that they would likely be affected by such challenges. There is little doubt, after all, that a similar legislative 'architecture' existed for both sets of individuals in both England and Hong Kong (see MacBeath, 2006), and that this agenda can be seen across much of the developed world (Levin, 2004). It is concerned with a much lower trust in professional judgements than previously, and with accompanying policies for standards and standardization, inspections, accountability, testing and markets. With such generalized legislative architecture, it would then have been remiss for the interviewers not to raise such issues, and so questions about them were normally asked. None of the interviewees raised objection to these questions, as these were issues which all recognized they faced to some extent. Nevertheless, it was clear that not all issues were perceived as 'challenges': head teachers who had just successfully negotiated Ofsted inspections, or principals who had more students applying for places than they had spaces were not normally troubled by issues of inspection or markets, for instance. In such situations, when leaders said that they didn't have a problem with an issue, and provided a reason, then that issue was not pursued (unless subsequent answers to other questions suggested that they had not realized that there remained a concern there). However, all the interviews contained other 'basket' type of questions, which allowed the interviewee to select issues they felt the most important. For example, *'What is your school like?' 'What gives you the greatest satisfaction in your job?' 'What would lead you to retire before a formal retirement date?'* were included to allow for individual interpretation. Interviews were then conducted in such a manner that individuals could identify and focus upon the things that mattered most to them. The interviews were intended, and were almost universally seen by individuals, as interviews about them **as a person,** not as an assessment of their performance. For many, this was an unexpected and refreshing change:

> *You go on a management course, fill in a profile about what you look like ... and it's going to feed that agenda and tell you or ask you if you are meeting that agenda ... and if you are, they tick boxes – as opposed to somebody who is coming in and saying, ok, where do you think you are going? Such as you did.*

> (Julian B., UK)

> *It's a good chance for me to be myself.*

> (Philip H., HK.)

We believe then that the focus on an individual as a person trying to cope with the demands of the job, rather than as a human resource being assessed on their functioning, was not only relatively novel for many interviewed; our results suggest that the focus was also seen as a relaxing, refreshing and informative exercise, from which many not only took pleasure but also gained considerable self-reflection.

The second P: The peer

The second P was that of being interviewed by a peer – someone knowledgeable of their situation, but not in a position of authority with respect to themselves, and therefore once again, not someone whose reason for being there was to appraise their performance in the job. Even though all of the interview team had doctorates, and two of them were full professors, the results from the interviews suggest that the possession of such qualifications did not negatively impact on the interviewees' responses – they were not intimidated by such professional titles. The process was sometimes helped when a member of the research team was known personally by an interviewee, and then the importance of formal titles receded even further. Probably more importantly, we were not seen as part of any inspectoral body, members of any hierarchy with power over them. Instead we seemed normally to be viewed as interested but dispassionate researchers – and in some cases as colleagues or friends – who were primarily concerned with their views for the purpose of academic research. On many occasions we became even more interested simply because these were almost always articulate, committed individuals with fascinating stories to tell. As noted in Chapter 3, one English head teacher, David G., thought that he '*would have been much more guarded to an Ofsted inspector ... because you know they have another agenda ... [but] I don't have to distrust you, because I don't think you would have other purposes in getting something from me*'.

So, just as being interviewed about themselves and how they as an individual coped with the job, was a refreshing change from the kind of assessment-based process they normally faced, being interviewed by an expert but non-involved peer also seemed to be enjoyable in its own right. The evidence suggests that being able to talk freely, knowing that anything said would not be used and taken down as evidence in an evaluation of their performance, definitely facilitated more relaxed conversations, and as the above quote suggests, seemed to have helped individuals to talk at length and in depth about things they probably would not have discussed if they had been interviewed by someone senior to them in a hierarchy. From an interviewer's perspective, the opportunity was equally enjoyable: we were in the privileged position of exchanging our largely research-based views – and academically based views with people actually doing the job – though it should be noted that all of the research team had formally been in senior positions in schools before moving into universities, and therefore spoke and asked questions informed by both perspectives.

Once again, then, we believe that the nature of the interaction – one between peers on an equal footing, rather than between individuals in a hierarchy where the educational leader is in the power-less position – was not only relatively unusual for many interviewed, because very few had been the centre of a research conversation about themselves conducted by skilled others, but was once again an enjoyable and non-threatening exercise in which nearly all felt they could talk freely about the challenges they faced – and therefore took pleasure in the process, and gained self-knowledge as they did so .

The third P: The private

Finally, and perhaps most importantly, the third P was that of Privacy, and our concerns were both pragmatic and ethical. At a simple pragmatic level, as researchers we were highly unlikely to gain any significant data about the personal concerns and the coping strategies of individual leaders if we did not promise full anonymity, full privacy for the individuals interviewed. So at the initial approach, all were told that they would be sent the questions before the interview, and could delete or change anything on the interview schedule. They were also informed that all comments, and all portraits would be anonymized, and nothing they said would be disclosed without their express permission. Finally, they were assured that they could alter or delete without question anything transcribed or written into a portrait. There is good evidence that adherence to these rules was a major reason for the depth of disclosure:

> *I know [with this interview] that it is not going ... to be reported to Ofsted, it's not going to reported to anyone else ... it's not going to be something for which I'm going to be held to account.*
>
> (James R. UK)

> *The appraiser was a lovely person, but I felt she came with an agenda ... ... [the portrait approach] made me much more comfortable about saying what I wanted to say rather than what she wanted to hear.*
>
> (Julian B. UK)

But there is a further, important ethical argument to be made here about the need for privacy. This transcends merely pragmatic concerns, and goes to the heart of the reasons for the research. As evidenced throughout the book, both by the researchers and the researched, we seem to be living in an age of the increasingly 'greedy' organization, where there is a growing demand for the alignment of personal values with those of the state and the organization, and of the viewing of privacy as an area to be curtailed. Most worryingly, perhaps, is the view of privacy as a luxury, and when performed by its 'leaders', as evidence of having something to hide. In so doing, we then begin to move from a society which views all individuals and all acts as innocent until proven guilty, to automatic assumption of guilt for both if any attempt is made to keep them private. So the focus in portrait methodology on assurances of privacy and anonymity was not merely procedural and pragmatic – it was seen as but one small expression of the need to assert the value of privacy as fundamental to the functioning of a 'good' and sustainable society. And from the responses by many of the individuals interviewed, their enjoyment and relief at and in the process seemed to come at least in part from the exercise of such concern.

The value of the personal in research

The focus upon privacy then, was more than a procedural device: it underpinned a view of how societies should treat individuals within them. And this therefore reflects back upon the nature of the research process itself. It values the contribution of the individual, and therefore points to the dangers of research attempts to identify sets of 'good leadership' characteristics, with the intention of engineering these into individual schools and individual leaders through a combination of training initiatives, quality checks and Ofsted inspections, to ensure that all institutions and individuals march to the same standardized designated tune. This research approach then supports critics of such approaches (e.g. Ouston, 1999) and echoes the critical views of those like Gronn (2003) with his concept of 'designer leadership'. Approaches like that of the School Effectiveness Movement (SEM) can be useful aids to reflection and action, but need to be viewed as problematic for leadership sustainability, because their approach not only can be abused by those who would like to see the individual turned into the unit, the human resource; but also because by its very nature it tends to ignore the critical ontological truth that human beings engage in complex social situations, which do not follow the simple causal rules of the physical universe. Instead, social encounters are different every time because different individuals react differently to different contexts; and because human beings 'make real' through their imagination situations which would not exist independently of such thought (Wallace and Fertig, 2007). The result of such reality is summed up by Plsek and Greenhalgh (2001, p. 625) who suggest that complex systems like education comprise sets of agents who are so interconnected that 'one agent's actions changes the context for other agents'.

Given this, other descriptions of educational engagement, which emphasize such complexity, seem much more realistic than human resource approaches. Approaches like those of Lave and Wenger (1991), who argued that much learning is the product of contextualized social and community engagement, and that of Schon (1983), who argued that procedural knowledge and reflection-in-action and reflection-on-action, are essential to sound professional practice, seem much better descriptions of what individuals do, rather than tendencies towards top-down impositions derived from large-scale surveys.

If this is the case, then attempts to engineer standardized practices into different contexts and individuals are not only poorly conceived, but also potentially dangerous, because they do not reflect the complex realities and contexts with which all individuals are faced. Bassey's (1999) notion of 'fuzzy' generalizations captures this concern well, as it argues that lessons can be learnt from other people, other organizations, but only if they happen to have the same characteristics, or have similar personalities. Even then, they will necessarily differ because no two individuals, or sets of people will be exactly the same. Such recognition would mean, at the very least, a dialogue between large data sets and the nature of individual contexts and personalities. Yet, the recognition of the importance of individual personality still seems, a little bizarrely, one step too far for many policy approaches which appear to assume that one should begin from large-scale quantitative approaches, and only then, and rather reluctantly, allow in qualitative input exemplifying the reality of the individual leader.

Many policy-makers then seem compelled to drive through measures which attempt to improve the whole of an educational system rather than to recommend the adoption of different approaches for different schools in different contexts. This may be understandable from their point of view: many need policies which are achievable within one term of office, and which are comprehensible to a non-specialist electorate. Yet these are political and personal career imperatives which may well run counter to educational requirements, as they seldom match the particular needs of individuals or particular contexts, because they do not utilize the kind of contextualized and procedural knowledge described above. As Scott (2002, p. 66) argued, perhaps we may need to move towards a form of knowledge 'which is embedded in specific contexts rather than simply being subsequently applied within these contexts'. This is a good description of the life-world of individual educational leaders, as they work in particular institutions, making differences to the life chances of particular pupils in their care. Educational leaders do require a knowledge of what large-scale research says about the general principles of good management and leadership, but they then need to be given the opportunity to dialogue this with a knowledge of the contexts within which they work, as well as a knowledge of their pupils, their colleagues and themselves.

General principles, then, should **not** be seen as the determining element in this dialogue, as immutable rocks around which the eddies and pools of context and personal knowledge swirl. In reality, general principles are no more than the adumbrated distillations of many different individual cases of context. While they may describe general trends, they never actually describe best solutions to particular cases. Policy-makers then may personally need generalizable prescriptions to meet political objectives, but such prescriptions need to be built precisely from the individual cases many seem to deride, for without such examples, there can be no generalizations. The portrait approach employed in this research is one part of the redressing of such a balance: it puts the importance of individual personality and context back into the policy equation.

Conclusion

This chapter then has argued that portrait methodology can generate significant and important data about individual experiences of leadership, but that perhaps the major surprise from using the approach was the varied impacts the process had on individuals. Many expressed their appreciation of being involved, and felt that both interview and portrait had been useful to them in a number of ways. The description in this chapter of different kinds of impact supports this view, and the evidence of reflections generated, insights provided and changes made as a consequence of being involved in such research, all strongly suggest that the process is not only an effective research tool, but can also work as a personal support exercise, allowing individuals to reflect upon their work and life. This chapter then suggests that it was probably the espousal and committed enactment of the '3 Ps' which most facilitated this. But there is more to this issue than just a methodological device for supporting educational leaders: the espousal of these '3 Ps' says something much more about the nature of the society in which we live, and if educational leaders are to be sustained, they need to work within sustainable contexts: they need to work within societies which espouse these 3 Ps.

CHAPTER TWELVE

The Contextualization of Sustainable Leadership:

No Simple Answers

Introduction

Q: How do you make God laugh? A: You tell him your plans.
This book has suggested that when discussing sustainability in educational leadership, a number of concepts and concerns need appreciating and working into measures for greater sustainability. A first is a proper understanding of 'sustainability' itself. As argued earlier, it is fundamentally a normative rather than a descriptive term, and it advocates rather than simply describes the continued well-being of values, practices, roles and people. The initial question then, with respect to the sustainability of educational leadership, is not: '*How do you make educational leadership more sustainable?*' but rather: '*What do you want sustainable educational leadership to look like?*'

Discussions about sustainability then should begin with questions about what is desired, with discussions about the role that we want education and educational leadership to perform, not with simple strategies for their improvement. Only when a clearly articulated view of these is reached, are we in a position to ask: 'How should the role of an educational leader be made more sustainable?'

Now some may agree with this, but still want to move swiftly on to practical 'how' questions. They may be fortunate, and find that their personal views about educational purposes are serendipitously aligned with the views of those advocating the means of achieving such sustainability. However, they may also find that they have adopted educational purposes with which, on further reflection, they strongly disagree. The caution is clear: the adoption of remedies for damaged sustainability which fail to recognize the value base of such remedies, may lead down very undesirable roads.

The importance of contexts

A second issue concerning the nature of sustainability is encapsulated in what a former UK prime minister, Harold Macmillan, is reputed to have said, when asked by a journalist what he thought was most, likely to blow his government off course. He paused, and then simply replied 'events, dear boy, events'. In this pithy phrase, he was simply saying that too much goes on in too many contexts for anyone to be aware of all, of even most of them, or to understand and control them. Moreover, the 'events' that cause threats to personal sustainability exist not just at one level, but at many different ones. Moreover, such factors will probably not be simply additive in their effects, nor are they all likely to combine to be completely threatening or completely facilitatory; they are much more liable to clash with each another. The reality of an educational leader, then, will likely be one with predictable features, surrounded by many unexpected and unpredictable elements. Leadership sustainability is then a complex function of the contexts surrounding it. Both threats to and support for leadership sustainability occur at all of the micro-, meso- and macro-levels.

At the micro-level, threats to leadership sustainability normally derive from personal issues, and relationships with other individuals and small groups. They may be displayed as a lack of preparedness for the role, overwork or communication problems. Paradoxically, in discussions on leadership sustainability, the micro-level is both over- and under-stressed. It is the level at which symptoms of unsustainable leadership are usually described, yet there is little in the literature which actually focuses on how individuals differ in their reactions to such sustainability pressures, and this is where the portrait approach can make clear that a 'pressure' is not necessarily a simple description of an external event, but more likely a negative reaction by a person in the leadership role to an event which may not be perceived by others in the same way. This points once again to the highly individual nature of the leadership role, and of the need for sustainability measures which take into account such singularity.

However, while it is important to recognize that individuals may react in very individual ways to external events, it is important to move beyond this perspective. Focusing on individual reactions to sustainability threats, and on their 'treatment', as a medical model does, all too easily becomes an approach limited to focusing on the victim, and then, perhaps, blaming them for the problem. Much attention needs to be focused on the origins of such pressures. To focus solely on diagnosing and remediating personal sustainability problems is rather like observing pollution coming downstream, and believing that sustainability measures should concentrate on cleaning up the pollution when it arrives. At least as important will be the identification of the origins of the pollution upstream, and the taking of preventative action there.

The 'upstreams' of leadership sustainability threats, then, are the higher contextual origins of impact that affect individuals. If the micro-level is a first point of examination, the second of these upstream influences is the meso-level, and we have already seen how different organizational elements can threaten or facilitate individual sustainability. Potential 'pollutants' or 'facilitators' of sustainability have been discussed: the metaphors describing an organization's activity, the nature of organizational focus, and the discourse used, were applied to two real organizations in different national cultures, in order to demonstrate how organizations can add to or reduce personal sustainability.

Yet even within the organizations discussed, it was clear that their sustainability could not be fully understood without appreciating the larger macro-contexts within which they were embedded. In the case of the UK organization, the political and legislative context, with its highly critical professional discourse, threatened not only the sustainability discourse used by the head teachers in dealing with schools they were 'healing', but affected their own personal sustainability, because they were increasingly prevented from developing strategies they felt were the most beneficial. In the Hong Kong context, the discourse of the principals and their organization met little critical resistance, though there was concern that the intense focus on caring for the children needed balancing by a similar focus on the care and development of staff.

Yet it also needs recognizing that these organizations exist within broader cultural contexts, which create different epistemological and value frames for understanding individual and organizational functioning, and which can lead to different views of the nature of leadership sustainability. In the highly communal society of Hong Kong, and indeed in many other societies in the Far East, the prioritization of cooperation, group well-being and communal harmony have historically been favoured over those of individual achievement and self-advancement, and likely have helped damp down the foci which pose real threats to the sustainability of many individuals and organizations in many Western societies.

However, the contexts requiring consideration do not end there. Many international and global pressures transcend particular political or cultural settings, create threats to their sustainability, and through the infiltration of their values, eventually put pressure on institutional sectors such as education, and on those working within them. While much globalization literature view economic forces as the dominant form, this book has suggested that other kinds may be at least as important in their influences on leadership sustainability, and particularly that of the globalization of information technology, in part because of the speed with which it facilitates financial, social and political change, but also because of the complex 'wicked' linkages that it creates between different globalization areas, which then impact on to the work of educational leaders, both overtly and covertly.

One important conclusion then is that the pressures on leadership sustainability are almost certainly more complex (and hidden) than many might recognise. There are likely to be very few simple one-action solutions to many leadership problems, and the desire to view many problems as 'tamer' than they actually are is likely to be a major threat to the sustainability of educational leaders, because by refusing to recognize the complexity of both the threats and the solutions to many issues, solutions may be imposed on educators which not only **don't** solve problems, but which may actually make them worse.

The range of wicked demands on educational leaders

There is then another important conclusion to be drawn from the preceding discussions, which also has major implications for individual sustainability. The combination of micro-, meso- and macro-impacts on education, and therefore ultimately on an educational leadership role, point to the fact that the complexity of demands and responses is almost certainly much larger than many realize. Table 12.1 provides a graphic illustration of the range of known and unknown impacts that an educational leader may face in the role. It uses Rumsfeld's classification, referred to in Chapter 2, of what we know and what we don't know: the *known knowns*, the *unknown knowns*, the *known unknowns* and the *unknown unknowns*, and it plots these not only against examples of micro-, meso- or macro-effects, but also against the interactions and combined effects of these different levels. An examination of Table 12.1 makes a number of things clearer concerning the challenges educational leaders face.

A first is that the initial column, that of 'known knowns' (what we know we know) is the only one where most people would probably want to claim confidence in understanding the implications of the various impacts on an individual leader and their role. Even then, any claim to certainty is likely to be restricted to the micro- and the meso-level contexts, as the potential number and complexity of the macro-effects, and interactions between these levels, would make it extraordinarily difficult to accurately predict future impacts: we are firmly back in Macmillan's territory of '*events, dear boy, events*'.

Second, there is always the likelihood that those things claimed to be known are nothing of the sort, but are actually 'unknown knowns' – things which were thought to be known, but about which we were wrong, resulting not in the predictable but in the unanticipated and surprising. A much-quoted remark by Popper (1982, p. 111) sums this for the scientific endeavour:

> The empirical base of objective science has ... nothing 'absolute about it. Science does not rest upon solid bedrock. The bold structure of its theories rises, as it were, above a swamp. It is like a building erected on piles. The piles are driven down into the swamp, but not down to any natural base ... . If we stop driving the piles deeper, it is not because we have reached firm ground.'
>
> We simply stop when we are satisfied that the piles are firm enough to carry the structure, *at least for the time being*.

A third thing to note from examining Table 12.1 is that the effects or impacts in 20 out of 24 of the boxes on this grid are likely to result in a number of unanticipated, surprising and unpredictable outcomes: many impacts will then be ones which educational leaders cannot anticipate, and even if they do, are unlikely to fully grasp the implications of such complex interactions. Many situations that impact on leaders (and indeed on everyone else) are then likely to contain a large measure of the unexpected, and are therefore likely to be difficult to manage.

Fourth, it might be assumed that the boxes within the grid contain equal numbers of potential events. It is, of course, impossible to definitively comment on this: three columns contain either events which we think we know about, but about which we may be mistaken; or which we know we don't know; or are composed of events of which we still don't know anything at all. It should also be added that many events may occur, but it may not be realized they are occurring, and so their impact is ascribed to other causes entirely. In such circumstances, it seems highly likely that events and impacts from the 'known knowns' category consist of a very small proportion of the things that actually confront educational leaders. This makes the leadership challenge much greater than a first inspection of Table 12.1 might suggest.

204

Table 12.1 The range of known and unknown impacts on educational leaders (and pupils, stakeholders, policy-makers, etc.)

	Known knowns: leaders think they know that they know: hence they expect to experience predictable Impacts. However, some of these may be unknown knowns	Unknown knowns: leaders think they know, but are wrong, and so experience unanticipated and surprising impacts	Known unknowns: leaders know that they don't know, and so experience unexpected but unsurprising impacts: this is 'normal science'	Unknown unknowns: leaders don't know that they don't know, and so experience highly surprising impacts: these are 'scientific revolutions'
Micro-effects only on leadership	e.g. broad leadership role; staff work; daily curriculum	e.g. school leader mis-reads a new chair of governor's character or intentions	Anything unpredictable or unexpected; e.g. large personnel changes cause instability	Unexpected impacts because previously unrecognized forces now in play. School leader diagnosed with long-term illness
Micro-meso interactions affecting leadership	Very broad, well-understood interactions	Misunderstanding the impacts of combined effects	Not knowing the impacts of combined effects; head teacher leaving causes change in school ethos	Unexpected impacts because previously unrecognized interactions now in play, e.g. school inspection destabilizes school leader
Meso-effects only on leadership	School rules and routines; well-known local inputs and interactions with other schools	e.g. misreading organizational intentions or inter-organizational relationships	Local changes; staff turnover; change in school ethos; large student turnover creates school instability	Unexpected impacts because previously unrecognized forces now in play. Changes in local population affect school intercultural relations

Meso-macro interactions affecting leadership	Very broad, well-understood interactions	Misunderstanding the impacts of combined meso-macro effects	Not knowing the impacts of combined effects	Unexpected impacts because previously unrecognized interactions now in play. New legislation changes school ethos
Macro-effects only on leadership	Existing legislation; broad cultural values	e.g. Misunderstanding macro forces and their impacts	Anything unpredictable or unexpected, e.g. new legislative demands	Unexpected impacts because previously unrecognized forces now in play. Sudden drop in birth rates affects school sustainability
Micro-meso-macro combined interactions affecting leadership	Very broad, well-understood interactions (very few between these levels?)	Misunderstanding the impacts of combined effects (many between these levels?)	Not knowing the impacts of combined effects (likely many?)	Unexpected impacts because previously unrecognized interactions now in play (likely man?)

Managing the impossible

Even when leaders do recognize some of these challenges and ensuing complexities, for sheer sanity's sake, they are unlikely to try and deal with all of them. Instead, they may adopt strategies which help them manage this situation in ways which don't threaten their personal sustainability. One strategy would be to simply ignore an issue. This is probably a dangerous strategy on many occasions, but is one which some leaders might feel is necessary in particularly demanding situations. Another approach is to triage presenting problems – to focus on what seems the most urgent at that moment in time, and to leave others until later. A third is to restrict focus to those problems presenting themselves most visibly, and the research in this book has suggested that leaders tend to focus and deal with local issues and people, or the effects on the local from other levels of effect. A fourth strategy is what Simon (1956) called to 'satisfice', a term derived from a combination of 'satisfy' and 'suffice', where one does the best that one can, even if the solutions adopted are recognized as incomplete.

'Satisficing' is quite similar to another strategy described by Lipsky (1980) on how many 'street level bureaucrats' ('SLBs') dealt with their most pressing dilemma: how do you manage a client workload which is simply too big to be dealt with in the manner you would ideally like to treat these clients? This sounds much like satisficing, but moves into the territory of how different people deal with this dilemma, and it is to the different kinds of approaches that individuals take to problems, that this chapter now turns.

Educational leadership typologies in market contexts

Lipsky (1980) argued that the sheer volume of work of these SLBs compromised the ability of many to fulfil their role to the degree and quality they desired. Instead, he argued, individuals adopt a range of different responses, in large part dependent on their character. The least worst of these responses, he suggests, is the development of individual coping strategies, designed to provide a sustainable degree of satisfaction in their role. However, such coping strategies may ultimately fail to satisfy the needs of some practitioners, and some practitioners may never manage to find this satisfactory level of coping, and then become dissatisfied with their situation; and some may become so cynical and disillusioned that they decide to leave the role completely.

Lipsky's description of different possible responses fits well with Fullan's (1991) judgement that many apparently excellent educational reforms have historically failed to achieve enthusiastic adoption by practitioners, not because the teaching profession is or was composed mostly of 'stone-age obstructionists', but because the implementation of new reforms may be viewed by practitioners as threatening to their individual coping strategies, a factor which many policy-makers may simply not have taken into account. Certainly, Bottery (1998) found this kind of strategic attitude to a largely new legislation in the UK quite prevalent: as noted earlier, one UK head teacher's approach to market-driven reforms varied from 'defy through subvert to ignore, on to ridicule, then to wait and see, and in some exceptional cases, to embrace'. In boxing terms, a lot of counterpunching then seems to be going on, as governments lead with new proposals and legislation, while professionals examine the consequences for their vision of education and what they can practically achieve, and then take up positions somewhere along the 'defy to embrace' spectrum and attempt to maintain them.

This description of the types of possible professional responses is helpful in exploring its diversity, but still has two main problems. One, as seen in Chapter 9, is that some insist that they don't attempt to satisfice their task, because there are some 'bottom lines' below which they will not go. As 'David G.' said, '*If you don't have a vision of every child coming through the school, succeeding to the best of their ability, and putting into place the bet that you can, then I don't think you should be a headteacher.*' A second issue is that Lipsky's work presents a rather linear view of practitioners' viewpoints, and seems to implicitly assume that professionals begin with an approach and stay with it. However, not only do people's views change, but as the specifications for the role and individual change, so institutions hire different kinds of people, ones who are more likely to embrace and implement such changes, and who are therefore more likely to be sustainable in new specifications of the role. Bottery (2016) suggests that a different kind of leader has therefore emerged, one more accepting of a role positioned within an increasingly marketized and centrally directed reform context. He therefore talks (pp. 84–5) of a different kind of professional and leadership spectrum. The first group he describes as '*educational entrepreneurs*', who in the new legislative architecture, are likely to be very sustainable in the role, as they are predisposed to embrace the nature of new reforms, even if they have to deal with threats from the demands of 'greedy' organizations, overwork and accountability measures. A second group, '*educational pragmatists*', may still harbour welfare state beliefs, but who also see value in newer positions, and have a mortgage to pay, a career to develop and a school to run. Finally, he suggests that there still remain committed '*welfare state advocates*', who try to keep alive the values of the greater communal focus, societal equality and public good aspirations of their youthful professionalism. These individuals' sustainability however is likely to be the most threatened, if they are working in low-trust/ high-achievement/ marketized contexts.

In similar manner, Banks (2004) also developed a leadership typology in her discussion of intra-professional working in the marketized and managerialist context of the UK, and suggested seven possible kinds of responses to the challenges presented, which she described as:

- The New Managerialist;
- The New Professional;
- The Professional Entrepreneur;
- The Reluctant Conformist;
- The Individual Challenger;
- The Radical Challenger;
- The Principled Quitter.

Banks' typology is useful in suggesting a number of different professional and leadership responses to changing educational conditions, and in advocating that such variety is not just because of different contexts, but because of the ways in which individuals react to these different contexts. Nevertheless, it is important to note that both her and Bottery's typologies are based on the same societal and policy context, both being concerned with describing how individuals hold, or move from welfare state professional positions to more marketized managerial positions within the public sector. The range of her typology, then, given its focus on a particular market-oriented context, might be more accurately described as moving from:

- The New Marketized Leader;
- The New Welfare State Leader;
- The Welfare State Entrepreneurial Leader;
- The Reluctant Marketized Leader;
- The Individual Welfare State Challenger;
- The Radical Welfare State Challenger;

To, finally:

- The Welfare State Leaver.

These need a little expansion.
Thus

1 The *New Marketized leader* is one who embraces new marketizing demands enthusiastically and relatively uncritically. Welfare state values are then seen as subservient to overarching corporate goals and targets in a competitive environment.

2 *The New Welfare State Leader* is an individual who also embraces the new changes as beneficial to the improvement of practice and service delivery; but who thinks that welfare state values may be used to challenge systems or modify targets not regarded as useful or worthwhile.

3   *The Welfare State Entrepreneur* is a leader who still regards some welfare state professional values as worthwhile, but whose public service ideals are now combined with private sector activities like marketing the school and fund-raising, and accepts the necessity of developing short-term projects with strict monitoring and accountability requirements.

4   *The Reluctant Marketized Leader* is an individual who is more likely to be seen at practitioner/senior practitioner level, who has worked in the field for some time, and who regards many new requirements as unnecessary or deleterious to his/her educational purposes. They might complain to colleagues, but seldom take overt action over new demands.

5   *The Individual Welfare State Challenger* is a leader who also sees many new requirements as harmful and unnecessary, but unlike the reluctant marketized leader, does take action by deliberately bending or ignoring rules, forms or procedures, sometimes publicly, more often covertly.

6   *The Radical Welfare State Challenger* is an individual who takes opposition one stage further by openly challenging the need or worth of particular requirements or new ways of working, and takes principled stands against a variety of legislation, arguing these cases openly with senior advisers and policy-makers.

7   *The Welfare State Leaver* is someone who may have been a radical welfare state challenger in the past, but who now sees that such challenge has borne no fruit, and/or is so worn down with the effort of challenge and reluctant conformity that they feel it is time to leave.

A further leadership type also needs to be added here, as the present typology suggests that the principal reason for or feeling that the role is no longer sustainable lies in the different purposes attributed to educational practice by educational leaders and their governments. There then seems an eighth position:

8   *The Exhausted Leader,* who may be either a welfare state leader or a marketized leader, but whose principal reason for leaving is physical and/or emotional exhaustion: the hours are seen as too long, the legislative demands too onerous, the implementation too difficult; they may plan to leave over a period of time, or something might have occurred which leads them to decide almost overnight to go.

Table 12.2 takes these eight types and examines how, in a marketized policy context, their sustainability in the role is affected by the stance they take. Unsurprisingly, perhaps, levels of sustainability correlate strongly with the degree to which values and purposes harmonize with neoliberal marketized

Table 12.2 Sustainability and educational leadership in marketized policy contexts

Leader type	Sustainability probably enhanced by	Sustainability probably threatened by
New Marketized Managerial	New policy directions, governmental support, alignment of personal and external values	Overwork due to personal commitment or policy demands
New Welfare State	Personal embrace of new challenges, use of welfare state values to critique purposes	Overwork due to personal commitment or policy demands
Welfare State Entrepreneur	Personal engagement with new challenges and projects	Overwork; possible personal conflict between market and welfare state purposes
Reluctant Marketized	Lack of overt resistance leaves room for quiet modification	Overwork; quiet internalizing of dissent
Individual Welfare State Challenger	Some covert, some overt resistance	Overwork, clash of performative and personal values
Radical Welfare State Challenger	Potential personal boost from overt resistance	Potential personal pressure and exhaustion from overt resistance
Welfare State Leaver	Disengagement leads to less physical commitment	Emotional exhaustion, clash between performative and personal values
Exhausted Leaver	Little adds to personal sustainability	Physical, emotional and spiritual exhaustion

values, with those most distanced being the most disaffected. Having said that, even the most ardent advocates of such positions are likely to feel, in an era of fast policies and greedy organizations, the work pressures from both personal commitments and/or policy demands.

The limitations of leadership typologies

Such analyses and typologies are very useful, because they move discussions of personal leadership sustainability away from simplistic and uni-dimensional descriptions of bodies of educational leaders, to more nuanced understandings of what endangers an *individual*'s sustainability in the leadership role. Such analysis can be further refined in a number of ways. One is to note that this typology is likely to work within only one policy context – the largely Western neoliberal context. While it may predict threats to educational leadership sustainability here, it cannot be assumed that such pressures will affect principals' sustainability in other settings. This is likely to be particularly relevant, as Chapters 8 and 9 argued, to leadership sustainability in different cultural and policy contexts. Even if some neoliberal educational measures are adopted elsewhere, it seems likely, as in the case of Hong Kong, for cultural values to counter or suppress the effects of these invading values. In other words, different typologies of leadership sustainability will very likely be needed in different contexts of culture and legislation. One cannot assume that the typology detailed in Table 12.2 could, or should be uncritically translated into other contexts. The development of other cultural sustainability typologies could then be an important area for future research.

Further, Table 12.2, like Morgan's organizational forms, is still only a typology: it should not be seen as reflecting the reality of individual responses. Thus, if one examines it again, it is quite possible that the sustainability of one 'radical welfare state challenger' may be boosted by speaking out publicly against market-based changes, particularly if they have the kind of extrovert personality that is nourished by active and vocal resistance; on the other hand, radical welfare state challengers of a more introvert disposition may find such public resistance physically and emotionally draining, with their personal sustainability depressed by such action. It would also be a mistake to assume that an individual permanently fits one of these types, as due to any number of factors, that individual and their context may change: due to unexpected ill health, a person may retire or move to more rewarding position, while another who takes on a new role may find it stressful and damaging to their health. It is therefore highly unlikely that *any* typology could encompass the range of possible impacts or decisions that an individual might make from year to year, and it is therefore unlikely that any typology could accurately predict how real individual leaders will actually change, and what this will do to their sustainability in the role. One cannot then be certain that if individual leaders in any particular 'typology box' of 12.2 do change, they will necessarily adopt the characteristics of the two bordering types: given a particular set of circumstances, an individual may move from being a *'reluctant marketised leader'* straight to either a *'welfare state leaver'* or *'exhausted leader'*, or a combination of them. Or, indeed, they may take on a project which so energizes them that they take on the characteristics (for a while at least) of either a *'welfare state entrepreneur'* or even a *'new welfare state'* leader. The point is that trajectories of real individuals are likely to be precisely that, highly individual ones; and discussions, remedies and policies on leadership sustainability need to reflect this.

Real individual leaders, as the portraits in this book also suggest, are much more multi-dimensional, nuanced and unexpected in development than any typology could hope to achieve. The portraits of 'John L.', mentioned in Chapters 9 and 11, for example, demonstrate this clearly: John initially enthusiastically embraced working a fourteen-hour day in order to keep his school open, but lost much motivation when he achieved that task, and then took on a more standard leadership role; he then thought of leaving education altogether, only to realize that there was much to motivate him in developing the musical abilities of young people in Hong Kong, and it was to this role that he moved. One can also mention the 'Harry C.' 'portrait of resilience' provided in Chapter 5. A subsequent portrait showed how he moved from initially being an uncertain and challenged if resilient young head teacher, to becoming a leading figure in his city's education leadership community. Both portraits demonstrate unexpected changes, and both illustrate the unpredictability of real life.

Sustainability and the leadership role

The individuality of leadership sustainability then implies an encouragement of the diversity of leadership approaches, rather than the encouragement of designer leadership. This is not only more acceptable ethically, it is also more acceptable pragmatically: in an era of constant change and challenge, when the emergence of the unpredictable is the most predictable thing likely, a variety of individual leadership approaches is probably the best survival strategy for its continued sustainability. Conformity to one model, or one typology, may be seen as safe and sensible in an era of stasis: it is a dangerous strategy to adopt in an era of change. Variety and differentiation not only permit individuals to practise and develop their best qualities: it permits the system within which they work to gain a better idea of the most sustainable approaches to the leadership role in such an era.

But this doesn't entail a leadership free-for-all, where anything goes. The preceding chapters have suggested that a sustainable leadership role needs to be underpinned by a number of understandings. A first is the need for educational leaders to appreciate a much more complex reality – and causality – than is normally accepted. This not only requires an understanding of limited predictability and control by them and by those senior to them: it also means a better understanding of how many problems need framing in a more wicked manner than is normally perceived. For the role to be sustainable it also requires the recognition that many problems are not solved with single, silver-bullet solutions, but instead require messier 'silver buckshot' solutions which may never completely resolve the issue.

Moreover, it is important to recognize that the leadership role does not sit outside a problem: real-life leaders are necessarily 'bricoleur' leaders (Grint, 2008), located in unique times and contexts, having to deal with existing messy problems, patching together with the perspectives of many others the best solutions that can be produced. This is not the glamour of the charismatic super-head, but much more the recognition of leadership reality, and is all the more sustainable for such recognition.

Ultimately sustainability will come not just from a diversity of leadership, but from a humility of it as well, as leaders recognize their and others' limitations, who don't feel the stress and pressure to provide charismatic visions to others in some quest for the fabled perfect school, and who don't feel the stress and pressure to personally provide permanent solutions to problems. It means that in an uncertain world, leaders need to adopt – and be allowed to adopt – a greater amount of 'negative capability', of remaining comfortable with uncertainty, with giving themselves and others the space and time to reflect upon problems rather than feeling they need to jump in quickly. They need to see themselves as creating the kind of conditions which permit as many as possible to contribute to finding the best ways forward – and therefore of being more the catalysts for wicked solutions rather than the providers of answers for others.

REFERENCES

Ainley, P. (2004), 'The new "market state" and education', *Journal of Education Policy*, vol. 19, no. 4, pp. 497–514.

Al-Omari, A. and Wuzynani, M. (2013), 'Factors influencing Jordanian and Saudi Arabian teacher decisions to pursue the principalship', *School Leadership and Management*, vol. 33, no. 5, pp. 473–85.

Amin, A., ed. (1994), *Post-Fordism: A Reader*. Oxford: Basil Blackwell.

Aquila, F. (1983), 'Japanese management in schools: Boon or bondage?', *Clearing House*, vol. 57, pp. 180–6.

Arendt, H. (2006), *The Banality of Evil*. London: Penguin Classics.

Ashton, D. and Sung, J. (1997), 'Education, skill formation and economic development: The Singaporean approach', in Halsey, A. H., Lauder, H., Brown, P. and Wells, A. S. (eds), *Education, Economy, Society*, pp. 210–26. Oxford: Oxford University Press.

Astiz, M., Wiseman, A. and Baker, D. (2002), 'Slouching towards decentralisation: Consequences of globalization for curricular control in national education systems', *Comparative Education Review*, vol. 46, no. 1, pp. 66–88.

Ball, S. (2007), *Education Plc*. London: Routledge.

Bangs, J., MacBeath, J. and Galton, M. (2011), *Reinventing Schools, Reforming Teaching*. London: Routledge.

Banks, S. (2004), *Ethics, Accountability and the Social Professions*. London: Palgrave.

Barber, M. (2007), *Instructions to Deliver*. London: Politicos.

Barineau, S. and Kronlid, D. O. (2014), 'Wicked Leadership education: On student-led higher environment and sustainability education', in Corcoran, P. and Hollingshead, B. (eds), *Intergenerational Learning and Transformative Leadership for Sustainable Futures*, pp. 103–13. The Netherlands: Wageningan Academic Publishers.

Barth, F. (1966), *Models of Social Organisation*. Occasional Paper no. 23. London: Royal Anthropological Institute.

Bassey, M. (1999), *Case Study Research in Educational Settings*. Buckingham: Open University Press.

Berliner, W. (2011), 'Teachers want to be treated as professionals', *Guardian*, 3 October 2011.

Binford, L. R. (1968), 'Post-pleistocene adaptations', in Binford, L. R. and Binford, S. R. (eds), *New Perspectives in Archaeology*, pp. 313–42. Chicago: Aldine.

Blake, R. and Mouton, J. (1985), *The New Managerial Grid*. Houston: Gulf.

Bobbitt, P. (2003), *The Shield of Achilles*. London: Penguin.

Bore, A. and Wright, N. (2009), 'The wicked and complex in education: Developing a trans-disciplinary perspective for policy formation, implementation and professional practice', *Journal of Education for Teaching*, vol. 35, no. 3, pp. 241–56.

Bottery, M. (1998), *Professionals and Policy*. London: Cassell.

Bottery, M. (2003), 'The end of citizenship? The Nation state, threats to its legitimacy and citizenship education in the twenty-first century', *Cambridge Journal of Education*, vol. 33, no. 1, pp. 101–22.

Bottery, M. (2004), *The Challenges of Educational Leadership*. London: Paul Chapman.

Bottery, M. (2007), 'Reports from the front line: English Headteachers' work in an era of practice centralisation', *Educational Management, Administration and Leadership*, vol. 35, no. 1, pp. 89–110.

Bottery, M. (2016), *Educational Leadership for a More Sustainable Future*. London: Bloomsbury.

Bottery, M., Wright, N. and James, S. (2012), 'Personality, moral purpose, and the leadership of an education for sustainable development', *Education 3–13*, vol. 40, no. 3, pp. 227–43.

Brown, P. and Lauder, H. (2001), *Capitalism and Social Progress*. Basingstoke: Palgrave.

Brundtland Report (1987), see World Commission On Environment and Development (1987), *Our Common Future*. Oxford: Oxford University Press.

Bryman, A. (2001), *Social Research Methods*. Oxford: Oxford University Press.

Bush, T. (2011), 'Becoming a school principal; exciting opportunity or daunting challenge?' *Educational Management, Administration and Leadership*, vol. 39, no. 5, pp. 514–15.

Bush, T. and Glover, D. (2014), 'School leadership models: What do we know?' *School Leadership and Management*, vol. 34, no. 5, pp. 553–71.

Bush, T. and Jackson, D. (2002), 'A preparation for school leadership: International perspectives', *Educational Management and Administration*, vol. 30, no. 4, pp. 417–29.

Carr, E. H. (1972), *What is History?* London: Pelican.

Carr-Saunders, E. and Wilson, P. (1933), *The Professions*. Oxford: Clarendon Press.

Ceulemans, C. (2017), 'How to move beyond the trust-control dilemma?' *Studia Paedagogica*, vol. 22, no. 2, pp. 33–50.

Chapman, J. (2005), *International Recruitment, Retention, and Development of School Principals*. UNESCO. http://www.iaoed.org/files/Edpol2.pdf.

Choi, P. K. (2005), 'A critical evaluation of education reforms in Hong Kong: Counting our losses to economic globalization'. *International Studies in Sociology of Education*, vol. 15, no. 3, pp. 237–56.

Clarke, S. (2015), 'School leadership in turbulent times and the value of negative capability', *Professional Development in Education*, vol. 42, no. 1, pp. 1–14.

Collins, D. (2011), *The Expectations and Experiences of First-Year Students in a Higher Education Institution*. EdD Thesis, University of Hull, England.

Collins, R. (1990), 'Market Closure and the conflict theory of the professions', in Burrage, M. and Torstendahl, R. (eds), *Professions in Theory and Practice*, pp. 24–43. London: Sage.

Conklin, J. (2006), *Dialogue Mapping: Building Shared Understanding of Wicked Problems*. Hoboken: John Wiley and Sons.

Creasy, R. (2017), *The Taming of Education*. London: Palgrave.

Davidson, J. D. and Rees-Mogg, W. (1999), *The Sovereign Individual*. New York: Touchstone.

Davies, B., ed. (2007), *Developing Sustainable Leadership*. London: Paul Chapman.

Day, C., Harris, A., Hadfield, M., Tolley, H. and Beresford, J. (2000), *Leading Schools in Times of Change*. Buckingham: Open University Press.

Dimmock, C. and Walker, A. (2005), *Educational Leadership: Culture and Diversity*. London: Sage.

Dixon, D. (2009), *Developing a Green Leader Model for Primary Schools*. EdD thesis. University of Lincoln, England.

Doyle, D. and Locke, G. (2014), *U.S. Lacking Leaders: The Challenges of Principal Recruitment, Selection, and Placement*. Washington: Thomas Fordham Institute.

Durka, G (2002) *The Teacher's Calling: A Spirituality for Those Who Teach*; New York: Paulist Press.

Durkheim, E. (1957), *Professional Ethics and Civil Morals*. London: Routledge and Kegan Paul.

English, F. (2008), *The Art of Educational Leadership*. London: Sage.

Eriksen, T. H. (2017), *What is Anthropology?* (2nd edn). London: Pluto Press.

Fabrizi, M. (2013), *The Use of Fantasy Literature in the Secondary School Classroom to Develop Critical Literacy Skills*. Kingston upon Hull: University of Hull.

Fergusson, R. (1994), 'Managerialism in education', in Clarke, J., Cochrane, A. and McLaughlin, E. (eds), *Managing Social Policy*, pp. 93–114. London: Sage.

Foucault, M. (1979), *Discipline and Punish*. London: Penguin.

Fox, K. (2014), *Watching the English*. London: Hodder.

Friedman, M. (1962), *Capitalism and Freedom Chicago*. Chicago: University of Chicago Press.

Fromm, E. (1942), *The Fear of Freedom*. London: Routledge and Kegan Paul.

Fromm, E. (2001), *The Fear of Freedom*. London: Routledge Classics

Fukuyama, F. (1991), *The End of History and the Last Man*. London: Penguin.

Fullan, M. (1991), *The New Meaning of Educational Change*. London: Cassell.

Fullan, M. (1997), *What's Worth Fighting for in the Principalship?* (2nd edn). New York: Teachers' College Press.

Fullan, M. (2004), *The Moral Imperatives of School Leadership*. London: Sage.

Fullan, M. (2009), 'Large-scale reforms comes of age', *Journal of Educational Change*, vol. 10, no. 2/3, pp. 5–28.

Fuller, E. (2012), *Explaining Principal Turnover*. National Education Policy Centre. http://nepc.colorado.edu/blog/examining-principal-turnover.

Galdames, S. and Gonzalez, A. (2016), 'The relationship between leadership preparation and the level of teachers' interest in assuming a principalship in Chile', *School Leadership and Management*, vol. 36, no. 4, pp. 435–51.

Gauss, N. (2011), 'Women and school leadership: Factors determining female teachers from holding principal positions in Elementary Schools in Makassar', *Advancing Women in Leadership*, vol. 31, pp. 175–88.

Giddens, A. (1984), *The Constitution of Society*. Cambridge: Polity Press.

Gold, A., Evans, J., Earley, P., Halpin, D. and Collarbone, P. (2003), 'Principled Principals? Values-driven leadership: Evidence from ten case studies of outstanding school leadership', *Educational Management and Administration*, vol. 31, no. 2, pp. 129–38.

Green, A. (1997), *Education, Globalisation, and the Nation State*. London: Macmillan.

Grint, K. (2008), 'Wicked problems and clumsy solutions', *Clinical Leader*, vol. 1, no. 2, pp. 11–25.

Gronn, P. (2003), *The New Work of Educational Leaders*. London: Paul Chapman.

Gronn, P. (2016), 'Fit for purpose no more?' *Management in Education*, vol. 30, no. 4, pp. 168–72.

Gunter, H. (2016), *An Intellectual History of School Leadership Practice and Research*. London: Bloomsbury.

Hackman, D. (2002), 'Using portraiture in educational leadership research', *International Journal of Leadership in Education*, vol. 5, no. 1, pp. 51–60.

Hallinger, P. and Kantamara, P. (2000), 'Leading at the confluences of tradition and globalization: The challenge of change in Thai schools', *Asia Pacific Journal of Education*, vol. 20, no. 2, pp. 46–57.

Handy, C. (1978), *Gods of Management*. London: Souvenir Press.

Handy, C. and Aitken, R. (1990), *Understanding Schools as Organisations*. London: Penguin.

Hargreaves, A. (2003), *Teaching in the Knowledge Society*. Milton Keynes: Open University Press.

Hargreaves, A. and Fink, D. (2003), *Sustainable Leadership*. San Francisco, CA: Jossey Bass.

Hayek, F. (1944), *The Road to Serfdom*. London: Routledge and Kegan Paul.

Heater, D. (2004), *A History of Education for Citizenship*. London: Routledge.

Heck, R. (2002), 'Issues in the investigation of school leadership across cultures', in Walker, A. and Dimmock, C. (eds), *School Leadership and Administration: Adopting a Cultural Perspective*, pp. 77–102. New York: Routledge-Falmer.

Hendry, J. (2016), *An Introduction to Social Anthropology* (3rd edn). London: Palgrave.

Hobsbawm, E. (1990), *Nations and Nationalism Since 1780*. Cambridge: Cambridge University Press.

Hodgen, E. and Wylie, C. (2005), 'Stress and wellbeing among New Zealand principals', http://www.nzcer.org.nz/research/publications/stress-and-well-being-among-new-zealand-principals-report-new-zealand-principa?cPath=130_131&products_id=1555.

Hodgkinson, C. (1978), *Towards a Philosophy of Administration*. Oxford: Basil Blackwell.

Hofstede, (2003), *Culture's Consequences*. New York: Corwin Press.

Homans, G. C. (1967), *The Nature of Social Science*. New York: Harcourt, Brace and Jovanovich.

Honig, M. (2009), 'What works in defining "what works" in educational improvement', in Sykes, G., Schneider, B. and Plank, D. (eds), *Handbook of Educational Policy Research*, pp. 333–47. New York: Routledge.

Hood, C. (1991), 'A public management for all seasons?' *Public Administration*, vol. 69, pp. 3–19.

Hoyle, E. and Wallace, M. (2006), *Educational Leadership: Ambiguity, Professionals, and Managerialism*. London: Sage.

Humphrey, H., Quoted in *Huffington Post*, 3 July 2011.

Huntingdon, S. (1988), *The Clash of Civilizations and the Remaking of the World Order*. London: Touchstone.

Huntingdon, S. (2004), *Who are We? America's Great Debate*. New York: Free Press.

Jackson, L. (2007), *Leading Sustainable Schools: What Research Tells Us*, p. 43. Nottingham: NCSL. Accessed at: www.ncsl.org.uk/media-24b-07-leading-sustainable-schools-report.pdf.

Karabel, J. and Halsey, A. H. (eds.) (1979), *Power and Ideology in Education*. Oxford: Oxford University Press.

Kelchtermans, G. (1993), 'Getting the story, understanding the lives: From career stories to teachers' professional development', *Teaching and Teacher Education*, vol. 9, no. 5/6, pp. 443–56.

Kellerman, B. (2004), *Bad Leadership*. Brighton: Harvard Business School Press.

Klare, M. (2004), *Blood and Oil*. London: Penguin.

Klare, M. (2008), *Rising Powers, Shrinking Planet*. London: Oneworld publications.

Klare, M. (2012), *The Race for What's Left*. New York: Picador.

Kluckholm, C. and Kroeber, A. (1952), *Culture: A Critical Review of Concepts and Definitions*. Cambridge, MA: Harvard University Press.

Knapp, M. and Feldman, S. (2012), 'Managing the intersection of internal and external accountability' *Journal of Educational Administration*, vol. 50, no. 5, pp. 666–94.

Korten, D. (1996), *When Corporations Rule the World*. London: Earthscan.

Kuhn, T. S. (1970), *The Structure of Scientific Revolutions*. Chicago: Chicago University Press.

Larusdottir, S. H. (2014), 'Educational leadership and market values: A study of school principals in Iceland', *Educational Management Administration and Leadership*, vol. 42, no, 4 (s), pp. 83–103.

Lauder, H, Jamieson, I and Wikeley, F (1998) '*Models of effective schools: Limits and capabilities*'. In School effectiveness for whom?, ed. R. Slee, G. Wiener, and S. Tomlinson, pp. 51–69. London: Falmer.

Lave, J. and Wenger, W. (1991), *Situated Learning*. Cambridge: Cambridge University Press.

Law, W. (2012), 'Educational leadership and culture in China: Dichotomies between Chinese and Anglo-American leadership traditions?' *International Journal of Educational Development*, vol. 32, no. 2, pp. 273–82.

Lawrence-Lightfoot, S. (1983), *The Good High School*. New York: Basic Books.

Lawrence-Lightfoot, S. and Hoffman Davies, J. (1997), *The Art and Science of Portraiture*. San Francisco: Jossey Bass.

Leeson, G. (2009), 'Later life and education: Changes and challenges', www.beyondcurrenthorizons.org.uk/later-life-and-education-changes-and-challenges/.

Leithwood, K., Jantzi, D. and Steinbach R. (1999), *Changing Leadership for Changing Times*. Buckingham: Open University Press.

Leithwood, K., Day, P., Sammons, P., Hopkins, D., Harris, A., Gu, Q. and Brown, E. (2006), *Seven Strong Claims about Successful School Leadership*. Nottingham: NCSL.

Levin, B. (2004), 'Educational policy: Commonalities and differences', in Davies, B. and West-Burnham, J. (eds), *Handbook of Educational Leadership and Management*, pp. 165–76. London: Pearson.

Levin, B. (2010), 'Governments and education reform: Some lessons from the last 50 years', *Journal of Education Policy*, vol. 25, no.6, pp. 739–47

Levi-Strauss, C. (1966), *The Savage Mind*. Chicago: University of Chicago Press.

Lipman-Blumen, J. (2005), *The Allure of Toxic Leaders*. Oxford: Oxford University Press.

Lipsky, M. (1980), *Street-level Bureaucracy*. New York: Russell Sage Foundation.

Lukes, S. (1974), *Power: A Radical View*. London: Macmillan.

Lukes, S. (2005), *Power: A Radical View* (2nd edn). London: Palgrave.

MacBeath, J. (2006), 'New relationships for old: Inspection and self-evaluation in England and Hong Kong', *International Studies in Educational Administration*, vol. 34, no. 2, pp. 2–19.

Management in Education. (2016) *Journal Edition on Leadership Sustainability*, vol. 30, no. 3. Special Issue: Sustainable Development Goals, Millennium Development Goals.

Marion, R. and Uhl-Bien, M. (2001), 'Leadership in complex organizations' *Leadership Quarterly*', vol. 12, no. 4, pp. 389–418.

Marriot, M. (1976), 'Hindu transaction: Diversity without dualism', in Kapferer, B. (ed.), *Transaction and Meaning*, pp. 109–42. Philadelphia: Institute for the study of human issues.

Marshall, T. H. (1950), *Citizenship and Social Class*. Cambridge: Cambridge University Press.

McGregor, D. (1960), *The Human Side of Enterprise*. New York: McGraw-Hill.

McSweeney, B. (2002), 'Hofstede's model of national cultural differences and their consequences', *Human Relations*, vol. 55, no. 1, pp. 89–118.

Meyer, E. (2015), *The Culture Map*. New York: Public Affairs.

Milgram, S. (1974), *Obedience to Authority*. London: Tavistock.

Mohamed, R. and Nor, C. (2013), 'The relationship between McGregor's X-Y Theory management style and fulfilment of psychological contract: A literature review'. *International Journal of Academic Research in Business and Social Sciences*, vol. 3, no. 5, pp. 715–30.

Moller, J. (2009), 'School Leadership in an age of accountability', *Journal of Educational Change*, vol. 10, no. 1, pp. 37–46.

Morgan, G. (1997), *Images of Organization* (2nd edn). London: Sage.

Morris, M. and Peng, K. (1994), 'Culture and cause: American and Chinese attributions for social and physical events', *Journal of Personality and Social Psychology*, vol. 67, pp. 949–71.

Morris, P. and Lo, M. (2000), 'Shaping the curriculum: Context and cultures', *School Leadership and Management*, vol. 20, no.2, pp. 175–88.

Munz, R. and Reiterer, A. (2009), *Overcrowded World? Global Population and International Migration*. London: Haus Publishing.

Murdock, G. P. (1945), 'The common denominator of cultures', in Linton, R. (ed.), *The Science of Man in the World Crisis*. New York: Columbia University Press.

Naisbett, J. and Aburdene, P. (1988), *Megatrends 2000*. London: Sidgwick and Jackson.

Nisbett R. (2003), *The Geography of Thought*. London: Nicholas Brealey.

Nozick, R. (1974), *Anarchy, State and Utopia*. Oxford: Blackwell.

O'Dea, C. (in process) *Changing Perceptions of Chinese Top Up Students Transitioning through a UK University*. University of Hull.

Ohmae, K. (1995), *The End of the Nation State*. New York: Free Press.

Ouston, J. (1999), 'School effectiveness and school improvement: Critique of a movement', in Bush, T., Bell, L., Bolam, R., Glatter, R. and Ribbins, P. (eds),

Educational Management: Redefining Theory, Policy and Practice, pp. 166–77. London: Paul Chapman.

Palan, R., Abbott, J. and Deans, P. (2002). *State Strategies in the Global Political Economy*. London: Pinter.

Park, V. and Datnow, A. (2009), 'Co-constructing distributed leadership' *School Leadership and Management*, vol. 29, no. 5, pp. 477–94.

Pawson, R. and Tilley, N. (1997), *Realistic Evaluation*. London: Sage.

Peters, T. and Waterman Jr., R. H. (1982), *In Search of Excellence*. London: Harper and Row.

Plsek, P. (2001), 'Why wont the NHS do as its told?', Plenary address to NHS conference, July.

Plsek, P. and Greenhalgh, T. (2001), 'Complexity science: The challenge of complexity in health care'. *British Medical Journal*, vol. 323, pp. 685–8.

Pollitt, C. (1993), *Managerialism and the Public Services* (2nd edn). Oxford: Basil Blackwell.

Popper, K. (1982), *The Logic of Scientific Discovery*. London: Hutchinson.

Porritt, J., Hopkins, D., Birney, A. and Reed, J. (2009), *Every Child's Future: Leading the Way*. Nottingham: NCSL.

Pounder, D. and Merrill, R. ((2001), 'Job desirability of the high school principalship', *Educational Administration Quarterly*, vol. 37, no. 1, pp. 27–57.

Preus, B. (2007), 'Educational trends in China and the United States', *Phi Delta Kappan*, vol. 89, no. 2, pp. 115–18.

Princen, T. (2005), *The Logic of Sufficiency*. Cambridge, MA: MIT Press.

Radcliffe Brown, A. R. (1957), *The Natural Science of Society*. Glencoe, IL: Free Press.

Rayner, S. (2006), *Jack Beale Memorial Lecture on Global Environment Wicked Problems: Clumsy Solutions – Diagnoses and Prescriptions for Environmental Ills*. Institute for Science, Innovation and Society, ANSW, Sydney, Australia.

Reames, E., Kochan, T. and Zhu, L. (2014), 'Factors influencing principals' retirement decisions: A southern US perspective', *Educational Management Administration and Leadership*, vol. 42, no. 1, pp. 140–60.

REf (2014). Accessed at: http://www.ref.ac.uk/2014/

Ribbins, P. and Zhang, N. J. (2006), 'Culture, societal culture, and school leadership', *International Studies in Educational Administration*, vol. 34, no. 1, pp. 71–88.

Rittel, H. and Webber, M. (1973), 'Dilemmas in a general theory of planning', *Policy Sciences*, vol. 4, pp. 155–69.

Ritzer, G. (1993), *The McDonaldisation of Society*. London: Sage.

Ritzer, G. (2004), *The Globalization of Nothing*. Thousand Oaks, CA: Pine Forge Press.

Robinson, S. (2009), *Primary Headteachers: New Leadership Roles Inside and Outside the School*. PhD thesis, Birmingham City University, England.

Robinson, V. (2007), *The Impact of Leadership on Student Outcomes: Making Sense of the Evidence*. Australian Council for Educational Research. http://research.acer.edu.au/research_conference_2007/5/.

Rorty, R. (1989), *Contingency, Irony, and Solidarity*. Cambridge: Cambridge University Press.

Rousseau, D. (1989), 'Psychological and implied contracts in organizations', *Employee Responsibilities and Rights Journal*, vol. 2, pp. 121–39.

Rumsfeld, D. (2002), U.S. Department of Defense News Briefing in February 2002.

Schein, E. (2013), *Humble Enquiry*. San Francisco, CA: Berrett-Koehler Publishers.

Schon, D. (1983), *The Reflective Practitioner*. New York, NY: Basic Books.

Scott, P. (2002), 'The future of general education in mass higher education systems'. *Higher Education Policy*, Vol. 15, pp. 61–75.

Shallcross, A. and Robinson, J. (2007), 'Is a decade of teacher education for sustainable development essential for survival?' *Journal of Education for Teaching*, vol. 33, no. 2, pp. 137–48.

Simon, H. (1956), 'Rational choice and the structure of the environment.' *Psychological Review*, vol. 63, no. 2, pp. 129–38.

Smith, A. (1976), *The Glasgow Edition of the Works and Correspondence of Adam Smith* (Raphael, D. D. and MacFie, A. L. (eds)). Oxford: Clarendon Press.

Starr, K. (2015), *Education Game Changers: Leadership and the Consequence of Policy Paradox*. Lanham, MD: Rowman & Littlefield.

Stern, N. (2006), *The Stern Review Executive Summary* (full) available at http://www.hm treasury.gov.uk/edia/9/9/CLOSED.SHORT_executive_summary.pdf

Stewart, J. and Clarke, M. (1987), 'The public service orientation: Issues and dilemmas', *Public Administration*, vol. 65, no. 2, pp. 161–78.

Stiglitz, J. (2002), *Globalization and its Discontents*. London: Penguin.

Studia Pedagogica (2016). *Special Edition on Intergenerational Education*. Masaryk University, Czech Republic.

Tawney, R. H. (1921), *The Acquisitive Society*. New York: Harcourt Brace.

Times Educational Supplement (16/5/13) '"Ratcheting up of pressure" drives worst primary headteacher recruitment crisis in 13 years', http://www.tes.co.uk/article. aspx?storycode=6334264&s_cid=tesmagazinehome.

Toffler, A. (1970), *Future Shock*. London: Bodley Head.

Troman, G. and Woods, P. (2000), 'Careers under stress: Teacher adaptations at a time of intensive reform', *Journal of Educational Change*, vol. 1, pp. 253–75.

Trompenaars, F. and Hampden-Turner, C. (1997), *Riding the Waves of Culture*. London: Nicholas Brealey.

Truong, T. D., Hallinger, P. and Sanga, K. (2017), 'Confucian values and school leadership in Vietnam: Exploring the influence of culture on principal decision-making', *Educational Management, Administration and Leadership*, vol. 45, no. 1, pp. 77–100.

Varey, W. (2008), 'Apithology: An emerging continuum', *Aspects of Apithology*, vol. 1, no. 1, pp. 1–5.

Verweij, M. and Thompson, M. (2011), *Clumsy Solutions for a Complex World* (Verweij, M. and Thomson, M. (eds)), pp. 1–31. London: Palgrave Macmillan.

Wacks, R. (2010), *Privacy*. Oxford: Oxford University Press.

Walker, A., Quian, H. and Zhang, S. (2011), 'Secondary schools principals in curriculum reform: Victims or accomplices?' *Frontier of Education in China*, vol. 6, no. 3, pp. 388–403.

Wallace, M. and Fertig, M. (2007), 'Applying complexity theory to public service change: Creating chaos out of order?' in Wallace, M., Fertig, M. and Schneller, E. (eds), *Managing Change in the Public Services*, pp. 36–56. Oxford: Blackwell.

Washington, H. and Cook, J. (2011), *Climate Change Denial*. London: Earthscan.

Waterhouse, J. (2007), 'From narratives to portraits: Methodology and methods to portray leadership', *The Curriculum Journal*, vol. 18, no.3, pp. 271–86.

Waters, M. (1996), *Globalization*. London: Routledge.

Weber, M. (1947), *The Theory of Social and Economic Organisation*. Oxford: Oxford University.

Wei-Ming, T. (2000), 'Multiple modernities: A preliminary inquiry into the implications of East Asian modernity', in Harrison, L. and Huntington, S. (eds), *Culture Matters*, pp. 256–67. New York: Basic Books.

Western, S. (2010), *Leadership: A Critical Text*. London: Sage.

Williams, R. (2001), *Unrecognised Exodus, Unaccepted Accountability: The Looming Shortage of Principals and Vice-principals in Ontario Public Schools*. Working Paper no. 24. Queens University School of Policy Studies.

Wright, N. (2011), 'Between "Bastard" and "Wicked" leadership? School leadership and the emerging policies of the UK Coalition government', *Journal of Educational Administration and History*, vol. 43, no. 4, pp. 345–62.

Yin, H., Lee, J. and Wang, W. (2014), 'Dilemmas of leading national curriculum reform in a global era: A Chinese perspective', *Educational Management Administration and Leadership*, vol. 42, no. 2, pp. 293–311.

Young, D. and Szachowicz, P. (2014), 'Responding to principals' rising responsibilities', *Education Week*, 4 February 2014.

Zhong, Q. (2006), 'Curriculum reform in China: Challenges and reflections', *Frontiers of Education in China*, vol. 1, no. 3, pp. 370–82.

INDEX